MW00355247

Witchcraft and Magic in Europe
The Period of the Witch Trials

WITCHCRAFT AND MAGIC IN EUROPE

Series Editors
Bengt Ankarloo
Stuart Clark

The roots of European witchcraft and magic lie in Hebrew and other ancient Near Eastern cultures and in the Celtic, Nordic, and Germanic traditions of the continent. For two millennia, European folklore and ritual have been imbued with the belief in the supernatural, yielding a rich trove of histories and images.

Witchcraft and Magic in Europe combines traditional approaches of political, legal, and social historians with a critical synthesis of cultural anthropology, historical psychology, and gender studies. The series provides a modern, scholarly survey of the supernatural beliefs of Europeans from ancient times to the present day. Each volume of this ambitious series contains the work of distinguished scholars chosen for their expertise in a particular era or region.

Witchcraft and Magic in Europe

The Period of the Witch Trials

BENGT ANKARLOO
STUART CLARK
WILLIAM MONTER

Edited by
Bengt Ankarloo
and Stuart Clark

PENN

University of Pennsylvania Press
Philadelphia

First published 2002 by
THE ATHLONE PRESS
A Continuum imprint
The Tower Building, 11 York Road, London SE1 7NX

First published in the United States of America 2002 by
University of Pennsylvania Press
Philadelphia, Pennsylvania 19104-4011

© 2002 The Authors

Library of Congress Cataloging-in-Publication Data
Ankarloo, Bengt, 1935–
  Witchcraft and magic in Europe : the period of the witch trials / Bengt Ankarloo, Stuart
Clark, William Monter; edited by Begnt Ankarloo and Stuart Clark.
    p.   cm.
  Includes bibliographical references and index.
  ISBN 0-8122-3617-3 (cloth : alk. paper); ISBN 0-8122-1787-X (pbk. : alk. paper)
  1. Witchcraft—Europe—History.   2. Trials (Witchcraft)—Europe—History.   I. Clark,
Stuart.   II. Monter, E. William
BF1584.E9 A55   2002
133.4/3/094—dc21   2002075051

Not for sale outside the United States of America and its dependencies and
Canada and the Philippines

All rights reserved. No part of this publication may be reproduced,
stored in a retrieval system, or transmitted in any form or by any means,
electronic, mechanical, photocopying or otherwise, without prior
permission in writing from the publisher.

Typeset by SetSystems, Saffron Walden, Essex
Printed and bound in Great Britain

Contents

Introduction

Bengt Ankarloo and Stuart Clark

With this volume the *History of Witchcraft and Magic in Europe* reaches the period of 'witch-hunting', from the mid-fifteenth to the mid-eighteenth centuries. This may be a label that is increasingly being questioned by historians but the fact remains that only at this moment in European history was diabolic witchcraft a criminal offence in most legal systems, secular and ecclesiastical, and only then were the vast majority of witches actually prosecuted for it. The numbers involved and the reasons behind the witch trials continue to be debated – and are debated again here – but no one denies that they belong to the early modern era as they belong to no other. One of the aims of this series is to balance this undeniable fact with an awareness of the role of witchcraft and magic in other societies that did not have the same general desire or legal capacity to punish them as thoroughly or even at all. Indeed, we want to demonstrate an enduring significance for these subjects that is independent of the phenomenon of legal prosecution, even during the age of witch-hunting itself. Another overall aim is to treat manifestations of witchcraft and magic before and after the early modern era on their own terms, rather than as the origins or aftermath of what happened during that time. Nevertheless, we still have to acknowledge that the period of the witch trials saw the high point not only of witchcraft as a criminal offence but also of magic as a serious intellectual pursuit.

Witchcraft and magic belong also to the historiography of the early modern era as to that of no other. It is extraordinary how, in the last thirty years, these subjects have come to occupy a commanding place in the scholarship devoted to this period of European history. Before that time many mainstream historians were clearly uncomfortable with them, finding them difficult or impossible to fit into the prevailing patterns of interpretation except as negatives – instances of irrationality, superstition and wrong-headedness to set against what was progressive in Renaissance and Baroque society and culture. The mood of ambiguity is caught perfectly in Hugh Trevor-Roper's famous essay on 'The European Witch-Craze of the Sixteenth and Seventeenth Centuries', its first versions dating from the 1950s and its final publication from 1967. Trevor-Roper obviously recognized the historical relativism of Lucien Febvre concerning witchcraft, referring to him as 'one of the most perceptive and philosophical of modern French historians' and quoting approvingly his view that only an intervening 'mental revolution' could account for the distance between modern rationality and the witchcraft beliefs of the sixteenth century. At the same time, he himself felt obliged to characterize witchcraft as the grotesque side of the Renaissance and describe acceptance of its reality as 'hysterical' and 'lunatic'. From the 1970s onwards, by contrast, the trend was away from this kind of rationalism and towards explanation – sometimes very grand explanation indeed. The tendency here was still to assume that societies that prosecuted witches must have something wrong with them – some pathology that accounted for what was obviously aberrant behaviour. But at least witchcraft history was accorded the benefits of interdisciplinarity before other fields were. Historical studies inspired by theoretical insights drawn from anthropology, sociology and social psychology began to turn witchcraft into a subject at the crossroads of the disciplines.

More recently still, explanation has given way to interpretation, and with this has come the desire to understand the history of witchcraft in more cultural terms – taking culture at its broadest and most inclusive. This kind of understanding makes different assumptions about both witchcraft and magic and is achieved more by the effort to contextualize than by the resort to grand theory. The worst excesses of the witch trials, described, for example, in the section of William Monter's essay in this volume on the German 'superhunts', will always strike us as abhorrent; so, too, the activities of the most notorious 'witch-hunters' of the period – like the officials who worked on the 'extirpation programme' of the Archbishop of Cologne, Ferdinand of Bavaria, in the late 1620s and 1630s. But under the influence above all of cultural anthropology, we have come to realize that the prosecution of witches may have rested on a culturally based rationality quite unlike our own, as in the case of other episodes in early modern European history that we once struggled or failed to comprehend.

This indeed was the suggestion that Trevor-Roper could not quite accept in Lucien Febvre's *Annales* essay of 1948 – 'that the mind of one age is not necessarily subject to the same rules as the mind of another'. It was the view of the Spanish anthropologist and historian, and pioneer witchcraft scholar, Julio Caro Baroja, that a different version even of reality itself was at work in witch-prosecuting societies. Even though contested in such societies, this helped to give those involved in witch-hunting the conviction that their beliefs and actions made sense. Religious and political requirements, ethical expectations and social norms, philosophies and cosmologies – even classification systems and taxonomies, as Ankarloo suggests in his essay – were likewise different and gave different meanings to the things they warranted. None of this can be appreciated unless witchcraft and magic are put back into the broadest possible context – including, of course, the poisonous hatreds and animosities, the fantasies and imaginings, that must so often have accompanied, and perhaps compromised, the giving of reasons for prosecuting witches. And this it is that has brought these two subjects into contact with the rest of early modern life and culture and, indeed, into the heart of early modern historiography.

The situation today, then, is that early modern witchcraft and magic are impossible to think about in isolation from the major developments of the age – the fundamental religious upheavals of the Protestant and Catholic Reformations, the transformation of political institutions and state systems, the competition for resources and the struggle for stability in agrarian economies, the development of medical and natural philosophical knowledge and so on. Indeed, if anything, the process of interpretation may be moving in the reverse direction, with early modern European history becoming impossible to think about without witchcraft and magic. There is a growing feeling that our understanding of such pivotal events as the religious Reformations and the Scientific Revolution will remain incomplete unless we relate them to the beliefs and experiences that encouraged (or inhibited) the prosecution of witches and the practice of magic. More broadly still, there is an emerging consensus that these may be the sorts of subjects that Robert Darnton had in mind when, in the final pages of his *The Great Cat Massacre and Other Episodes in French Cultural History* (1984), he spoke of finding access to strange cultures in the past at the points where they initially seemed most opaque. He wrote: 'When we run into something that seems unthinkable to us, we may have hit upon a valid point of entry into an alien mentality' (p. 262). It is no longer clear, in other words, whether we are only making better sense of witchcraft and magic by looking at them 'through' early modern history. We may, in addition, be making better sense of early modern history by looking at it through them.

Whichever is the case, it says something about the capacity of these subjects to act in the way Darnton described that they have attracted the attention of some of the most innovative and influential early modern historians. One thinks not only of Trevor-Roper himself – and, indeed, of Febvre and Caro Baroja – but, in subsequent years, of Frances Yates, Keith Thomas, Erik Midelfort, Michel de Certeau and Carlo Ginzburg, and more recently of Robert Muchembled, Gábor Klaniczay, Robin Briggs and Wolfgang Behringer. For example, the impact of Thomas's *Religion and the Decline of Magic* (1971) on the writing of the general social and cultural history of sixteenth- and seventeenth-century Britain has been incalculable. This first scholarly ethnography of English witchcraft and magic (and allied beliefs) was inspiring not simply for the subjects it dealt

with but for its ability to reconfigure British history in the light of them –
for the *kind* of interpretation it was. The other authors mentioned, too,
have all seen in witchcraft and magic opportunities that would not
otherwise exist to explore and illuminate their broader concerns as
historians. Arguably, no other aspects of early modern historiography have
acted in quite this manner as avenues for approaching and vehicles for
expressing the major themes of the period.

The sheer scale of advanced research on these subjects in recent years,
together with their presence on countless syllabuses, are themselves a
testimony to their current significance. Especially important have been the
initiatives to pool research and promote collective enquiry in the field of
witchcraft studies, often arising from groups of scholars at the forefront of
historical innovation in their respective countries. In the Netherlands,
beginning in 1982 and continuing for about a decade, collaborative and
interdisciplinary studies were co-ordinated under the auspices of a study
group entitled 'Witchcraft and Sorcery in the Netherlands'. In Germany,
exactly the same development occurred – and still continues – in the form
of the AKIH (*Arbeitskreis Interdisziplinäre Hexenforschung*). In Hungary, a
witchcraft research team has existed for fifteen years, consisting of historians and folklorists, and dedicated to the exhaustive documentation of the
Hungarian witch trials and the study of popular mentalities. In the case of
France, the *Annales* tradition itself paid little attention to the history of
witchcraft, despite Febvre's essay and Le Roy Ladurie's brief incursion
into the subject in his *Les Paysans de Languedoc*. It was left instead to those
more influenced by the old Vème, not the VIème section of the original
École des Hautes Études, like Robert Mandrou, Jean Delumeau and
Robert Muchembled. Even so, witchcraft studies flourished in the 1990s
among the *équipe* associated with the École Normale Supérieure de
Fontenay/Saint-Cloud, working under the title '*Histoire critique de la
sorcellerie*'. In the same period and since, in French-speaking Switzerland,
the University of Lausanne has been the focus of an entire series of
publications on witchcraft published as part of the *Cahiers Lausannois
d'Histoire Médiévale*.

The outcome of all this intense interest, stretching back to the 1970s
and beyond, has been a truly enormous amount of scholarly publishing of
monographs, essays and archival materials. This present volume cannot
hope to take account of anything but a small portion of this total output
but it can indicate in broad terms how the subject currently stands in the
light of the most up-to-date research. As with the other volumes in the
series, it aims to present the salient features of the history of witchcraft and
magic in Europe, in the form of long essays devoted to some of the main
topics in the field. In this case, we, the series editors, are ourselves authors,
joined by another of the experts whose work on witchcraft originated in

the 1970s, William Monter. It seemed essential to give attention to the witch trials themselves and to offer a round-up of what can presently be said about their incidence and scale and the way they were handled judicially in the various regions of Europe. As Monter himself writes: 'Much confusion persists about just how extensive witch-hunting actually was and even more about where it was concentrated.' The other main aim of the volume is to look at witchcraft and magic as components of the broader culture of the period and as the inspiration for various kinds of published writings and intellectual debates. This means that we have avoided explaining the history of our subject in terms of theory, feeling, as Ankarloo points out, that it has probably been overtheorized in the past and mainly in reductive ways.

The first essay, by Monter, considers those areas where, broadly speaking, inquisitorial procedure was adopted in the courts, whether they were secular, where Roman or civil law predominated, or religious, where canon law was used. After looking at a typical continental witch trial from Montgaillard (southern Languedoc) in 1643, he eventually concentrates on the Holy Roman Empire, whose Germanic core experienced the 'epicentre' of European witch-hunting and which, when extended to its fullest notional extent to include, for example, Switzerland, Alsace and Lorraine, accounted for six out of every seven executed witches. Monter considers in turn the situation in the Empire in 1560, the huge witch-hunts conducted in the lands of Catholic prelates (especially in the Rhine basin and in Franconia in the late 1620s and 1630s), the witch trials in the best-studied large secular principality, the duchy of Bavaria, and the regional features of prosecutions in the western borderlands, in Switzerland and in the Low Countries. He then surveys the story in the largest, most populous and most centralized state, the kingdom of France, suggesting remarkable contrasts and comparisons with the many disparate jurisdictions of the Empire. Finally, he looks in the revisionist terms made familiar by recent scholarship (amongst which is Monter's own) at the caution and moderation shown by the various tribunals of the Mediterranean Inquisitions, again provoking striking comparisons with the secular jurisdictions of central, southern and western Europe.

The second essay, by Ankarloo, focuses on northern Europe, where in countries like England and the Scandinavian nations an accusatorial style of justice was still in use, at least up to the end of the sixteenth century. He offers a description of the witchcraft prosecutions in this region, and an analysis of the procedures adopted in them, ranging from England and Scotland in the West to Finland and Livonia in the East. Ankarloo concludes that legislation in these northern territories was directed mostly against *maleficium*, and that, while a fully diabolical notion of witchcraft took hold in Sweden and Finland, especially during the great panic of the

1670s, it remained foreign to the peoples of regions like Denmark and Livonia. Indeed, northern Europe probably never fully integrated the perennial sorcery believed in by its peoples and the new diabolism that dated only from fifteenth-century demonology.

The last essay, by Clark, concentrates not on trials or legal procedures but on the realm of beliefs and ideas. It examines the character of beliefs in witchcraft and magic both in terms of the material culture of the general population of Europe and also in relation to the book culture of its intellectual élite. A first chapter describes the magical practices actually adopted by ordinary men and women, the meaning which they appear to have had for them, the role which fears of *maleficium* played in their lives and the clerical reactions to these various aspects of popular culture once the major European churches had entered their 'reforming' phase. Then, the essay looks at the history of demonology – the expression in print of theories about witchcraft, magic and diabolism – both as a genre and as a problem for intellectual historians today. It seeks, in particular, to locate witchcraft texts according to both the wider interests of their authors and the broader debates of the age, especially in the field of politics, and not simply according to the patterns of the legal prosecutions. Finally, Clark turns to 'high' or 'Faustian' magic – to the more philosophical and scientific aspects of beliefs in magical powers and forces shared by Neoplatonists, 'Hermeticists' and natural magicians in the late Renaissance period. Again, consideration is given to their wider role in the development of Renaissance and seventeenth-century intellectual life, notably in the area of the Scientific Revolution. During the early modern centuries, this kind of intellectual magic was at its highest level of influence – an influence that was political as much as anything else. Later volumes in the series indicate its continued appeal in modern societies but, by then, the creation of conceptual and institutionalized borderlines between 'science' and 'magic' prevented precisely the kind of eclecticism and hybridity that enabled Renaissance natural philosophy, in particular, to flourish.

An important overall theme of this volume is the way it confirms the correctives that have recently been at work in witchcraft scholarship – correctives which, hopefully, will prevent the historiography of early modern Europe from finding *too* prominent a place for witchcraft in its pages. After all, the successful recognition of a topic's significance always runs the risk of exaggerating that significance. It is worth asking, therefore, whether contemporaries were always quite so caught up in the subject of witches and witchcraft as the sheer weight of recent scholarship sometimes seems to imply. In this respect, Monter's answer to his own question about the 'confusion' surrounding the extensiveness and scale of the witch trials is of fundamental importance. He shows just how concentrated they were in a relatively few specific territories and areas and how in the rest of Europe – across huge expanses of it, in fact – they were sporadic, scarce or had a negligible role. This does not diminish the ferocity with which they could and did occur, nor the historian's need to confront such outbreaks for what they were – 'witch-hunts'. Nor should we neglect the more continuous part played by *maleficium* in the lives of communities where episodes of witchcraft were never or rarely brought to the attention of the courts. Nevertheless, if we are to gauge the presence and impact of witchcraft prosecutions over the whole continent of Europe – and to continue to label the age as one of 'witch-hunting' – then we clearly need to show extreme caution and geographical awareness. For example, in England, the United Provinces and southern Scandinavia, as Ankarloo strikingly remarks, witchcraft cannot have been perceived as a major problem in comparison with other crimes.

A related corrective concerns the way witch trials originated – whether in the charges and accusations brought by ordinary people against their neighbours or among the policy-makers and opinion formers of the churches and states of the period. Here, our essays confirm the impression gained from much recent research that the main pressures for prosecutions came 'from below', with local officials carrying on the process, sometimes enthusiastically, but not usually instigating it. Indeed, this volume presents instance after instance of how, as witchcraft cases moved upwards through the judicial system, greater and greater caution was displayed and more and more reservations were expressed. Monter's opening case stands as emblematic of this – a case in which the charges against the five accused ended up being dismissed or left unresolved once they reached the appellate jurisdiction of the Parlement of Toulouse. Everywhere in Europe, the higher reaches of the judiciary, ecclesiastical as well as secular, usually showed the most reluctance and often fought for control over witchcraft cases with their colleagues at the lower or local levels. Everywhere, it seems, appellate jurisdictions acted in a restraining capacity. The corollary – also displayed in this volume – is that those states or territories where judicial systems were more centralized had very different witch trial profiles from those where they were decentralized. Weak regimes, lacking strong legal or political control, always seem to have spelled disaster for witches. This does not close the old debate about 'top-down' witch-hunting, especially as most of Europe's witch trials occurred during what Monter calls 'the confessional century', when the repression of religious deviance became a clerical priority. But clerical priorities were not necessarily judicial ones, as both the English 'Puritan' and many French Catholic demonologists complained. Once again, we have to be careful, at the very least, before attributing hostility to witches simply to Church or state-sponsored acculturation.

The intellectual history of witchcraft and magic underlines these correctives, for despite its links with the actual prosecutions it also maintained a life of its own. There has been an assumption in the past that witch-hunting was fuelled by books – by demonology – and thus by yet further members of the European 'élite'. There are certainly instances of publications and sermons calling loudly and violently for witch trials or written by men who had taken part in them. These must have had some impact. But, as Clark shows, there was also (and always) a debate within demonology in which many writers criticized or denounced the trials. In addition, there were countless others who made witchcraft the occasion for reflections that could be unrelated to the legal prosecution of witches. Here is an example, indeed, of how our understanding of early modern European history might actually be slightly skewed by the focus on witchcraft *trials*. With 'high' magic, especially, we enter a world of thought and practice that those involved would certainly have never associated with diabolism, even if some of their critics did. It seems important to recognize, therefore, that both witchcraft and magic could feature – and feature centrally – in the minds of contemporaries without them necessarily exhibiting what might be called the 'witch-hunting' mentality.

PART 1

Witch Trials in Continental Europe 1560–1660

William Monter

In the autumn of 1643, as the largest witch-hunt in French history spread across southern Languedoc, an aged widow named Jeanne de Biau, known to her neighbours as Nane de Mathieu, was arrested in the village of Montgaillard, in the foothills of the Pyrenees. Her trial and five others which subsequently emerged from her confession rank among the most fully documented cases that we possess from Europe's largest state.[1] Two men had denounced Nane de Mathieu as a notorious witch. When first interrogated on 9 October, she firmly denied that she was a witch, had ever attended a sabbat, had ever been tempted by the Evil Spirit, or had ever killed children at night by 'arts and malefices'. Answering other leading questions, Nane also denied having given some poisoned cheese to a woman three weeks before her arrest; that she threw objects into fountains in order to 'create tempests and storms which destroy the fruits of the earth'; that she had any unusual marks on her body; that she had ever served poisoned figs to people; that she had poisoned both her husband and her son. Questioned about the 'unguents for casting spells' which had been found in a box at her home, she said they were cosmetics. Finally, she denied going to cemeteries in order to dig up the bodies of freshly buried children.

However, in the overheated local context, the charges against her sufficed for Montgaillard's public prosecutor to appeal to the archdeacon of the Bishop of Pamiers at nearby Foix, who on 11 October approved three successive ecclesiastical summons or *monitoires* to be read from the pulpit at Montgaillard in order to unearth all evidence of witchcraft against this defendant and anyone else similarly suspected of practising witchcraft. A legal certificate dated 2 November verified that these *monitoires* had been carried out, and they had produced a harvest of several additional suspects. Montgaillard's village clerk had recorded testimony from six men and three women on 26 October and from three more men on 29 October. The first additional suspects to be denounced were two sisters, Marie and Germaine Dalabert. An old man recalled an incriminating episode 23 years previously involving Marie (nicknamed 'the Cat') who, he said, 'was already suspected of being a witch back then, as she is now'.

Marie's nephew, Jean Allabert, recalled an incriminating episode two years previously and accused his aunt of killing her own son through witchcraft. Two men and a woman accused Françoise Prat, known as 'la Boubellotte'; two women accused Antoinette de Donac, called 'the Duchess', of lifting a spell she had cast on them ten years previously. The most important witness on 29 October was the local notary, Maître Mathieu Tappie, who had employed la Boubellotte as a wet-nurse exactly 30 years earlier; his child died suddenly in bed a month after he had discharged her. The notary's daughter had quarrelled with the Cat, who first bewitched and then cured her in 1626. Another man charged Catherine d'Astoré with poisoning his father ten years before, but he stood alone. On 29 October, the four women with two or more accusers – the Cat, her sister la Fustière, the Duchess and la Boubellotte – were ordered to be arrested.

We hear next about the interrogations of all four women in early November. Each faced slightly different charges and reacted differently to them. La Boubellotte, a widow with five children who finally gave her age as 58, was asked first about the old wet-nursing episode: she said that the notary's sister-in-law took the baby away from her and that it had smothered in its crib. Asked about attending sabbats with Nane de Mathieu, she 'responded deeply troubled' that she never attended the witches' dances because she had to care for three young girls. She denied curing spells, and explained that one accuser was her husband's nephew, with whom she had quarrelled five years ago. By her second and third hearings on 7 and 10 November, she shifted into flat denials of all charges and maintained the same stance at her final hearing on 7 December.

The Duchess, aged about 60, was questioned on 7 and 9 November. Proud that her six children had grown up well, 'come to a good port' as she put it, she similarly brushed aside all charges of malefice. The prosecutors seemed more interested in Nane de Mathieu's accusation that the Duchess danced with a red devil at the local sabbats; they also asked if she had a diabolical mark, although there is no evidence that she was ever checked for one by local surgeons or midwives. We learn that Nane de Mathieu had also accused a man named Vincent Dieumidou and several others (his wife, another man and two other women) as participants at sabbats. Apparently some of them, including Margeurite Labarde, nicknamed 'the Dove', were also arrested about this time.

The Dalabert sisters fared less well than the other defendants. Germaine, la Fustière, who finally gave her age as 60, with nine children, began very badly on 7 November by refusing to take the customary oath. Then 'she pretended to weep, but only a single tear came from her eyes'. When she did finally take the oath, she irritated the judges by denying that she had ever met Nane de Mathieu. At her second interrogation, 'after thinking about it for some time', she still denied any acquaintance with Nane de

Mathieu. The judges then questioned her closely about three specific malefices against babies. At her third hearing she finally admitted knowing Nane de Mathieu, 'not that she has done any evil with her', and denied that she had been marked by the devil.

Her sister did no better. The Cat, who gave her age as 55 and claimed no fewer than eleven children, began on 6 November by 'remaining a long time without answering' the judges' questions. Next day, she denied a raft of charges about the sabbat, where, helped by her sister and Nane de Mathieu, she reputedly helped to 'cook a little child on a spit and eat it afterwards'. She tried to defend herself against a half-dozen charges of malefice with poison, among which one dated back 23 years and another only six weeks. 'Denies the said allegation as false and calumnious,' reads the final comment on this session. But she had the largest collection of specific grievances to refute.

On 10 November, with five other women jailed, Nane de Mathieu, aged 65, made her full and final confession of witchcraft and was then personally confronted with all five in order to sustain her accusations face-to-face. Her meeting with la Fustière, 'she about whom she had spoken in her hearings', was predictably stormy. Under oath, the older Dalabert sister denied having said that Nane 'deserved to be burned already, because she could have saved herself and save those whom she accused' and that Nane 'had three bastards by different fathers'. Under oath, Nane maintained that she had said exactly that. Nane's confrontations with the other four women passed without insults, but each defendant denied Nane's charges. Other accusers were also present on 10 November. Confronted by the man with the 23-year-old grievance, the Cat attacked his character; she objected to another accuser 'because he hit her with his stick, and she knew well that he could only testify falsely' – and he admitted the incident. When she objected to another accuser as a 'bad man' whose brother had beaten her, he denied that he had ever litigated against her.

Over the next nine days, Montgaillard's officials continued to ratify accusations against the five women who refused to confess. Three more men and three women, including the parents and the village midwife, testified about the Cat's most recent exploit involving the death of a baby. On 16 November, a notary testified about an odd charge from 1639, when the Cat reputedly wounded a man in his sleep after he had threatened her with his sword. But overall, Montgaillard remained relatively calm until 3 December, when Nane de Mathieu was finally sentenced to death. Both she and her trial (which apparently has not survived, apart from the extracts which accused her 'accomplices') were sent to the Parlement of Toulouse for confirmation.

Montgaillard saw a final flurry of legal depositions over the next nine days as the village prepared its cases against the five prisoners and others whom Nane had accused. On 9 December, fresh (but very old) charges were levelled against both Dalabert sisters. A man had taken Germaine to court nineteen or twenty years previously for causing his child's death; she claimed she could not recall the episode. Similarly, she could not remember curing a spell which she had cast fifteen years earlier with an onion. But Marie, as always, had the most difficult time. Three old men recalled that a very odd hailstorm had struck Montgaillard back in August 1618 and ruined the wine harvest, and wondered if she had caused it. There were further ratifications and a confrontation with the parents of the 7-week-old girl who had died the previous November.

On 12 December 1643, Montgaillard wrapped up its cases against everyone accused of witchcraft. Maître Vital Dufere, Doctor of Civil Law, who charged the hefty sum of ten *écus* for his services, convinced the village officials to pronounce death sentences against both Dalabert sisters. They were to make official apologies for their crimes at the parish church, each barefoot and holding a large candle, before being strangled and their bodies burned. The Duchess, with a shorter list of malefices on her record, was to be whipped and banished for five years. La Boubellotte and the Dove, both charged by Nane de Mathieu with attending sabbats but without sustained accusations of malefices, were spared whippings but similarly banished for five years. The property of all five women was to be confiscated. Minor charges against two other women and two men were handed over to the Parlement of Toulouse, accompanying the five women who were physically sent to Toulouse for final judgement.

The Dalabert sisters and their Montgaillard companions were relatively fortunate, because their cases were judged at a moment when this appellate court was practising damage control on witchcraft accusations. The Parlement's appointed judge, Maître Delaporte, pronounced their final sentences on 28 January 1644.[2] All charges against la Boubellotte, the Duchess and the Dove were dismissed (in legal language, *hors de cour et de procès*). The Parlement ruled that evidence against the Dalabert sisters was insufficient to convict them and prolonged their case for a fortnight in order to produce further proofs. Apparently no conclusive evidence was forthcoming, because no further rulings were made in their cases, leading one to presume that they, like others at this time, were quietly discharged or at worst banished briefly from their parish.

FEATURES OF CONTINENTAL WITCH TRIALS

This cluster of cases at Montgaillard in late 1643 contains many features which illustrate major aspects of continental witch trials as they reached their peak during the century after 1560. First, these trials were often closely linked. A single arrest in early October led directly to four further imprisonments; after the original suspect made a full confession, a fifth person was arrested and four more were accused. Second, all of those imprisoned, and eight of the ten persons involved, were older women living in a remote village. Third, the original pressure to arrest suspected witches came from within the village; local officials maintained the hunt, but they did not start it. We never learn the names of Nane de Mathieu's original accusers, but the subsequent *monitoires* at the village church soon coaxed accusations from both young (the first recorded witness was a girl of 19) and old (the loudest witness against the Cat was at least 60). Fourth, many of those accused were not arrested and many of those arrested were not sentenced to death, even at the local level. Fifth, many of the penalties decreed against witches by local authorities, even with careful and expensive legal help, were likely to be overturned if they reached an appellate court: the Parlement of Toulouse, which supervised Montgaillard, upheld fewer than one sentence in ten against accused witches during the panic of 1643–5 (Vidal 1987) – and only because their written trial records had to be sent to Toulouse together with the prisoners can we learn anything about these cases. Let us consider each of these general aspects in turn.

Because Languedoc, like many other parts of continental Europe, conducted its criminal trials under principles of Roman or 'civil' law, the village of Montgaillard had to hire an expensive expert before presenting its cases against these five women to the Parlement of Toulouse. Both the village and the Parlement followed what is technically known as inquisitorial procedure, and concluded most trials with 'arbitrary' rulings. It is important for people raised under the Anglo-American system of adversarial justice and jury decisions to realize two things: first, that inquisitorial rulings did not strip the accused of her or his rights to a full defence against specific accusers; and second, that 'arbitrary' rulings by judges were not inherently less fair than a decision by a jury of one's peers. Indeed, in the specific context of continental witch trials, one could easily argue that arbitrary decisions were overall more lenient towards defendants than jury decisions.

Inquisitorial justice meant that investigations, arrests and hearings were carried out through an official inquiry, or *inquisitio*, rather than being the legal responsibility of a private accuser. If a French judge could not name individual accusers, he was assumed to have acted from some personal vendetta and therefore suffered heavy penalties (at Montgaillard, everyone arrested had at least two unrelated accusers). Defendants charged with witchcraft normally had ample opportunity to impugn their accusers. The most serious charges had to be maintained under oath in face-to-face confrontations which often generated high drama; at Montgaillard, when

Nane de Mathieu faced the five imprisoned women whom she had accused of attending sabbats with her, she had a bitter exchange with Germaine Dalabert, while Marie Dalabert vituperated the spiteful old man who so clearly recalled an evil spell which she had cast on him more than twenty years ago.

Arbitrary justice in witch trials offered a method for letting the punishment fit not the crime but the degree of proof. Nane de Mathieu apparently made a full and 'voluntary' confession without being tortured, which obliged her judges even at Toulouse to decree the maximum punishment. However, no one else at Montgaillard confessed to attending sabbats; none was searched for the devil's mark; and none admitted casting any evil spells. Under such circumstances, 'arbitrary' justice attempted to tailor the punishments to the seriousness of the evidence against each subject. At the village level, this situation created four levels of punishment ranging from hanging and burning, to public whipping with banishment, on down to simple banishment and finally to suspending judgement because of insufficient evidence. But at the appellate level in Toulouse, the same evidence produced a two-tiered set of equally arbitrary rulings, postponement for those most seriously accused and dismissal for the others.

The essential charges against accused witches involved two different but complementary aspects, malefices and sabbats. The former, evil spells cast and sometimes lifted by witches, was the older element, virtually omnipresent across villages in western and central Europe long before 1560 and long after 1660. At Montgaillard, the original charges against Nane de Mathieu revolved around two suspected malefices, and the subsequent *monitoire* unearthed additional charges against three other women. But specific malefice was very hard to prove under Roman law; precisely because its effects were supernatural, they could not be demonstrated by ordinary rules of evidence. At best, one could use bits of physical evidence in the possession of accused witches; but if Nane de Mathieu claimed that the substances confiscated from her private chest were cosmetics, no one could really prove the contrary. Suspects were rarely caught with genuinely poisonous substances or bits of magical writings in their possession – but those unlucky few almost invariably suffered the full penalties of the law.

If malefice was difficult to prove, attendance at sabbats was even harder, unless the suspect confessed. Sabbats were nocturnal, often distant, vague events for which no possible physical corroborative evidence existed, apart from testimony by those who had attended one. As *ipso facto* confessed witches, such people also suffered the full penalties of the law, unless they happened to be children – and then, under Roman law, their testimony should not be believed. The concept of the witches' sabbat, still little known at the time of the *Malleus Maleficarum* (*Hammer of Witches*), became a central feature of witchcraft doctrine among such subsequent western European demonologists as Bodin (1580), Binsfeld (1589), or Rémy (1595). At about the same time, it also seems to have become increasingly important in witch trials. Before 1587, the Parlement of Paris, Europe's most prestigious court, questioned over half of those accused witches whom it eventually ordered executed about the sabbat; afterwards, questions about sabbats occurred in nearly 90 per cent of cases where it sentenced accused witches to death. Among the much larger group of accused witches whom the Paris Parlement failed to execute, questions about sabbats appeared in only 20 per cent of cases before 1587, subsequently rising above 50 per cent (Soman 1993). The importance of the sabbat at Montgaillard is obvious. As many scholars have pointed out, it was an expedient way to multiply accusations and trials for witchcraft; here, in 1643, it turned one trial into six. However, it also seems worth emphasizing that increased stress on the concept of the witches' sabbat did not necessarily imply increasing severity in judging the resulting witch trials; at the Parlement of Paris, only twelve among the hundreds of accused witches whom it questioned about sabbats after 1610 were ordered to be executed. Interest about the witches' sabbat increased after 1580, at the same time as witch trials and executions were multiplying across much of central and western Europe. But the cause–effect relationship was far from being automatic.

The huge differences in trials and executions of witches between the two largest regions of western Europe – the kingdom of France and the 'Holy Roman Empire of the German Nation' – masks major similarities between them. In both places, the impulse to hunt witches came primarily from beneath, from prominent people in local villages. Such local agendas were easily and willingly accommodated by local courts, but not by regional governments; higher court systems, as at Toulouse, were frequently critical of the primary-level village courts which they supervised. For a legal scholar, the major difference between France and the Empire is that the former had a court system which was thoroughly centralized, while the latter was extremely decentralized. One example should suffice to illustrate the enormous difference in practical consequences between local self-government and appellate justice. At the opposite extreme from French parlements, which generally rejected village testimony, stood the 550 villages and eleven small towns which today comprise Germany's Saarland. During the half-century after 1580, these virtually autonomous rustics executed 450 per cent more witches than the Parlement of Paris, in a corner of the Empire divided among four principal overlords, two Protestant and two Catholic (Labouvie 1991). Throughout the Saarland, witch-hunting remained firmly controlled by village authorities, usually operating through a system of special committees or *ausschüsse*, which a recent historian (Rummel 1991) has aptly labelled 'village Inquisitions'. In this region, testimony about witches' sabbats remained uncommon until the late sixteenth century, being employed first by younger people; but it spread quite rapidly after 1600. Thus the importance of the sabbat increased sharply at the village level in both central France and western Germany precisely when witch trials began to multiply around the end of the sixteenth century. We cannot say to what extent these French and German villagers grasped the theological implications of the concept of witchcraft as devil-worship which regional demonologists had been vigorously promoting since 1580; but it is painfully obvious just how eager they became around this time to learn about their neighbour's dealings with the Evil One.

WITCHCRAFT AND THE REFORMATIONS

It is frequently claimed that witch trials multiplied across much of central and western Europe because of the religious fanaticism engendered by both the Protestant and Catholic Reformations, which disastrously exacerbated the fears of an ignorant and suspicious peasantry. While it is difficult to deny some kind of connection between these movements, which had such profound effects on all layers of European society, and the concurrent wave of witch trials across much of western and central Europe, the exact relationship between these phenomena remains elusive. It is undeniable that both Protestant and Catholic governments sponsored witch-hunting. Sometimes, as in the Saarland, Catholic overlords (the Duke of Lorraine and the Archbishop of Trier) were more likely to sponsor witch-hunts than Protestant sovereigns (in this case, the Lutheran Count of Nassau and the Calvinist Count of Zweibrucken). But in other regions, for example French-speaking western Switzerland, Protestant rulers were more severe than Catholic overlords in prosecuting witches (Monter 1976). The majority of Europe's witch trials and executions took place in the century after 1560, coinciding with Europe's wars of religion in France and the Low Countries, and frequently rose to a crescendo during the Thirty Years War. It has therefore been tempting to conclude that Europe's great witch-hunt was simply one tragic social consequence of its religious conflicts (Trevor-Roper 1967). However, any correlation between these two phenomena is far from direct. In the first place, the outbreak of warfare, whether or not religiously motivated, temporarily ended witch trials whenever and wherever it occurred. War disrupted all normal government activity. In the Saarland, for example, witch-hunting ended abruptly in the mid-1630s and did not resume for 30 years, because the region was so badly devastated that it lost up to four-fifths of its population. Subtler connections must be found.

Let us rethink the problem, starting from the fact that the two greatest leaders of the Protestant Reformation, Luther and Calvin, both explicitly approved the conduct of witch trials in their respective residences of Wittenberg and Geneva in the early 1540s. Since the papacy had officially approved the *Malleus Maleficarum* 60 years previously (or so its authors and publishers claimed) and Holy Scripture apparently threatened witches with death (Exodus 22:18), there was no reason for any major sixteenth-century theologian to doubt the reality of witchcraft, although no socially responsible theologian would deliberately provoke witch-hunts. So what, if anything, connects the Protestant Reformation, which occupied centre stage in most of Europe after 1520, to the rapid increase in witch trials in most of Europe during the century after 1560?

If we reconceptualize the religious history of western Europe after 1560, traditionally known as the age of religious warfare, under its newer general label as the age of confessionalism, we can sketch a different picture. Long after Luther's defiance of the papacy in 1520, the Protestant Reformation remained essentially a movement which was often repressed vigorously by major governments in western Europe. While thousands perished for heresy across western Europe between 1520 and the early 1560s (Monter 1999), governments rarely sponsored witch trials. But the movement evolved into several organized churches, each with elaborate dogmatic codes designed to separate itself from the unorthodox. Protestant confessionalism seems to have flourished most vigorously around 1560, just when Catholicism was redefining itself through the Council of Trent. Confessionalism meant well-trained clergy systematically indoctrinating precisely defined creeds. The Reformation transformed itself into well-organized and well-disciplined churches, most of which were under state control. These Protestant governments soon entered into long and ultimately inconclusive armed conflict with Catholic states. Both kinds of states relied heavily on their clergy to support their respective war efforts, and both sets of clergy responded enthusiastically.

Regardless of whether or not their governments were officially at war, Europe's rival confessions competed constantly with each other in demonstrating religious zeal. The need to discipline members who failed to meet confessional norms created a climate in which overt repression of religious deviance increased. Witchcraft – an extremely dangerous form of Christian apostasy – now became a much-feared form of religious deviance, in addition to the social dangers which maleficent magic had always posed. Under such conditions, theologians of all confessions warned about an alarming increase in witchcraft; a few of them, for example the Calvinist

Lambert Daneau or the Jesuit Martin Del Río, even composed demonologies, while a great many others preached sermons on the subject. Although the role of confessionalism in encouraging witch-hunting remained indirect, mainstream Protestant and Catholic Churches exerted much energy across the 'confessional century' after 1560 in catechizing their membership and reinforcing an awareness of sin and diabolical temptations in both oneself and others (Delumeau 1978). Parishioners' fears of immoral activities, among which witchcraft occupied a uniquely powerful place, increased; as we have seen in the Saarland and northern France, awareness of the witches' sabbats spread at the local level. Overt warfare between confessions, however, was extraneous to this process and actually interfered with it.

THREE-QUARTERS GERMAN? EUROPEAN WITCH TRIALS 1560–1660

All regions of western Europe and all confessions proved able and willing to conduct trials and executions for witchcraft after 1560, but much confusion persists about just how extensive witch-hunting actually was and even more about where it was concentrated. Although the actual figures are ghastly enough without embellishment, the temptation to exaggerate the size of Europe's witch-hunts has proved almost irresistible. Even the best recent syntheses (Muchembled 1993: 73–6; Levack 1995: 21–6) continue to mislead readers with inflated estimates. Although serious historians have repeatedly demolished the figure of nine million executed witches – originally proposed by an eighteenth-century German author extrapolating from a single incident, which he misread (Behringer 1998b) – it still reappears from time to time in sensationalist accounts.

Meanwhile, even the best experts continue to recycle such wildly exaggerated numbers as the fifteen thousand supposed trials and ten thousand executions for witchcraft in the kingdom of Poland. This fantastic estimate was created, much like the general figure of nine million, by arbitrary and implausible extrapolations from a small sample of preserved witch trials (Klaniczay 1994: 219). The one aspect of this sample that seems useable is its chronology, which suggests that Poland's record was essentially similar to that of its carefully studied southern neighbour, Hungary, with recorded trials and executions peaking in both places around 1700. Neither kingdom ever produced a witch-hunt of international notoriety, and both contained a comparable proportion of Germanophone subjects, who tended to hold the earliest witch trials in east-central Europe. If the pre-1750 kingdom of Poland (substracting its Jews and its Orthodox Christians, neither of whom produced witch trials) was roughly twice as populous as the kingdom of Hungary, one might reasonably expect about twice as many executions for witchcraft in Poland as in Hungary – which had about five hundred. This revised estimate for Poland lowers the original estimate by about 90 per cent.

Although few other estimates must be downsized so radically, the totals proposed in our best-known recent synthesis – about 110,000 trials and 60,000 executions for witchcraft in all of Europe (Levack 1995: 21–6) – should be reduced by at least one-third. The epicentre of European witch-hunting lay overwhelmingly in the Germanic core of the Holy Roman Empire. Here, using SS files (which we shall discuss shortly), cross-checked against surviving documentation, Germany's leading expert has established a baseline figure of about 15,000 confirmed witchcraft executions within contemporary Germany; after allowing for lacunae in his sources, he arrived at an estimated total of somewhere between 20,000 and 25,000 executions for witchcraft in the area corresponding to present-day Germany, of which 90 per cent occurred between 1560 and 1660 (Behringer 1994). Although our most reliable estimate therefore proposes 22,500 executions from 1560, it should probably circulate at a modest discount, since this author occasionally rounds an estimate upwards.[3] But even when shrunk by perhaps 10 per cent, this German figure dwarfs the number of witchcraft executions between 1560 and 1660 in other parts of Christendom.

Everywhere outside the Holy Roman Empire, these totals seem relatively modest. Several other parts of Christendom have been very well studied in this respect; we have reliable numbers of witches tried and executed in such places as Hungary (but almost nowhere else in east-central Europe), Portugal (but nowhere else in southern Europe), Scandinavia, the Netherlands, some parts of France and most of the British Isles. There were more than a thousand executions for witchcraft apiece in the kingdoms of Denmark and Scotland, but only a few hundred executions apiece in the kingdoms of England or Sweden, and fewer than 500 in Norway, Finland, Estonia-Livonia and Iceland combined. All of northern Europe executed about three thousand witches, many of them in major witch-hunts after 1660 in Scotland and Sweden. Hungary also executed most of its 500 witches after 1660. These figures are 'pre-shrunk' by allowing for lacunae in the available evidence, and, apart from Denmark, far below what we formerly believed. But they do not cover much of western, southern or eastern Europe between 1560 and 1660.

What happened in the largest and most populous state of early modern Europe, the kingdom of France? We know that the Parlement of Paris, which supervised justice in half of the kingdom and whose records are complete, ordered barely a hundred witches executed (Soman 1992). Although some other French provinces, such as Normandy (Monter

1997), hunted witches more zealously, the total number of witches legally executed throughout the kingdom of France before 1650 remained under five hundred. Levack's estimate of 10,000 trials and 5,000 executions in the regions comprising present-day France needs to be cut by about half, while the vast majority of these 'French' trials and executions need to be moved inside the western boundary of the pre-1648 Holy Roman Empire, where they may be added to bring Behringer's slimmed-down figures for 'German' executions back to his original level of 22,500.

What of southern Europe? We have precise figures only for Portugal, which executed a grand total of exactly seven witches, six of them in 1559–60 (Bethencourt 1990: 406). We know that witch-hunting was endemic along the Spanish Pyrenees, with more than a hundred witches executed in Catalonia between 1610 and 1625; however, the Spanish Inquisition, which vigorously battled local lay courts for control of such trials, displayed a consistently sceptical attitude towards all aspects of witchcraft and permitted barely two dozen executions for maleficient witchcraft or *brujería* between 1498 and 1610 (Henningsen 1980; Monter 1990). The situation in Italy was broadly comparable, with small numbers of witches executed sporadically in subalpine regions, but virtually none by order of the Roman Inquisition. In eastern Europe, there is no evidence of extensive witch-hunting until after the mid-seventeenth century (and almost all of its early trials occurred in German-speaking enclaves). Overall, therefore, we should probably add about a thousand executions for witchcraft between 1560 and 1660 from western, southern and eastern Europe to the nearly 3,000 instances from northern Europe (whose single largest pre-1660 cluster, we recall, came from Denmark).

What remains is central Europe, *Mitteleuropa*, most of it loosely housed under the political umbrella of the Holy Roman Empire. This ramshackle polity included every European region extensively involved in witch-hunting before 1660, except Denmark (which of course bordered it) and Scotland. Most regions from the first Reich were incorporated into Hitler's Third Reich (along with traditionally Germanophone enclaves in east-central Europe) and therefore had the dubious privilege of having their judicial records surveyed for witch trials by one of the strangest Nazi creations, the *Hexen-sonderkommando*. It remains unclear whether Himmler started this special SS branch primarily in order to accumulate anti-Christian propaganda against both Evangelicals and Catholics, or whether he wanted to learn what insights witch trials might offer into Germany's 'natural' pre-Christian beliefs; the Nazis were Europe's first 'pro-witch' government, using 'witches' as cheerleaders to accompany their massive rallies of the 1930s (Behringer 1998b). In any event, the SS produced an investigation of unique breadth into Germany's surviving witch trials, accumulating over 30,000 dossiers of trial summaries which survived the war, slumbering undisturbed in Poland until a West German scholar revealed their existence (Schormann 1981: 8–16). Although full of repetitions, errors of all sorts, and useless remarks about the 'race' of witches, these SS dossiers provide an unparalleled mine of information about the extent and geographical distribution of witch-hunts within the first German Reich.[4]

However, these figures exclude many significant parts of the old 'Holy Roman Empire of the German Nation'. An especially important case is the Swiss Confederation, which did not sever its legal connections to the Empire until 1648. While Levack's estimate for Switzerland – over 5,000 witches executed – also needs to be downsized by about one-third, this small country, the apparent birthplace of European witch-hunting in the first half of the fifteenth century, continued to be disproportionately active in executing witches throughout the century after 1560 and well beyond. Before they too formally broke all ties to the Empire in 1648, the seventeen autonomous provinces of the formerly united Low Countries executed several hundred witches, mostly in its southern, French-speaking provinces after 1592. Although Switzerland's eastern neighbour, present-day Austria, the patrimonial base of the Habsburgs, also belonged to the Empire, its most intensive witch-hunts took place only after 1660. However, the western edges of the Holy Roman Empire which have become parts of France since 1648 (principally, but not exclusively, Alsace and Lorraine) seem extremely important from the perspective of witch-hunting, adding nearly 3,000 executions for witchcraft between 1560 and 1660. Together, these additional regions of the pre-1648 Holy Roman Empire add almost 7,000 pre-1660 executions to Behringer's slimmed-down 'German' estimate.

This enlarged definition of the old Holy Roman Empire includes every known major centre of witch-hunting in Christendom until the mid-seventeenth century, except Scotland and Denmark. When added to Behringer's estimate of 20,000 witchcraft executions in present-day Germany between 1560 and 1660, these 7,000 victims make the volume of witch trials in this enlarged version of the Holy Roman Empire during the confessional century completely dwarf those across the remainder of Christendom. The rest of Europe combined – the great monarchies of England, France and Spain, all of Scandinavia, all of Mediterranean Europe, all of eastern Europe – probably executed fewer than 5,000 witches between 1560 and 1660. Demographers generally estimate the total population of Europe around 1600 as a hundred million people, of whom about twenty million apiece lived in the kingdom of France and the enlarged version of the Holy Roman Empire, with most of the remainder clustered in southern Europe rather than the more thinly populated North and East.

Conventional wisdom among the experts therefore seems emphatically correct. Present-day Germany, particularly when enlarged to include other parts of the pre-1648 Holy Roman Empire of the German Nation, truly was *tot Sagarum Mater*, 'mother of so many witches', as Friedrich Spee, the great Jesuit critic of witch trials, wrote in 1631. Or, as Germany's leading expert observed more recently, 'witchcraft is as "German" as the Hitler-phenomenon, and will similarly occupy our attention for a while longer' (Behringer 1989: 639). Despite the notorious inaccuracy of early modern statistics, these estimates – between 25,000 and 30,000 witches executed in the Empire and fewer than 5,000 in the rest of Christendom during the confessional century (1560–1660) – contain a margin of error no greater than 20 per cent. To put it differently: three of every four witches executed in Europe between 1560 and 1660 spoke some dialect of German, while six of every seven lived – and died – within the boundaries of the pre-1648 Holy Roman Empire, a region holding about 20 per cent of Europe's population.

A GERMAN *SONDERWEG*?

How did this situation develop? Germans sometimes describe their history as a *sonderweg*, a path different from other, more ordinary European states. But every country's history is different from every other's; no part of Europe can legitimately claim to be normal or standard. This sprawling Empire, known to contemporaries under the plural form of 'the Germanies', was actually a federation of more than 300 autonomous governments under the largely ceremonial leadership of its elected Kaiser. At first glance, locating the main features in the history of witch-hunting within this daunting political labyrinth – filled with secular princes of various ranks and sizes, an almost equal number of ecclesiastical princes of various sizes and titles, nearly a hundred free cities and many more autonomous knights, an empire in which many territories were riddled with enclaves and where condominiums (jointly ruled districts) abounded – seems a hopeless task. But a few of its major features with respect to witch trials have begun to swim into focus. Two aspects deserve particular attention. First, there is no evidence that the German core of the Holy Roman Empire played a dominant role in witch-hunting before 1560. Second, the massive trials and executions for witchcraft which occurred after 1560 were distributed extremely unevenly over the Empire; almost half of Behringer's estimated 20,000 executions took place in a handful of its territories. Five governments accounted for almost 8,000 deaths; if we add two small ecclesiastical principalities ruled simultaneously by the same prelate from 1612 to 1636, we approach 9,000.

All these territories at the apex of German witch-hunts shared key features. They were headed by the three western archbishoprics (Mainz, Cologne and Trier), whose rulers were also the Empire's three ecclesiastical electors. If Trier began Germany's first general campaign against witches in the 1580s, the seventeenth-century persecutions of witches in the lands of the Elector of Cologne probably outstripped anything else in the Empire, or indeed in the rest of Christendom. The other four states of heaviest witch-hunting also belonged to ecclesiastical princes. But it would be naïve to assume that these Catholic prelates governed their secular subjects with anything approaching the bureaucratic thoroughness of Germany's major secular states. In other words, the most severe witch panics during the confessional century correlate not only with regions ruled by Counter-Reformation prelates, but also – and probably more importantly – with areas of notoriously loose government control.

Moreover, the worst witch-hunts among secular (often Protestant) princes or among Imperial free cities also occurred in smaller or medium-sized territories which similarly lacked strong central authority. Back in 1972, Erik Midelfort pointed out that among the immensely complicated chequerboard of autonomous governments within today's south-western German *Land* of Baden-Württemburg, neither the very largest nor the very smallest territories conducted important witch-hunts. Instead, 'trials that executed ten or more in one year occurred in middle-sized territories', whose rulers included Catholic prelates, Protestant lords and some of the region's small free cities (Midelfort 1972: 80–1). A generation later, this observation remains valid. The Prince-Abbot of Ellwangen alone accounted for one-ninth of the 3,229 known executions for witchcraft throughout Baden-Württemburg. Two other smaller Catholic prelates also instigated genuine witch-hunting panics: the monastery of Obermarchtal (whose territory of ten tiny settlements contained barely 350 adults) executed over 50 witches between 1586 and 1588 and 30 more afterwards; the Teutonic Knights at Mergentheim executed 114 witches between 1628 and 1630 during a panic inspired by developments in the neighbouring bishopric of Würzburg. But if a handful of Catholic prelates compiled the highest death totals in south-western Germany, a few self-governing cities, ruling territories no larger than the Teutonic Knights at Mergentheim, were not far behind. Rottenburg executed at least 150 witches between 1578 and 1609; Rottweil executed 113 in thirty different years between 1566 and 1648.

However, as Midelfort also saw, witch trials were comparatively rare among the largest secular principalities in the Empire. Not only does this statement apply to such large and relatively well-governed Protestant states as the duchy of Württemburg in the south-west and to all three Protestant electorates (Brandenburg, Saxony and the Palatinate), but it also extends to the largest Catholic duchies such as Bavaria and most of the hereditary Habsburg lands comprising present-day Austria. In north-western Germany, the large duchy of Cleve-Mark, Jülich and Berg, home of Europe's best-known sixteenth-century critic of witch trials, seldom prosecuted witches even after becoming Catholic after 1600. As Wolfgang Behringer noted, this record in Germany's largest secular territories was 'completely independent of their religion, their economic structure, of relations between the sexes, or other divergent determining phenomena; in these large states, witch trials were invariably controlled by secular jurisdictions, known by a variety of titles but performing essentially the same functions' (Behringer 1994: 87–8). Like their counterparts in the great monarchies of western Europe, such institutions normally behaved with exemplary caution when confronted with the phenomenon of witchcraft.

In order to explore the history of witch-hunting from 1560 to 1660 across the sprawling political labyrinth of the Holy Roman Empire, where this phenomenon was so heavily concentrated, we shall begin by examining the situation in the Empire with respect to witchcraft and witch trials around 1560. We will focus next on the huge witch-hunts conducted in the lands of Catholic prelates, concluding with the paroxysm of such hunts in the Rhine basin from 1627 to 1632. We will then contrast the history of witch trials in the best-studied large secular principality, the duchy of Bavaria. After a brief look at confessionalism and appellate justice in the Empire, we will turn to the history of witch trials along its western (and often French-speaking) borderlands, including its autonomous south-western and north-western corners, the Swiss Confederation and the Low Countries.

1563: WEYER AND WIESENSTEIG

When investigating the history of continental European witch trials after 1560, one must remember that the German core of the Holy Roman Empire had no tradition of priority in witch-hunting before 1560. We are reasonably confident today that the 'classical' doctrine of witchcraft crystallized during the middle third of the fifteenth century, shortly after the Council of Basel, primarily within a western Alpine zone centred around the duchy of Savoy (Ostorero *et al.* 1999). Geographically, it soon spread as far north as the Low Countries in the famous *Vauderie* of Arras and as far east as Austria, where Institoris did the fieldwork for his infamous *Malleus Maleficarum*, published in 1487. By the end of the fifteenth century, scattered trials for witchcraft by both secular and ecclesiastical courts occurred in many places from the Pyrenees, where the Spanish Inquisition had become involved, to the North Sea. Germany was emphatically not the centre of this activity; Institoris encountered enormous hostility in the Austrian Alps, and absolutely no evidence exists that the publication of his *Malleus* started any chain of trials anywhere in the Empire.

Furthermore, during the first sixty years of the sixteenth century, witchcraft was not the most significant concern of public officials in the Empire. Instead, Martin Luther and his Reformation movement, soon to become a new type of church, occupied centre stage. In addition, radical Anabaptists, who frightened Luther and his Catholic opponents alike, provoked repressive measures of unprecedented severity; they were hunted with zeal and rage by several governments in the aftermath of the 1525 Peasants' War. Almost a thousand of them were executed in the Empire between 1527 and 1533, mostly by Habsburg officials, near those same regions where Institoris had met so much opposition two generations earlier (Clasen 1972: 373ff). Immediately afterwards, Anabaptists were also executed in large numbers in the Low Countries. Meanwhile, however, one hears little about prosecutions of witches.

Where were witch trials being held in Christendom during the zenith of the Reformation era between 1520 and 1560? Small numbers of them were conducted in many different places. Several regions where witches had been tried before 1500 continued to hold them; for example, the Spanish Pyrenees, where a witch-hunt in the recently conquered kingdom of Navarre provoked a major policy debate and, ultimately, intervention by the Spanish Inquisition. Similar developments in northern Italy also generated considerable debate in the 1520s. Meanwhile, new regions were affected; for example, the kingdom of Denmark held a spate of such trials in the late 1540s and executed the relatively large total of 60 witches.

Between 1520 and 1560, witch trials seem to have been relatively frequent in the two autonomous western corners of the Empire, Switzerland and the Low Countries. The largest known groups of witch trials during Charles V's reign occurred in such obscure provinces of the Low Countries as Namur (117 trials, with 34 burned and 33 banished) or Gelderland, where twenty witches were executed in the Ommelanden in 1547. The Gelderland panic ranked among the worst of its kind in Europe – certainly in the Empire – during these years. One also finds witches executed in some major cities of the Low Countries, for example Utrecht (four, in 1533) or Amsterdam (four, in 1555).

In Switzerland, the rustic 'forest cantons' of the original Confederation apparently remained unaffected by witch trials until after 1560. Meanwhile, Zwingli's Zurich saw 29 witch trials and eight executions between 1500 and 1539. There were at least ten executions for witchcraft at Bern in the first half of the sixteenth century; the Catholic capital of the Confederation, Lucerne, had a comparable record. Basel, the city of

Erasmus, executed six witches in eight trials between 1500 and 1550. In the largely Protestant regions which today form French Switzerland, witch trials, already traditional in such places as the Pays de Vaud, moved smoothly from ecclesiastical courts in the 1520s to secular courts in the 1530s; however, only a handful of executions have been recorded during these decades. Geneva, for example, recorded only nine deaths for witchcraft between 1520 and 1560, despite Calvin's personal intervention in 1545 urging the magistrates to 'extirpate the race' of witches from a rural district governed by the Republic of Geneva.

If witch trials occurred before 1560 at both ends of the Rhine in the Low Countries and the Swiss Confederation, they happened relatively rarely in between. Although there were trials to the west (eighteen known executions in the duchy of Lorraine between 1545 and 1552) and as far north as Denmark, very few witches were executed in the German heartlands of the Empire during the Reformation era. Meticulous tabulations list barely 30 deaths across south-western Germany, with the largest group occurring between 1547 and 1555 on the Swiss border, in the former Imperial Free City of Constance (Midelfort 1972: 201–2). Farther east (and farther from Switzerland), equally careful research on Bavaria lists only two or three confirmed executions for witchcraft before 1560 (Behringer 1987: 433–4).[5]

Against this chronological and geographical background we must now place two fateful German events of 1563. From the Netherlands border came the huge, magnificent summa of Johann Weyer, *De Praestigiis Daemonum* (*On the Tricks of Devils*), Europe's most comprehensive attack on the witch-belief and witch-persecutions. Although first printed at Basel in 1563, Weyer's work must be set against the background of current witch-hunting in the Low Countries. Meanwhile, from the small county of Helfenstein in south-western Germany came an anonymous pamphlet, *The True and Horrifying Deeds and Activities of Sixty-three Witches, Who Have Been Executed by Fire in Wiesensteig*, also printed in 1563. Renaissance Europe's most important attack on the doctrine of witchcraft and Reformation Germany's first major witch-hunt arrived simultaneously. Curiously, both would remain relatively isolated events in Germany for nearly twenty years.

This is not the place for an appreciation of the novelty and merits of Weyer's arguments, which may be found in Part 3 of this volume. But it is appropriate to look briefly at the practical consequences of these arguments within the Holy Roman Empire. First, it is noteworthy that Weyer proved something of a prophet in his own country, which in his case meant the united duchy of Cleve-Mark, Jülich and Berg, a scattered chunk of lands with a population of nearly 400,000, spanning the Rhine as it entered the Low Countries. This state, ruled from 1539 to 1592 by

Weyer's employer, the Erasmian Duke William V, remained immune to witch-hunting even after passing to zealously Catholic overlords after his death. Although its southern neighbour, the electorate of Cologne, staged the largest witch-hunt in the Empire around 1630, Weyer's old duchy remained quiet.

Printed as the Council of Trent was closing, Weyer's work belonged to a preconfessional age which was rapidly overtaken by events across the Empire. Both its Latin and German versions had come from Basel, at that time one of the largest centres of Reformed-Church printing in Europe and certainly in the Empire. Its persuasiveness in the Empire during the confessional century correlates less with Weyer's own religious stance than with the limited adoption of the Reformed confession within the Empire. The largest and most important Reformed state in the Empire, the Palatinate, consistently followed Weyer's advice about witch trials. So, subsequently and in more general fashion, did the United Provinces of the northern Netherlands after consolidating their fragile independence in the 1590s. Since the Low Countries had been among the European regions most affected by witch trials when Weyer composed his treatise, the fact that his arguments ultimately carried more weight downstream from Cleves than up the Rhine is not without importance. In Switzerland, despite an influential Reformed Church, Weyer's impact was apparently nil outside the city of Basel.

The significance of the panic at Wiesensteig, where 40 more witches subsequently died long after the first huge persecution, remains elusive. Like Weyer's masterpiece, it remained an isolated event; no comparable outbreaks occurred elsewhere in the Empire around this time. However, it seems noteworthy that the first known witch-hunt in the kingdom of France began in the northern Pyrenees in the spring of 1562, a few months before the outbreak at Wiesensteig. Between April 1562 and February 1563, the Parlement of Toulouse judged on appeal at least three dozen accused witches from the diocese of Couserans.[6] The first two women were ordered hanged and burned; a third subsequently followed, while six early sentences (probably banishments) were also upheld. Sixteen women were subsequently ordered to make public apologies and banished for a few years, while another eleven women were ordered released. The results of the first known cluster of witch trials judged by a strongly Catholic sixteenth-century French appellate court – executing three witches, one at a time, and banishing two dozen others – contrasts sharply with Ulrich of Helfenstein's reported 63 executions. Both episodes, moreover, closely coincide with the first official criminalization of witch-craft in 1563 by the English Parliament. Apparently, witch-hunting revived in some Lutheran, Catholic and Anglican states almost simultaneously.

GERMANY'S 'SUPERHUNTS' (1586–1639)

A handful of huge witch-hunts, sponsored by the three archbishop-electors of western Germany and a few other prelates, accounted for over one-third of all executions for witchcraft in present-day Germany, and for almost a quarter of all such executions in Europe, during the century after 1560. This phenomenon was noticed by at least one seventeenth-century contemporary, himself a fugitive from the largest witch-hunt of all. 'The Roman Catholic subjects, farmers, winegrowers, and artisans in the episcopal lands are the most terrified people on earth,' noted Hermann Löher, 'since the false witch trials afflict the German episcopal lands incomparably more than France, Spain, Italy, or Protestants' (Schormann 1991: 108). These huge witch-hunts began in the lands of Johann VII von Schönenberg, Archbishop of Trier, in the mid-1580s and ended in the lands of Ferdinand of Bavaria, Archbishop of Cologne, in 1639. Between these dates, and almost midway between Trier and Cologne, several cycles of witch-hunting under consecutive Archbishops of Mainz between 1593 and 1631 resulted in approximately 1,500 deaths for witchcraft in this Electorate, surpassing the overall total for Trier and not far below the total for Cologne (Pohl 1988; Gebhard 1989).

What made some Catholic landed prelates, and especially their leaders, the three archbishop-electors, such remarkable witch-hunters? Not their religion. Seventeenth-century Germany's two most prominent and equally devout Catholic brothers, Maximilian and Ferdinand of Bavaria, took diametrically opposed positions on witch-hunting. After some hesitation, Maximilian effectively stifled witch-hunts in Germany's largest Catholic duchy during his long reign, while Ferdinand orchestrated the single largest witch-hunt in European history. The most persuasive explanation for such differences is that Catholic landed prelates were 'prisoners of their situation' (Rummel 1991) within the Empire. Their political weaknesses stemmed from two main causes. First, unlike secular princes, they had no heirs and thus no continuity in office. Second, their authority was often stymied by their chapters, who were permanent, irremovable and frequently pursued interests opposed to theirs. Thus the central governments of the great ecclesiastical princes were proverbial for their inefficiency, and their control over the large blocks of territory owing allegiance to them tended to be haphazard. At the same time, these prelates were spiritual as well as temporal lords: their moral obligation to improve the spiritual as well as the material environment of their subjects was more direct and more intense than for even the most paternalistic and zealous secular rulers. The resulting combination of inefficient government and heightened moral obligation defined the parameters within which these great landed prelates operated.

Of course, the material needs of their subjects also played a vital part in precipitating and sustaining witch-hunting. The Lutheran ruler who began Germany's first large witch-hunt had been enraged by the ruin of Wiesensteig's 1562 wine crop through a sudden and severe hailstorm which he and some of his subjects imputed to witchcraft. The archbishopric of Trier, located along the Mosel valley, included important wine-growing regions, vulnerable to hailstorms which could destroy a harvest within an hour. The remarkably lengthy and severe witch-hunts which afflicted the archbishopric of Trier during the 1580s and 1590s coincided with a prolonged cycle of extremely poor grain and wine harvests; in the eighteen years of Archbishop von Schönenberg's reign since 1581, noted a local chronicler, Trier had seen only two good harvests (Behringer 1993: 195–6).

Germany's first 'superhunt', unrolling against this gloomy backdrop of chronic dearth, seems noteworthy for several reasons. First, its scale was unprecedented; this was the first occasion in European history where we know the exact names and locations of hundreds of accused witches tried and executed in one small region within a few years, although unfortunately it would not be the last such instance. Second, it produced some peculiar twists in the social history of witchcraft and witches' sabbats. Last but not least, it generated theoretical treatments of witchcraft with significant consequences for German Catholicism in this confessional age.

The sheer scale of the persecutions in the lands of the Archbishop of Trier between the mid-1580s and early 1590s can best be approached through the elaborate register of suspects made for Claudius Musiel, a highly placed official, available in a recent critical edition (Voltmer and Weisenstein 1996); it lists over 6,000 accusations resulting from over 300 executions scattered across several districts of the electorate in a few years. Complementing it are more than a hundred surviving trial dossiers, including many names not found in Musiel's register. Although lacunae make exact totals impossible to calculate, it seems certain that no fewer than 500 and no more than 1,000 people were executed on charges of witchcraft in the electorate of Trier during von Schönenberg's reign. A 'spillover effect' from this witch-panic also affected neighbouring territories. In the duchy of Luxembourg, which shared a long frontier with the electorate of Trier, five Germanophone districts belonging ecclesiastically to the Archbishop of Trier tried over 150 witches between 1580 and 1599, while two Francophone districts within the same diocese tried only 23 witches and two other districts in the diocese of Liège tried only eight (Dupont-Bouchat 1978).

Because of its sheer scale, Europe's first 'superhunt' reached unusually far up the social ladder in searching out suspected witches. Musiel's register includes the names of some priests who were indicted and burned as witches; one of them, it seems, became the principal accuser of the most prominent victim of this panic – or, for that matter, the most prominent person executed for witchcraft anywhere in sixteenth-century Europe. Doctor Dietrich Flade, vice-rector of the University of Trier and former electoral councillor, was probably arrested because he and a few magistrates in the city of Trier had tried to obstruct the witch-hunters. A carefully orchestrated campaign produced numerous accusations by convicted witches that they had seen Dr Flade at the sabbat. Moreover, many of them insisted that he and his influential cronies flaunted their social rank at these diabolical assemblies. Instead of the broomsticks used by ordinary witches, they arrived in horse-drawn carriages, wearing expensive silks and furs, and enjoyed front-row seats while the devil exhorted his audience to do as many evil deeds as possible (Biesel 1993: 193–5). Under torture, Dr Flade made a full confession and was burned in 1587. His fate remained exceptional; although one encounters several wives of officials and even an occasional magistrate among the victims of subsequent German witch-hunts, this elaborate vendetta and the accompanying accusations about social discrimination at witches' sabbats found no real echo in the subsequent history of witch-hunting in the Empire.

The official orchestrating this 'superhunt' was not Trier's archbishop, but his vicar, Peter Binsfeld. In order to justify such an extensive prosecution and the burning of such prominent people, Binsfeld composed a short *Tractatus de confessionibus maleficorum et sagarum* (*Treatise on the Confessions of Witches and Sorcerers*), which he had printed at Trier in both Latin and German between 1589 and 1591. Although he claimed that the guilt of witches was 'clearer than the noonday sun', Binsfeld desired a more comprehensive and effective refutation of the heretical sceptic, Weyer, and hired a Dutch Catholic scholar named Cornelius Loos to compose one. However, Loos decided after reading him that Weyer was essentially correct, and he had begun printing his treatise at Cologne in 1593 when his furious patron managed to stop the presses and have all copies of the book destroyed. Loos was arrested and shipped to Trier, where he was compelled to perform a public abjuration in Binsfeld's presence. A stubborn man, Loos was soon imprisoned again at Brussels for his outspoken criticisms of witch trials (Behringer 1993: 205–7). The official silencing of this Catholic intellectual inadvertently solidified a Catholic confessional position about a previously unresolved issue, much as Galileo would subsequently do with Copernicanism.

From the archbishopric of Trier, which continued to prosecute witches sporadically until the 1630s, the pattern of major witch-hunts soon spread north-east to the archbishopric of Mainz. In this region, where executions for witchcraft were almost unknown before 1590, four main cycles of persecution occurred in 1593–8, 1601–5, 1611–18 and 1627–31, under five consecutive archbishops. As at Trier, much evidence from Mainz suggests that 'village Inquisitions' which indicted, tortured and convicted witches were primarily responsible for these trials, leaving the archbishop's officials with little to do except organize executions. At Mainz, the earliest prosecutions were directed overwhelmingly against women (only five men and 61 women were executed here in the 1590s), while men were more common among the final group of victims (30 per cent of the 141 people executed at Dieburg from 1627 to 1630).

As at Trier, there was a 'spillover effect' from Mainz into condominiums ruled jointly with secular lords and even into such Lutheran lands as Büdingen. In fact, the worst outbreak under Archbishop Adam von Bicken (1601–5) occurred in the condominium of Alzenau, comprising thirteen small villages east of Frankfurt which he ruled jointly with the Calvinist Counts of Hanau: in 40 months, no fewer than 139 witches (thirteen of them men) were burned at Alzenau – almost one adult in ten and one adult woman in every six. However, the persecutions in the archbishopric of Mainz apparently peaked only after 1626, lasting until Swedish troops captured Mainz in December 1631. An outbreak of plague then severely depopulated the archbishopric and effectively paralysed witch-hunting for over a decade.

The habit of 'superhunts' ultimately spread downstream from Mainz into the electorate of Cologne, which was ruled for over 30 years by Ferdinand of Bavaria, who became its vicar in 1607 and its archbishop in 1612. To a greater extent than at Trier or Mainz, the Cologne witch-hunts of the late 1620s and 1630s were instigated by a deliberate campaign from the archbishop's government in Bonn. General regulations governing witch trials were issued for both major sections of the archbishop's lands in 1629, and we have records of eleven special commissioners working in one district and ten more working in the other during the next few years. One of them, Heinrich von Schultheiss, published a 500-page *Instruction* for hunting witches in Cologne in 1634. The author had worked for the Archbishop of Mainz before transferring to Cologne in 1616; he remained involved in witch-hunting, principally in the eastern 'Sauerland', the duchy of Westphalia, for almost a decade after publishing his legal guide (Schormann 1991: 59, 69, 79–80).

Despite a greater degree of government initiative, it was as true of Cologne as of Trier or Mainz that no large-scale witch-hunt could be conducted successfully without full co-operation from village authorities. Ferdinand's electorate offers vivid testimony for this proposition, since one of his most zealous special commissioners, Dr Kaspar Reinhard, narrowly escaped assassination while working in the duchy of Westphalia (his colleague Schultheiss subsequently punished the assassins with suitable ferocity). Even near the capital at Bonn, the archbishop's orders were obeyed only after repeated injunctions and mostly when they coincided with the agendas of local officials. For example, a village reluctant to burn witches could protest, as some did in March 1631, that no wood was available for this purpose (Schormann 1991: 63). Because of unusually poor documentation from half of the Archbishop's possessions, we cannot be certain that Ferdinand's 'extirpation programme' for witches truly was the most drastic of its kind anywhere in Europe; but current estimates, extrapolating from nearly 600 deaths from the duchy of Westphalia between 1628 and 1631 and 400 known deaths from the Rhineland districts, suggest about 2,000 deaths for witchcraft in the electorate of Cologne during Ferdinand's rule. The other two western archbishoprics governed comparably sized patchworks of lands, but executed fewer witches than Ferdinand's Cologne over a longer period of time.

The most important reaction to Ferdinand's witch-hunting excesses came not from the electorate but from the nearby bishopric of Paderborn, one of his lesser possessions. Here the Jesuit Friedrich Spee observed the abuses of Ferdinand's officials towards accused witches, above all the savage and unregulated tortures inflicted on them in order to coerce confessions. Here he composed his *Cautio Criminalis* (*A Warning on Criminal Justice*) in 1629, publishing it anonymously two years later in a Lutheran town. Spee began by asking 'whether there were more witches and sorcerers in Germany than elsewhere'. He admitted this was apparently so, but his real concern was that 'Germany smokes everywhere with execution pyres which are supposed to cure this plague.' Spee condemned much of German society, from princes, advisers and judges down to ordinary subjects, for their brutality and blindness in handling witch trials. His criticisms subsequently influenced Swedish policy in northern Germany, where witch trials were prohibited by royal edict in 1649, soon after a Swedish court preacher published a German translation of this still anonymous work. It is even more reassuring to learn that by 1650 Spee's warnings were also being heeded in the two other German electoral archbishoprics, Trier and Mainz.

Unfortunately, the three archbishoprics do not exhaust the list of 'superhunts' conducted by Catholic prelates in the Empire. Two large Franconian bishoprics, Bamberg and Würzburg, executed nearly a thousand witches apiece. Witch-hunts struck both places simultaneously in two waves, the first lasting from 1616 to 1618. followed by even greater persecutions lasting from 1625 to 1630. Printed pamphlets listed hundreds of burnings in these contiguous bishoprics. Like the first 'super-panic' at Trier, these Franconian witch-hunts were co-ordinated by an episcopal vicar, Dr Friedrich Förner, who served both bishops simultaneously. Förner also published a devotional aid in 1626 which contained a sermon about witches for every Sunday of the year. These localities became so well known for their crusades against witches that Cologne's witch-commissioner, Dr Schultheiss, called his activities in the 1630s a 'Würzburgish work'. Once again, neighbouring Protestants were impressed. When those at Wertheim petitioned their count at Christmas 1628 to increase his prosecution of witches, 'since many places, especially Bamberg and Würzburg, are beginning to uproot this weed', he listened; three dozen executions followed within five years.

Fulda, which bordered Würzburg, was the largest territory in the Empire ruled by a prince-abbot. Here, even more than at Cologne, witch-hunting was instigated by a Catholic prelate rather than his subjects, but under unusual circumstances and with unexpected results. Abbot Balthasar von Dornbach was deposed in 1576 by a rebellion of his chapter and his Lutheran subjects, both of whom objected to his Counter-Reformation policies; he was not restored by Imperial edict until 1602. Upon his return, von Dornbach commissioned a faithful minister, Balthasar Nuss, to eliminate witches and other troublemakers. Nuss began a large-scale witch-hunt, arresting many of the abbot's prominent enemies and some crypto-Protestants on charges of witchcraft alongside more typical victims. Within three years, he had executed over 200 people (his accusers claimed 239; Nuss admitted to 205) when his patron died early in 1606. The new prince-abbot quickly jailed Nuss for his judicial excesses; all sources agree that Nuss tried cases extremely rapidly and employed torture with exceptional brutality. But the former witch-commissioner defended himself ably, counter-suing his Fulda enemies in the *Reichskammergericht*, the Imperial appellate court, in 1609. By 1615, the law faculty of Würzburg proposed that Nuss be fined heavily and banished; but his accusers then approached the Bavarian jurists of Ingolstadt, who they knew had recently recommended the death penalty for another judge who had used illegal methods when trying witches. Ingolstadt's jurists recommended that Nuss be executed for his misdeeds; after twelve years in prison, the old judge, now aged 73, finally mounted the scaffold at Fulda in December 1618.

Ranking among the very worst Catholic witch-hunting prelates of seventeenth-century Germany, Johann Christoph von Westerstetten combined the offices of Prince-Prior of the abbey of Ellwangen and Prince-Bishop of Eichstätt between 1612 and 1636. During his tenure, Ellwangen registered the largest cluster of witch trials in the modern German *Land* of Baden-Württemburg and Eichstätt in the modern *Land* of Bavaria. Although incomplete in both places, the recorded death totals – nearly 400 at Ellwangen from 1611 to 1618, plus almost as many at Eichstätt during those years and again in the late 1620s (concurrently with the 'superhunts' just to the north at Bamberg and Würzburg) – seem huge, given the relatively small size of each of his territories. During his quarter-century of rule, von Westerstetten therefore patronized almost a thousand executions for witchcraft.

Apart from the handful of 'superhunts', when and where was witch-hunting most severe in the Empire? In south-western Germany, Midelfort identified one region affected by severe witch-hunting between 1628 and 1632, just before it was seriously depopulated by plague: it comprised several contiguous territories along the Rhine in central Baden, including the margravate of Baden-Baden, two free cities (Offenburg and Gengen-bach), a Habsburg possession and a district owned by a bishop. Within five years, these five places (one of which, formerly Protestant, had become Catholic, while another was officially Catholic but was adminis-tered by a Lutheran duke) executed almost 600 witches, or over one-sixth of the entire regional total (Midelfort 1972: 121–38). Central Baden offers an exact chronological fit both with the great 'extirpation' programme of electoral Cologne and with the crescendo of persecutions by other prelates at Würzburg, Bamberg and Mainz.

Historians of the Thirty Years War also note that this apogee of witch-hunting between 1628 and 1632, largely confined to Catholic areas and zealously promoted by a few Catholic prelates, corresponds closely to the zenith of Catholic euphoria, the moment when Protestantism had appar-ently been crushed militarily, thus enabling religious 'restitution' (the unmaking of the 1555 Peace of Augsburg in favour of Catholics) to proceed rapidly in many districts. A handful of these newly 'restituted' places experienced their first witch-hunts before plague decimated their population and military setbacks destroyed Catholic optimism; for example, 190 witches were executed in the County of Nassau-Diez, newly forfeited to the Archbishop of Trier, between 1629 and 1631.

Other small territories which remained Protestant also conducted important witch-hunts between 1580 and 1630. Working partly from the SS collections, scholars have identified the counties of Schaumburg, Lippe and Büdingen as having somewhere between 250 and 500 executions for witchcraft apiece. Some smaller Protestant territories, for example Wal-deck and Saxe-Coburg, each accounted for more than a hundred execu-tions. Although we still know far too little about the history of witch trials in such staunchly Lutheran states, located in the geographical heartland of this phenomenon, it seems clear that their attitudes about witch-hunting were not confessional. For example, in Saxe-Coburg the Lutheran clergy tried to stimulate more arrests of suspected witches in the late 1620s by pointing to the example of their Catholic neighbours of Würzburg, while the court jurists who opposed them pointed to the example of careful restraint in the equally Catholic duchy of Bavaria; on this occasion, Duke

Johann Casimir sided with his clergy, and nearly a hundred recorded executions for witchcraft soon followed (Behringer 1987: 432 n. 17).

A BAVARIAN *SONDERWEG*?

Saxe-Coburg's jurists pointed to the most prominent and best-known example of moderation and effective control of witch-hunting by a major German state: the duchy of Bavaria, the largest secular Catholic state in the Empire outside the Habsburg possessions, had only 271 known executions for witchcraft, nearly all of them before 1615 (Behringer 1987). Located east and north of the earliest centres of witch-hunting, Bavaria seems to have been relatively little troubled by this problem until the late 1580s, when echoes of the massive Trier persecutions rolled across much of southern Germany; a ruler on Bavaria's western border, the Prince-Bishop of Augsburg, had a male witch-finder arrested in 1586, and his remarkable testimony both started a local witch-hunt and inspired a superb recent micro-history (Behringer 1998a). Around 1590, more than a dozen places in today's Bavarian *Land* each executed more than twenty witches (three of them had more than 50 executions apiece), while four more places held ten or more executions and eighteen other places (including the Bavarian capital, Munich) had at least four. Witch trials were also held in the region's largest cities (Nuremberg, Augsburg, Ulm) in 1590, but no one was executed. Meanwhile, the German translation of Binsfeld's witchcraft treatise was reprinted at Munich in 1592.

The duchy of Bavaria, justly famous at this time as the pilot-state of the Catholic Reformation, wrestled with the problem of witchcraft for a quarter of a century after 1590, with unexpected results. In 1589, the most savage witch-hunt ever conducted in Bavarian territory had terrorized the district of Schongau, an apanage ruled by the duke's half-brother. The following spring, Duke William V issued the first Bavarian regulations governing witch trials; his chief advisers were jurists from the Bavarian university of Ingolstadt, a city where 28 witches had been tried and 22 executed between 1589 and 1592. Few Bavarian authorities were satisfied with these 'General Instructions': they seemed too lenient to the Ingolstadt jurists, too harsh to some of the duke's councillors and too vague or even contradictory to local judges attempting to apply them.

For the next twenty years, partisans of two diametrically opposed approaches to witch trials confronted each other at the summit of Bavarian government. On one side sat the 'zealots' or *zelanti*, a group of highly devout jurists and theologians who emphasized both the material and spiritual dangers posed by diabolical witchcraft and urged the ducal government to greater severity. Their highly placed Bavarian opponents, whom they derisively labelled 'politicians' (*politici*), refused to consider witchcraft as an 'exceptional' crime to be judged by special rules. Neither side possessed decisive advantages, but the Bavarian 'zealots' had the disadvantage of being mostly foreigners, including some converted Protestants; their only important native Bavarian, Dr Johann Wagnereckh, who became chancellor in 1606, came from a modest provincial family (Behringer 1988: 138–40). On the other hand, the pragmatic 'politicians' were led by well-trained Bavarians of noble birth. Their leader, Dr Johann Georg Herwerth (head of Bavaria's state chancellory in the 1590s), had sat on the Imperial appellate court or *Reichskammergericht*, which, like similar courts throughout Europe, consistently exercised a moderating influence in its rulings about witchcraft. Herwerth was also interested in science, a patron of Kepler (for whom he acted as godfather, despite their religious differences), and contributed to the development of logarithmic tables. Although the 'politicians' usually controlled most key offices, the 'zealots' received powerful support from court theologians; Bavarian policies towards witch trials therefore fluctuated unpredictably.

Although Bavarian witch trials decreased and punishments became less severe in the 1590s, the 'zealots' briefly seized the initiative in 1600 through a remarkable show trial at Munich centred around witchcraft (Kunze 1987). They attributed a fantastic number of felonies to the Pappenheimers, a family of vagrant cesspool-cleaners, applied torture relentlessly in order to extract lurid confessions and inflicted gruesome public atrocities on their bodies, while intensive debate raged inside the Bavarian court. However, even this dramatic spectacle failed to goad Duke Maximilian's councillors into any general campaign against witches, or even into revising their ambiguous edict about witch trials. Only long after Wagnereckh's promotion to chancellor could the 'zealots' finally push through a revised code governing witch trials.

The 40 printed pages of Bavaria's official *Regulations against Superstition, Sorcery, Witchcraft and Other Punishable Diabolical Arts*, issued in 1611, make it the longest and arguably the most severe legal code in this genre. After a seven-page justification for these laws, its first and lengthier section described no fewer than 52 separate forms of superstition, sorcery and witchcraft; it concluded with sixteen articles ordering appropriate punishments for such misdeeds. It was elaborate, comprehensive and 'rigorous' in every sense of the word. But, like the Pappenheimer case, this masterpiece of Bavaria's 'zealots' failed to start any witch-hunts in the duchy. Even after this code had been printed, Bavaria's privy council managed to delay its distribution for over a year and then issued it in a 'corrected' form which blunted its practical effects.

Instead of inaugurating a new spurt of Bavarian witch-hunting, the 1611 code soon turned from the monument of Bavaria's 'zealots' to their tombstone. In the summer of 1612, Bavaria's 'politicians' ordered the arrest of Dr Gerhard Sattler, a university classmate of Wagnereckh, who had executed ten witches in the district of Wemding. Sattler and two of his associates were tortured at Munich for their misdeeds and excesses in conducting these witch trials; they were banished and he was sentenced to death on the advice of jurists from Ingolstadt, his own university. After much manoeuvring by both court factions, Duke Maximilian finally approved Sattler's execution, and he was publicly beheaded at Munich in May 1613. This was an unprecedented event in the history of witch trials, sufficiently well-known to become a weapon against the old judge of Fulda a few years later, and a stinging humiliation for Bavaria's 'zealots'. Subsequently, they obtained some measure of revenge. The 1611 code (in its expurgated 1612 version) was officially renewed in 1625 and again in 1629, during the general climax of witch-hunting in Catholic regions; dozens of witches were once again executed in Sattler's old district of Wemding during Bavaria's worst such episode in 40 years. But this outbreak remained confined to Wemding. One member of Maximilian's privy council, Dr Bartholomew Richel, undoubtedly helped contain it; eight years earlier, he had resigned as Chancellor of the bishopric of Eichstätt after his wife had been burned for witchcraft.

CONFESSIONALISM AND APPELLATE JUSTICE IN THE EMPIRE

Starting from Midelfort's pioneering investigation in the south-west, scholarly research on German witch trials has moved north, lingering on the heavily afflicted territories of the 'priests' alley' along the Rhine and Main rivers with their strong local initiatives, and then east to the instructive history of Germany's pre-eminent Catholic state, the duchy of Bavaria. Our picture of the subject seems relatively clear across nearly all of western and southern Germany, where the majority of the *H-Sonderkommando*'s 15,000 verifiable executions occurred. But the recent achievements of German witchcraft scholarship seem curiously unbalanced; we know so much about the Empire's Catholic regions that many of its Protestant parts remain in shadow. Yet over half the old Reich had turned Protestant by the time the witch-hunts began, and the first panic occurred in a small Lutheran state.

We still know too little about witch-hunting in the almost solidly Lutheran zones which comprised the former German Democratic Republic, including the duchy of Mecklenburg, from which more than a thousand legal opinions about witch trials survive. Similarly, we know too little about detailed developments in smaller Protestant territories near the centre of the Empire, some of which conducted extensive witch-hunts.

We need to learn more about witchcraft theory and legal practice in the Lutheran 'pilot-state' of electoral Saxony, which dominated the north-central region as much as Bavaria dominated the Catholic south-east. We know Luther's response to witches executed at Wittenburg; we know the important precedent of Saxon legislation providing death penalties even for white magic in 1572; and we know the notorious boast of Saxony's most famous seventeenth-century jurist, Benedict Carpzov, about the severity of its witch trials. But until we have a Lutheran counterpart to Behringer's work on Bavaria, our knowledge of witch-hunting in Germany's 'confessional century' will remain unbalanced.

Meanwhile, we have learned that appellate justice played a role in moderating witch-hunting even in that chaotic political labyrinth called the Holy Roman Empire. Its original appellate court, the *Reichskammergericht*, sitting mostly at Speyer since 1495, was complemented by the emperor's newer Aulic court or *Reichshofrat*, sitting at Vienna since 1559. Like other major European courts, the *Reichskammergericht* insisted on clearer standards of proof than those used by local witch-hunters, and it invariably opposed abuses of torture; however, any general assessment of its overall record on witch trials is extremely difficult, because its archives, unlike those of the *Reichshofrat*, were dispersed to almost 40 different locations in the mid-nineteenth century (Schormann 1992). No witches were executed in Speyer, where the *Reichskammergericht* sat. It intervened in witch trials more often than most scholars have assumed and its rulings had some positive effects (Oestmann 1997).

Probably the greatest weaknesses of the *Reichskammergericht* were that it was distant, expensive and cumbersome for non-experts, although some very ordinary plaintiffs found it helpful. During some severe panics, such as those at Ellwangen, it was never asked to intervene. Although, contrary to a long-held belief, it could make witchcraft rulings swiftly (Oestmann 1997: 520), its decisions could be difficult to enforce. For example, in 1611 a plaintiff from the duchy of Sachsen-Lauenburg appealed to it, but his mother was convicted and executed before it could nullify her trial. Highly placed plaintiffs suffered similar consequences: in 1627, during the worst of Bamberg's witch-hunts, the episcopal chancellor travelled to Speyer in order to protect his wife and daughter, who had been arrested for witchcraft; he returned with a ruling to liberate them, but they had both been burned in the interval. The furious bishop immediately imprisoned him and his son (who had also gone to Speyer), tortured both of them until they confessed on the basis of accusations made by his wife and daughter, and burned them also. Three years later, an appeal to the *Reichshofrat* by the city of Nuremberg on behalf of a prominent refugee from Bamberg, followed up by three Imperial orders and pressure from the College of Electors, culminated in the evocation of all Bamberg's witch trials to the emperor in 1631. Bamberg's bishop protested vigorously, but no longer dared imprison witches in the special prison he had built for that purpose.

Next year, the *Reichskammergericht* sharply censured the Elector of Cologne when ruling in favour of a plaintiff accused of witchcraft, but could not curb Cologne's 'extirpation' programme. The *Reichshofrat* was not asked to intervene in Ferdinand's electorate until 1639, although its actions proved as decisive here as they had at Bamberg; only ten days after learning of Vienna's decision, Cologne flatly refused a local petition to renew witch-hunting. Such examples suggest that the newer Imperial appellate court could act with somewhat greater effect than its predecessor, but it had different shortcomings. Because the *Reichshofrat* had been created in order to arbitrate disputes between autonomous Imperial governments, individual subjects could not appeal to it against witch-hunting zealots; the Imperial Free City of Nuremberg had to bring a formal complaint against the Bishop of Bamberg, or the Free City of Cologne against the Archbishop-Elector of Cologne, in order to involve it. Moreover, since the emperor was a partisan Catholic, Protestant governments were often reluctant to appeal to it. But each court did what it could to curb the worst excesses of witch-hunting in the Empire, and the *Reichshofrat*'s most important ruling in these matters was yet to come.

The bizarre history of the small Alpine land of Vaduz, nestling between the Swiss Confederation and Austrian Voralberg, illustrates how, long after 1648, appellate justice could still play a decisive role in the history of witch-hunting in the Holy Roman Empire. Witch-hunting began in Vaduz around 1648, simultaneously with outbreaks in nearby Prättigau. This hunt ended in 1651, but an even more severe burst of witch trials erupted in Vaduz a quarter of a century later. By 1680, it was claimed that nearly 300 people – approximately one-tenth of the entire population of the county of Vaduz – had been executed as witches since 1648. When prominent families among the Count's victims (whose confiscated properties helped pay his huge debts) complained to Habsburg officials in Tyrol, Emperor Leopold I appointed the Prince-Abbot of Kempten to investigate their accusations. Supported by the University of Salzburg, the prince-abbot successfully pressed charges of extortion and sadistic tortures in witch trials against Franz Carl von Hohenems, *Reichsgraf* of Vaduz, before the *Reichshofrat* or Aulic appellate court in Vienna, which in 1684 declared him deposed. His accuser, aided by soldiers from the Tyrolean government, thereupon captured the Count of Vaduz and kept him prisoner at Kempten until Franz Carl died sixteen years later; his lands were forfeited to his accuser. After the count's death, the prince-abbot sold Vaduz to the distinguished Austro-Moravian house of Lichtenstein with the blessing of Emperor Leopold I, who raised it to a *Fürstentum* or principality in 1712. The House of Lichtenstein have ruled in Vaduz ever since, outlasting even the Austrian Empire. Thus a late and brutal Alpine witch-hunt helped create one of the smallest sovereign states in contemporary Europe.

THE 'LOTHARINGIAN CORRIDOR' AND FRANCOPHONE WITCH-HUNTS

In order to complete our survey of witch-hunting in the Holy Roman Empire of the German Nation, we need to cross modern frontiers and inspect this record in several places which do not belong to present-day Germany, often places where German has never been a hegemonic language, but places which acknowledged the legal overlordship of the Empire until 1648 and consequently followed its legal guidelines – the famous law code of 1532 known as the *Carolina* – in conducting witch trials. Extending southwards from the Rhine delta to the Alps, these regions had formed the 'Lotharingian corridor' between the kingdoms of France and Germany when Charlemagne's empire was divided in 843. By the high Middle Ages, these regions, many of which spoke some dialect of French, formed the western boundary separating the Empire from the kingdom of France. During the century after 1560, these regions were responsible for the overwhelming majority of witch trials and executions in present-day France, not to mention present-day Switzerland, Luxembourg and Belgium. Together, these western borderlands of the Empire (which included many places involved in hunting witches during the fifteenth century) executed even more witches than Germany's three greatest 'superhunts' combined, although they were scattered across the entire 'Lotharingian corridor' during a far longer period of time. We shall briefly sketch their witch-hunting history between 1560 and 1660, moving from north to south, from the briefly united Seventeen Provinces of the Low Countries to the thirteen cantons of the Swiss Confederation.

In Weyer's time, as we have seen, the Low Countries – both southern and northern, French and Flemish-speaking – ranked among Europe's most active witch-hunting zones. When the region first split into two confessional blocs during the 1580s, witch trials and executions could still be found in many provinces, with the largest hunt occurring in Gelderland, in the north-east. However, not long after seven rebellious northern provinces formed the Union of Utrecht in 1579 and the Habsburgs solidified their control over the remaining provinces two years later in the Union of Arras, a 'witchcraft watershed' – the only true confessional frontier about witch-hunting in Europe – appeared abruptly in 1592–3 between the Protestant north and Catholic south, amidst the unusually bitter and prolonged religious warfare which afflicted this region. In the southern provinces, Philip II promulgated a decree in 1592, subsequently expanded in 1595 and 1606, extending the right to execute witches down to the level of seigneurial justice. Not surprisingly, the pace of witch-hunting accelerated throughout both French and Flemish-speaking districts of the Habsburg Netherlands. But in July 1593, the Supreme Council or *Hoge Raad*, the highest appellate court of the United Provinces, overturned a witchcraft conviction from Schiedam in Holland, a town where five women had been executed as witches as recently as 1585 (Gijswijt-Hofstra and Frijhoff 1991).

This 1593 decision abruptly ended executions for witchcraft in Holland, the largest and most influential of the seven provinces. The remainder soon followed: Utrecht after 1596, Groningen after 1597, finally Gelderland after 1603. After 1610, prosecutors throughout the United Provinces stopped demanding death sentences against accused witches. By the mid-seventeenth century, Dutch jurists were remarking smugly that, after the Reformation triumphed in the northern Netherlands, 'all imagined illusions of witchcraft . . . are considered to be a curious deception and rejected as false accusations. Since then nobody has been found to be truly guilty thereof' (*Ibid.*: 62). Similar self-congratulatory motifs can be found in popularizations as early as the 1630s. The Dutch *zonderweg* in witch trials was celebrated early and often, centuries before such scholars as Huizinga labelled it as one aspect of the triumph of a bourgeois spirit in the heavily urbanized northern Netherlands. Meanwhile, in the Catholic south, trials and executions of witches increased from Artois and Flanders in the west to Namur and Limburg in the East: fifteen executions at Peeland in Brabant in 1595, 40 at Roermond in Limburg in 1613 and, worst of all, almost 90 executions at Bouchain in the Cambrésis between 1611 and 1615, including nearly two dozen children put to death.

To the south, Philip II's 1592 decree similarly affected his more remote provinces of Luxembourg and Franche-Comté. Both were large (between 250,000 and 400,000 people), deeply Catholic and rural. Perhaps more importantly, each bordered a region to the east which was heavily infested with witches, one Catholic and Germanophone (Trier), one Protestant and Francophone (Vaud). As we have seen, Luxembourg's witch trials in the 1580s and 1590s were strongly affected by relative proximity to Trier. Using financial records which are about two-thirds complete, 316 trials with 82 per cent executions have been counted in Luxembourg's Germanophone districts between 1580 and 1635, compared to 231 trials with only 41 per cent executions in its approximately equal-sized Francophone districts (Dupont-Bouchat 1978). Men comprised about 30 per cent of all executed witches in Luxembourg's Germanic zone (roughly the same share as in the Saarland), but they formed a negligible share of victims in its Francophone parts.

Like Luxembourg, the Habsburg province of Franche-Comté would be devastated by war and plague in the 1630s. Its witch trials started later than Luxembourg's, reaching a first peak between 1603 and 1614, following the publication of a witch-hunting manual by a local judge, Henri Boguet, in 1602. A second wave of trials spread over this entirely Francophone province between 1627 and 1632, exactly simultaneous with the 'superhunts' in Catholic Germany at Mainz, Cologne, Würzburg-Bamberg, or in central Baden. Overall, about 800 witch trials have been located from seventeenth-century Franche-Comté; just over half of the defendants were executed, mostly after being judged by the provincial appellate court or *parlement* (Rochelandet 1997). Unlike its regional neighbours, Franche-Comté experienced a final wave of witch-hunting from 1658 to 1661, long after the Thirty Years War ended, in which hundreds were put on trial and dozens executed.

Between the Habsburg provinces of Luxembourg and Franche-Comté lay the independent duchy of Lorraine. Separating the German Empire from the kingdom of France, it was not only the largest buffer state in western Europe, but also the western European state most heavily affected by witch trials (Biesel 1997; Briggs 1996). Lorraine's witchcraft executions were spread fairly evenly over a long time period but distributed unevenly across its three principal parts – the Germanophone *bailliage d'Allemagne* in the north-east, its Francophone heartland *bailliages* of Nancy and Vosges and the western duchy of Bar, partly under French suzerainty. Lorraine's total of around 1,500 witchcraft executions[7] matched or even exceeded the estimated totals from most of the 'superhunts' sponsored by Catholic prelates in western Germany. There are several explanations for this dubious achievement.

In the first place, this bicultural but solidly Catholic state had the unfortunate distinction of producing a well-known demonologist, Nicolas Rémy, who published his witch-hunting manual after being appointed Lorraine's Attorney-General or *procureur général* in 1591. No other author on witchcraft could match his practical experience. But although Rémy's 1595 preface boasted that he had prosecuted 900 people who had been executed as witches during the previous fifteen years, he actually named about 125 defendants, only a few of whom can be found in Lorraine's well-preserved fiscal archives, including some who were not burned. Instead, Rémy's significance lies in the fact that he and his son Claude-Marcel occupied the post of *procureur général* of Lorraine for 40 consecutive years after 1591, thereby making it the largest European state where an appellate court system consistently encouraged, rather than curbed, witch-craft prosecutions throughout the worst period of witch-hunting in western Europe.

Lorraine's remarkably complete local financial records, supplemented by hundreds of trial fragments, enable us to see that witch trials began in its Francophone heartlands between 1544 and 1552 and resumed in the 1570s, when they averaged about six executions annually. They accelerated to about thirteen executions per year during the 1580s; after Rémy's appoint-ment, they increased to about eighteen executions per year in the 1590s and remained at approximately this level throughout the 40 years when the two Rémys ran Lorraine's prosecutorial apparatus. Witchcraft trials and executions from Lorraine's Germanophone districts add another five or six executions per year in the 1580s; during the Rémy era (1591–1630), the sparsely populated *bailliage d'Allemagne* averaged close to ten executions per year (Hiegel 1961). Germanophone Lorraine, like Germanophone Lux-embourg, seems proportionately more heavily affected by witch trials than its Francophone regions, although the differences are not dramatic. Mean-while, sketchier records from the western duchy of Bar, a separate possession of Lorraine's dukes, where the Rémys had no authority, suggest a probable total of fewer than four witchcraft executions per year between 1580 and 1630 for a region midway in size and population between Lorraine's Germanophone districts and its Francophone heartland.

In the duchy of Lorraine, witchcraft persecutions became as notable for the quality of the accused as for their quantity. In 1604, a minor court official was burned for bewitching the duke's second son, a cardinal and papal legate. In the 1620s, as Lorraine's annual averages of witchcraft executions slowly began to drop, two more prominent men were burned for this offence. The first was a physician attached to the ducal family, convicted of causing the demonic possession of an extremely devout noblewoman (she also accused a high-ranking Franciscan, who fled Lorraine to avoid arrest). In 1625, a prominent courtier was burned soon after his patron's death, charged by the new duke with bewitching his marriage to the previous duke's heiress.

Lorraine's new ruler soon confronted the novel problem of a demoni-cally possessed village, Mattaincourt. Its parish priest is now venerated as a saint, but he had to resign in 1632 because neither he nor anyone else could control the devil's public scandals in his church whenever Mass was celebrated. Before the scandal ended, it evolved into the largest single witch-hunt in Lorraine's history, with three dozen people burned for witchcraft, mostly accused of attending sabbats by demonically possessed adolescents. In order to stop this panic, eight under-age witches, too young to be executed, were quarantined for over a year in a special dwelling. In some important ways, Mattaincourt's tragedy foreshadows the all-too-famous developments at Salem Village, Massachusetts, 60 years later.

Directly east of Lorraine lay Alsace. Like the present-day German *Land* of Baden-Württemburg, located directly opposite it along the Rhine, this region formed an intricate mosaic of small secular and ecclesiastical states sprinkled with ten Imperial free cities; however, no recent scholar has tried to unravel the formidably complicated pattern of its witch-hunts. Nonetheless, we possess sufficient evidence to suggest that they were quite extensive. One chronicler counted over 150 local deaths for witchcraft in his local district, Thann, between 1571 and 1630, and estimated about 800 deaths for all of Alsace during this period (Behringer 1993: 154–6). Moreover, we know that although witch-hunting affected many places throughout Alsace and frequently peaked around 1630, it also affected some parts of Alsace considerably later. Overall, there is good reason to accept Behringer's estimate of approximately a thousand executions for witchcraft in Alsace.

South of Lorraine and Alsace lay some small autonomous territories, usually Francophone, Protestant, nominally ruled by absentee princes and politically allied with the Swiss. Unlike their larger Catholic neighbours, they generally managed to avoid the horrors of the Thirty Years War, but were instead infested with witch trials during a much longer period; for example, Lutheran Montbéliard held about 150 executions for witchcraft between 1580 and 1660, and Reformed Neuchâtel had over 250 deaths during the same period. While this region's large provinces like Luxembourg or Franche-Comté executed one or two witches per thousand population, and Lorraine between three and four per thousand, these smaller places sometimes executed eight or ten per thousand. Worst of all in this respect were the three or four thousand Francophone Protestants, nominally subjects of the Bishop of Basel, who executed more than 120 witches between 1600 and 1660.

The Pays de Vaud, ruled after 1536 by the Swiss Protestant canton of Bern, holds the unenviable distinction of being the witch-hunting capital of Francophone Europe, and probably of Protestant Europe as well. Both the natives and their Swiss rulers were aware of this situation. Bern, in a 1609 edict, blamed the exasperation of Vaud's peasants, 'driven by poverty, despair and denial of God', for the 'envy, hatred, [and] spirit of revenge . . . which unfortunately these daily trials prove abundantly'. Later, a pastor noted that French Catholics marvelled at 'the quantity of witches whom they say are burned . . . in the Pays de Vaud, inferring that our religion was the cause of it'. These remarks were not exaggerated. No fewer than 971 executions have been counted in Vaud between 1580 and 1620, scattered across 91 local jurisdictions (Kamber 1982). Exactly one-third of these victims were men. Executions occurred every year. Only five years (four of them before 1590) recorded fewer than ten executions, although only four years between 1597 and 1616 surpassed 50 executions; until 1595, Vaud (which was about one-third the size of Lorraine) averaged fifteen executions for witchcraft a year; afterwards, they doubled to around 30 per year. Of course, witch-hunting in Vaud continued long after 1620; the library of Lausanne's Reformed Theological Faculty holds 40 witches' confessions from one district, Moudun, between 1647 and 1671. In all, the Pays de Vaud probably executed more than 1,200 people for witchcraft.

The independent republic of Geneva, despite a tradition of witch trials dating from the fifteenth century and Calvin's urging of greater severity against rural witches in 1545, showed much greater restraint in conducting witch trials than its Protestant neighbour Vaud. Although Geneva conducted well over 300 witch trials between 1537 and 1660, barely one-fifth of them resulted in executions, compared with more than 90 per cent in Vaud (Monter 1976). Geneva behaved much like its Swiss Protestant allies, Bern and Zurich, who executed about one accused witch in every three. But so did the staunchly Catholic and bilingual canton of Fribourg, bordering both Germanophone Bern and Francophone Vaud, and several other Catholic cantons.

Within the Swiss Confederation, the most significant differences in witch-hunting lay between the sovereign cantons, which generally followed careful legal procedures, and their subject territories which were vulnerable to gross miscarriages of justice. Bern never regulated the use of torture among its Francophone subjects with the same care that they or their Swiss neighbours used on themselves. In Fribourg, the most southwesterly canton and thus farthest from Germany, prison registers provide unexpected testimony that Switzerland still respected the Empire even after 1648: they continued to specify that accused witches must be tortured 'exactly according to the provisions of Imperial law', meaning the 1532 criminal code. Consequently, as many witches were probably executed in the French-speaking 20 per cent of present-day Switzerland as in the German-speaking 70 per cent, which included all thirteen cantons.[8] However, Switzerland also executed witches both earlier and later than other parts of the Continent, and, although our information remains imperfect, it probably contributed about 3,000 executions to the European totals between 1560 and 1660.

WITCH-HUNTING IN THE KINGDOM OF FRANCE

We cannot understand the history of witch trials in continental Europe without an adequate grasp of developments in its largest, most populous and probably most centralized state, nor can we make useful comparisons with the sprawl of jurisdictions across the pre-1648 Holy Roman Empire. However, despite a premature attempt at synthesis (Mandrou 1968), the history of witch-hunting in the kingdom of France remains poorly known, and few reputable scholars have dared to estimate the total number of witches executed here. We know that the Parlement of Paris, flagship of the French legal system and appellate court for half of the entire kingdom, authorized the deaths of barely 100 witches between 1568 and 1625, although a larger number of witches was probably executed without its approval in its vast district (Soman 1992). Developments in the other half of this vast kingdom, divided among regional appellate courts in Normandy, Burgundy, Dauphiné, Languedoc, Guyenne and Provence, can furnish the outlines of an answer.[9]

Although Montaigne, a seasoned judge, claimed in his *Essays* that 'we have more laws in France than in the rest of the world put together', the kingdom of France – unlike England, such major imperial states as Saxony or Bavaria, or the Spanish Inquisition – never produced a statute defining and punishing the crime of witchcraft. However, Montaigne's very next phrase rings true with respect to witchcraft: 'so much is left to the opinion and decision of our judges that never was their liberty more unshackled'. Every judge in France knew that witchcraft ranked among the most dangerous crimes, an offence to God and man alike. But without any specific procedural guidelines, every accusation of witchcraft had to be decided by the judge's 'arbitrary' discretion; the monarchy required only that the hierarchy of courts be respected and that justice be done.

Before 1560, a time when other French parlements reduced the occasional death sentence for witchcraft proposed by lower courts, one finds traces of a few witches executed within the huge district controlled by the Parlement of Paris (with roughly half the population of the Holy Roman Empire), but without the court's knowledge or approval: four people at Beaujolais (1539), two suspected witches lynched near Lyon (1542, 1551), a Faustian magician executed at Poitiers (1553) and three people near Nevers (1558). Until 1560, the pattern of witch trials across France resembles that of southern Germany; the first cluster of witch trials handled by a French parlement, when at least three death sentences were upheld at Toulouse, coincided with Wiesentsteig's outbreak in 1562. Soon afterwards, a witch was executed by order of the Paris Parlement in 1568, followed by several more in 1572. Adequate precedents were available by the time Jean Bodin, working in a royal prosecutor's office in north-eastern France, began composing his *De la Démonomanie des Sorciers* (*On the Demon-Mania of Witches*) in 1578.

Bodin's book, published in 1580, became a cornerstone of early modern demonology, both because of the author's prestige in other fields and because he was the first trained jurist to offer guidelines for trying witchcraft in secular courts. His main point was that witchcraft should be judged as an 'exceptional' crime, one whose peculiar danger and secrecy required relaxing the normal rules of evidence and proof in criminal cases. Although the *Démonomanie* was Bodin's second most popular work, enjoying many editions, translations and imitations (always the sincerest form of flattery), it never convinced the Paris Parlement to regard witchcraft as an 'exceptional' offence. Instead, the Paris judges took vigorous action in 1588 to quash illegal witch-hunting methods in north-eastern France, not far from Laon. They intervened again in 1601 by arresting the hangman of Rocroi, a notorious witch-finder responsible for the deaths of more than 200 people; although only eight of his victims were French subjects, the parlement ordered him to the galleys for the rest of his life. They subsequently intervened in the same region in 1623 by punishing local judges who approved the custom of 'ducking' witches, and followed in 1624 by ordering that all condemnations for witchcraft throughout their vast district be automatically appealed to Paris (Soman 1992).

By 1625, the Parlement of Paris had condemned over a hundred people to death for witchcraft or magic; but this figure represents fewer than one-fifth of the death sentences appealed to it for such offences. Europe's premier secular court ordered 58 such executions between 1587 and 1610, but never more than six in a year. Between 1611 and 1620, its ratio of executions for witchcraft fell to only 4 per cent of cases appealed, while one-sixth of such defendants was released without punishment. Apart from one extremely late incident, the Parlement of Paris stopped sentencing witches to death after 1625, exactly when it also required that all witch trials be appealed before it; as Soman has emphasized, this date began the de facto decriminalization of witchcraft in the kingdom of France.

Meanwhile, in 1608, Henri IV granted an appeal from the kingdom's far south-western corner to send a special commission from the Parlement of Bordeaux in order to root out witchcraft among the Basques. One commissioner, Pierre de Lancre, inspired by simultaneous developments in Provence, where a prominent priest had been unmasked and burned by another parlement for black magic, and across the Spanish border, where the Inquisition had just staged a famous *auto de fe* against other Basque witches, published the only demonology by a French appellate judge: the *Tableau de l'inconstance des mauvais anges et demons* (*A Display of the*

Inconstancy of Evil Angels and Devils) (1612). His primary target was the persistent scepticism of his parlementary colleagues, which subsequently provoked him into publishing a second book on the subject at Paris ten years later. Much confusion, compounded by the disappearance of criminal *arrêts* from Bordeaux for this period, surrounds de Lancre's activities among the Basques. Three priests and probably about a dozen others were executed in 1609 during his special commission; it was the worst witch-hunt in the Bordeaux district and probably the worst record compiled by any judge in any French parlement, but de Lancre remained frustrated by his inability to overcome the persistent doubts of his colleagues, either at Bordeaux or Paris, about the reality of this crime.

During the half-century after 1580, parlements throughout France ordered witches to be executed, but mostly in small numbers: for instance, only ten at Aix-en-Provence, probably even fewer at Grenoble or Rennes, perhaps twenty at Dijon, and about two dozen apiece at de Lancre's Bordeaux or at Toulouse, seat of France's second-largest appellate court. During this period, only one provincial parlement, Rouen, executed relatively large numbers of witches, about 90 in all (Monter 1997). All told, the hundred witches executed after 1572 by order of the Paris Parlement probably represent about one-third of the totals for the entire kingdom. Of course, one must add in executions of witches who were never judged by French parlements; but this number is probably relatively small, since appeals from death sentences cost defendants nothing and required only four words ('I appeal to Parlement'). Overall, France provides impressive support for Brian Levack's insight (1995: 93–9) that centralized court systems inhibited witch-hunting, at the same time that it radically deflates his estimate of French witchcraft executions (*ibid.*: 21–6).

A remarkable feature of these French executions is that half of the victims were men. Although such peripheral regions as Iceland or Finland reveal a preponderance of male witches, France offers our richest evidence about the role of men in European witch trials. Neither Bodin nor de Lancre discussed the role of men in witchcraft, because neither worked in regions such as Normandy where male witches predominated. It was emphatically true that men, like women, were not randomly accused of witchcraft. In France, two occupational groups were remarkably predominant: clerics and shepherds. Between them, these categories accounted for close to half of the men executed as witches at Rouen and Paris. And clerics, although less numerous among this group than shepherds, can be found among men tried for witchcraft in nearly every French parlement between 1590 and 1650.

Basque priests figured prominently in de Lancre's demonology; in 1609, he had ordered three of them executed and arrested five others. Gaufridi, the priestly *magus* executed at Aix in 1610 for causing demonic possession in several women, was only the best known among a squalid phalanx of French priests condemned by parlements for witchcraft and black magic. At Aix, only two other priests were tried for Gaufridi's offence and both were liberated; but in Provence, between 1598 and 1625, two other clerics were hanged and two others given life sentences in the galleys for 'impieties' involving sacrilegious magic; another, charged with magic, had his paraphernalia burned. There were lurid cases involving priests at Paris, resulting in at least four executions between 1604 and 1609. A Franciscan *magus* was hanged and his corpse burned at Grenoble in 1606; a sacrilegious priest was hanged at Dijon in 1613 and another in 1625. At Rouen, over twenty priests were tried for illicit magic between 1594 and 1620; five of them were hanged. By the time the all-too-famous Urbain Grandier was burned at Loudun in 1634, French clerical magicians were in decline, but he was not the last such case: two priests were executed for illicit magic in Brittany and another in Normandy in the 1640s.

However, shepherds formed the largest group of France's male witches. The largest cluster came from Normandy, a cheese-producing region where two shepherds had been executed back in 1540 for stealing hosts from a church. Over 60 shepherds were tried for witchcraft by the Parlement of Rouen between 1590 and 1635; over twenty of them, and two of their wives, were executed. Shepherd-witches from eastern or southern Normandy appeared in Rouen's records nearly every year. Unlike women accused as witches, shepherds were almost never charged with putting spells on people; instead, they employed magical arsenals ranging from stolen Eucharists to toad venom in order to protect, or harm, livestock. Blacksmiths, another male occupational category which produced a disproportionate share of witches, similarly used home-made magic in order to sustain (or afflict) an indispensable kind of livestock.

A third type of Frenchman, the witch-finder, was responsible for clusters of witch trials, though not himself accused of witchcraft. They usually operated in the Pyrenees, where they played a major role in spreading France's largest witch-panic in 1643–4. Before dying out in 1645, it had spread as far north-west as Poitiers and northeast through Burgundy to a few flurries in the Ardennes, leaving behind an ugly trail of over a hundred lynchings from Guyenne to Burgundy. Early in the panic, about two dozen witches were sentenced to death by the Parlement of Toulouse, followed by three more at the Parlement of Dijon in 1644. By November 1643, the Parlement of Toulouse was trying to capture a group of witch-finders who were carrying the panic to previously unaffected parts of Languedoc. In June 1644, they hanged three of them, bogus surgeons who claimed to be working under its licence. Their Burgundian counterpart, 'a young shepherd whom stupid villagers called the "little prophet"', who identified witches by looking into their eyes, was banished early in 1645 by the Parlement of Dijon. But the greatest witch-finder of all was surely the fictional hero of the *Marvellous History of the Sabbat and Witches*, published in 1645 at Barcelona (then under French occupation). Born near the Languedoc villages where this panic began, 'Señor Barbasta' held a general commission from the Pope to find magicians and witches and hand them to the courts; readers were assured that he had been responsible for the deaths of 3,000 witches throughout France, including his own wife. Although the 1643–5 panic was the last of its kind in France, other witch-finders turned up in south-western France around 1670, but the affair ended quickly after Louis XIV put one 'expert' in the Bastille.

WITCHCRAFT AND THE MEDITERRANEAN INQUISITIONS

Friedrich Spee, a patriotic German, noted in 1631 that 'the Italians and Spaniards, who are naturally more inclined to [magical practices], nevertheless seem able to ponder and repress such things, which would doubtless cause the deaths of innumerable innocent people if they wished to imitate the Germans' (Schormann 1991: 108). Agreeing with Spee, a Portuguese historian entitled his recent introduction to witchcraft in Mediterranean Europe 'a universe saturated with magic' (Bethencourt 1994: 159). But Spee also pointed out that few witches were executed in southern Europe, and a great nineteenth-century anticlerical historian attributed this development to an unlikely source: 'only the wisdom and firmness of the Inquisition', noted H. C. Lea, rendered the witch craze 'comparatively harmless' in Spain (Monter 1990: 262). Lea's remarks could be extended to the Roman and Portuguese Inquisitions as well.

Before 1525, however, no thoughtful observer would have predicted that witch trials would become relatively rare in southern Europe, or that the Mediterranean Inquisitions would be primarily responsible for curbing their spread. The earliest preserved trial containing a full description of the sabbat (1428) comes from the Papal States. Later fifteenth-century Italian witch trials were conducted entirely by ecclesiastical judges; in the Alps, the Inquisitor of Como ordered 41 witches burned at Bormio in 1485, and the Bishop of Brescia reportedly executed 64 witches at Val Camonica in 1518, despite the veiled scepticism of the Venetians. Between 1505 and 1525, at least seven witchcraft treatises were composed by Italian theologians and lawyers, arguing about the reality of witches' flight to the sabbat. Meanwhile, the new Spanish Inquisition began trying witches in the Pyrenees by 1494. It executed four or five of them around 1500, while Spanish authors argued the same issues as their Italian colleagues and

Francisco de Rojas, a Spanish humanist, produced Europe's first great fictional portrait of a witch, *La Celestina* (1499).

During the Italian high Renaissance, art imitated life. At Mirandola in the Po basin, 60 witches were investigated and ten of them were executed in 1522–3 in the tiny principality ruled by Gianfrancesco Pico della Mirandola, nephew of the great philosopher (Burke 1977; Biondi 1984). This humanist prince promptly celebrated the episode in a dialogue about witches, published at Bologna in 1523. 'When you listen to the witch speaking,' he noted, 'you are hearing an accurate account, which I have in part seen with my own eyes and in part heard with my own ears, when the records of the trials were read to me.' In Pico's dialogue, the sceptic gradually becomes convinced that witches really do exist and sometimes fly to their nocturnal gatherings. Unlike the theological and legal treatises of his contemporaries, Pico's *Strix* was quickly translated into Italian and frequently reprinted.

However, the most important Mediterranean development in this decade was the Navarrese witch-hunt of 1525, an episode never properly set in context (Idoate 1978: 23–50, 249–79).[10] It recorded the first appearance of the professional 'witch-finder', a Pyreneean specialty during the next century and a half. When the Navarrese government sent a special commissioner 'to visit the mountains, where for a long time they have not known what temporal or spiritual justice means', he took along at public expense 'two girl witches (*brujas*) who know how to discover witches', sisters aged 9 and 11. Lodged in separate houses, they inspected villagers who presented themselves voluntarily, 'as if they were gaining indulgences', examining their eyes for evidence of a secret witch's mark. Among 400 people, only ten women and two men tested positive, with two doubtful cases. Meanwhile, the commissioner scoured north-eastern Navarre, arresting many witches, confiscating their livestock and executing an unknown number in five different places; he also purchased a hundred Masses from their confiscated property in order to ask God's blessing for his mission.

However, this Navarrese witch-hunt provoked decisive intervention by the Supreme Council of the Spanish Inquisition. By August 1525, after a sharp conflict at the Spanish court, they had apparently won jurisdiction over Navarre's accused witches; 30 of them, in shackles, were handed to the local inquisitor and moved to his prison. The Inquisition's headquarters insisted that no final judgements be made until they had a chance to inspect some of the trials. By February 1526, four trials had been sent to them, accompanied by local theological opinions. After prolonged discussion, a special junta of the Suprema decided, by a 6:4 vote, that witches attended sabbats in reality rather than imagination. In December 1526 they issued a set of guidelines for Navarre, soon extended to such other regions as Sardinia where Spain's Holy Office confronted other episodes of witchcraft. As many historians have noted, the 1526 guidelines paid more attention to re-educating witches than to punishing them; they affirmed the Inquisition's right to try witches, but maintained great scepticism about the malefices or evil spells which justified most death sentences. Several guidelines, such as that forbidding the confiscation of property in witchcraft cases, seem designed to prevent inquisitors from condemning witches to death.

Operating under these 1526 guidelines, which were occasionally evaded, only about two dozen witches were ever sentenced to death by the Spanish Inquisition (including those who died in prison). Only five condemned witches, none of whom was executed, appeared among the 3,600 people sentenced at 90 public *autos de fe* in Pyreneean Spain between 1550 and 1600. After this trend was broken at Logroño in 1610, one stubborn inquisitor, Alonso de Salazar y Frías, dubbed the 'Witches' Advocate' (Henningsen 1980), conducted some remarkable experiments to determine the medical properties of witches' powders, and single-handedly prevented further prosecution until the Suprema decided in 1614 to summon two witches 'in great secrecy' for direct questioning, after which it reverted to its traditional lenient policies.

Of course, the Spanish Inquisition could not always prevent Spanish secular courts from implementing death sentences against witches, particularly in Navarre, where the events of 1525–6 were repeated exactly half a century later. Again the denunciations came partly from children, but this time only three witches were executed before the Inquisition intervened. After a sharp dispute, Logroño's Holy Office took jurisdiction over 50 arrested witches. On this occasion, Philip II, by ruling in favour of the Inquisition, probably saved the lives of over 40 women (five others died in prison). Twenty years later, the story ended differently. Once again an adolescent girl examined suspects' eyes, exactly as her predecessors had done 70 years before, but those whom she identified as witches soon revoked their confessions. Navarre's inquisitors complained that 'this witch business has ordinarily given the Inquisition much work, expense, and bother, but little benefit comes from it, as experience has shown'; with death sentences unlikely, the Supreme Council told them they need not intervene. Eight women subsequently died in Navarrese jails, but none was executed.

While the Spanish Inquisition usually kept witch-hunting contained in the Pyrenees after 1525 (Tausiet 2000), their Italian counterparts confronted a confusing situation without clear guidelines from Rome (Romeo 1990). Before 1600, relatively few witches were executed by Italian secular courts (for example, ten at Bologna between 1498 and 1579), but Italian clerics were probably responsible for more witchcraft executions than the Spanish Holy Office. After Trent, St Carlo Borromeo became a zealous and influential witch-hunter in the Alpine parts of his Milanese arch-diocese, while a vicious witch-hunt afflicted Avignon (which belonged to the Roman Inquisition) in 1582. In 1588, Rome's Holy Office ruled that its officials could not prosecute someone accused by another witch of attending sabbats; but this development could not prevent local inquisitors from executing witches at Siena, Perugia and Mantua soon afterwards. A curious parallel connects the Roman Inquisition with the Parlement of Paris, which also legislated against witch-hunting excesses in 1588 but could not prevent its subordinates from ordering further executions for witchcraft.

Our picture of Mediterranean witch trials after 1600 is dominated by secular rather than ecclesiastical justice. To their credit, both great Inqui-sitions were applying restrictive (and almost identical) guidelines for witch trials before 1620, thereby stopping public executions for this offence almost as early as the most 'enlightened' secular court in Europe, the *Hoge Raad* of the United Netherlands. Unfortunately, witches were still being executed in Italy and Spain, because neither Inquisition was always able and willing to prevent it. In Milan, for example, nine witches were publicly executed between 1599 and 1620. The worst known witch-hunt in Spanish history ravaged Catalonia from 1618 until 1620, resulting in almost a hundred deaths, while smaller outbreaks afflicted other parts of northern Spain until mid-century. The Spanish Inquisition did nothing in Catalonia until a direct plea from the viceroy spurred them into condemn-ing a notorious witch-finder to the galleys (he was a French immigrant; his Catalan counterpart went unpunished). Later, other witch-finders were questioned and released by inquisitors in Aragon.

The refusal of the Spanish and Roman Inquisitions to execute anyone for witchcraft after 1610 tells only half of their story. The other half, described in monographs from all three Mediterranean Inquisitions (Bethencourt 1987; Martin 1989; Romeo 1990; Fajardo Spinola 1992; Di Simplicio 2000), chronicles their preoccupation with condemning a wide range of traditional but illicit magical practices, the sort of activities in which La Celestina had once engaged. In 1580, the papal nuncio in Venice reported that the matters 'which have taken up most of the time' of the Venetian Inquisition concerned incantations, 'generally accom-panied by activities which made them matters for the Inquisition, such as the adoration of demons'. The nuncio added that 'the incantations did not arise from any inclination towards heresy; rather they were directed towards two ends, love and gain, which wield great power over empty-headed people' (Chambers and Pullan 1992: 236–7). His remarks could easily be extended to cover all of Mediterranean Europe during the next century and even beyond.

Cases of illicit magic proliferated between 1580 and 1660 in every Italian tribunal with extensive records, but declined thereafter. Reggio Emilia alone conducted over 200 trials for such practices within five years after 1597, devoting over 60 per cent of its efforts to controlling illicit and diabolical magic during its busiest period; Siena investigated over 600 cases of magic and diabolical arts between 1580 and 1640, just over one-third of its total, with a peak in 1600–4. However, prosecutions for similar offences developed much later in remote Spanish tribunals such as the Canary Islands, where they accelerated only after 1660; in Portugal, they did not reach their peak until the eighteenth century.

In all three Inquisitions, the frequent, relatively mild but well-publicized punishments for sorcery had unintended and unwelcome results. On the one hand, professionals regarded them as free advertising; a Neapolitan monk boasted in 1623 that 'he was the best necromancer in the world and had had twenty-five trials by the Holy Office'. On the other hand, the public believed that some of these offenders were being punished too mildly and took vigilante justice. At Reggio Emilia, a woman was stoned to death after her public abjuration in 1599; something very similar occurred in the Canary Islands almost a century later. By 1754, the Canariot inquisitors explained to their superiors that they no longer punished well-known sorceresses in public, because long experience had taught them that they either provided free advertising for such women or else risked public riots by sentencing them.

All three Mediterranean Inquisitions proved sufficiently powerful to prevent secular officials from launching major witch-hunts; Catalonia in 1618–20 serves as the exception which confirms the rule, and the Spanish Inquisition was less respected there than anywhere else in the kingdom. In Italy, where witches' activities had been demonized by ecclesiastical courts before 1400, canon law never relinquished its pre-eminent jurisdiction over such crimes. By 1525, the Spanish Inquisition had wrested primary control over witchcraft cases from secular authorities and established unusually cautious guidelines for judging them, which in turn were largely copied by the Roman Inquisition. These Mediterranean inquisitors were preoccupied not with witches' maleficia or evil spells, but with their apostasy to the devil. They were reluctant to employ torture as a means of eliciting confessions, and sceptical about accusations of accomplices seen at witches' sabbats – although searching for networks of heretical accomplices was an essential part of their work. They were always merciful with those who confessed. De Lancre, the French parlementary judge and demono-logist, censured the Logroño inquisitors for executing only those witches who refused to confess at their 1610 *auto de fe*, while pardoning all those who had confessed: this procedure, he knew, was the exact reverse of proper justice.

WITCH-HUNTING AFTER 1650: NEW AND OLD PATTERNS

By the mid-seventeenth century, witch trials had declined steeply almost everywhere in western Europe. After the Thirty Years War ended and confessional rivalries began their gradual decline, only a handful of places conducted large-scale witch-hunts. In north-western Europe, there is the well-known case of Scotland, whose worst witch hunts began in 1649 and peaked in 1661–2. But England and France experienced only a few minor outbreaks after 1645, and there were almost no trials for maleficent witchcraft in the Iberian peninsula or Italy after 1650. Even within the western half of the Holy Roman Empire, which had clearly been the centre of the storm between 1560 and 1660, relatively few serious outbreaks now occurred. In the Protestant north, there was a final bloody outbreak at Lemgo in 1666–7, during which over 50 witches died. But it seems exceptional and almost anachronistic, the final episode in a local tradition which had seen even worse cycles of trials and executions, rather like the final few confessions from the 1660s in the Swiss Pays de Vaud.

The geography of European witch-hunting shifted after 1650. Apart from Scotland, most places which now occupied centre stage lay east of the fifteenth meridian. It was only after the mid-seventeenth century that witch trials and executions reached their peak in the kingdom of Sweden, including Finland; along the Baltic coast from Danzig to Estonia; in Silesia and neighbouring Moravia; and especially in the great kingdoms of Poland and Hungary, where they apparently peaked only after 1700 (Klaniczay 1990). Here we catch a glimpse of 'cultural lag' in the eastern frontiers of Latin Christendom, although admittedly much work remains to be done, particularly in Poland and in other regions which bordered Orthodox eastern Europe.

In Switzerland, as in Germany, witch-hunts generally moved from west to east around the middle of the seventeenth century. The clearest local example comes from the 'Gray Leagues' or Graubunden, an autonomous Alpine federation south-east of the thirteen Swiss cantons. Here the valley of Prättigau freed itself from vestigial dependence on Austria in 1648 and immediately celebrated by holding its first big witch-hunt, known locally as *die grosse Hääxitöödi*, where 100 people were tried and most of them executed within a few years. At the same time, Austrian officials success-fully prevented the neighbouring valley, which failed to secede, from holding any witch trials, despite local requests. However, witch trials spread south from Prättigau to other parts of the biconfessional and trilingual Gray Leagues, culminating with a savage outbreak in the Italophone valley of Poschiavo, during which almost 5 per cent of the population were put on trial for witchcraft in the 1670s and at least 60 people were executed.

In the heart of central Europe, witch-hunting also reached its apogee in the hereditary Austrian lands between 1660 and 1700. The single worst outbreak occurred not in Austria proper but in an episcopal enclave, the bishopric of Salzburg. The most remarkable feature of the Salzburg outbreak of 1677–81, known as the 'magic-coat' or *Zauberjäckl* scare, was the nature of its archetypical victims. Two hundred people, over 90 per cent of them sturdy young beggars, were accused of various magical practices under a mysterious leader with his 'magic coat', who was never caught despite huge rewards offered by several governments. During Salzburg's scare, 140 people were executed; more than 70 per cent of them were less than 22 years old, and over 70 per cent of them were male. Its victims exactly reversed the venerable old-woman archetypical witch-figure which had predominated in Austria as well as elsewhere in western and central Europe. Repercussions from the *Zauberjäckl* 'conspiracy' spread across much of Austria in the 1680s and 1690s, and its aftermath can be traced in southeastern Germany for 50 years. In a witch-scare from 1720–2 in the Bavarian bishopric of Freising, for example, all the old women who were accused were liberated, while three middle-aged female beggars were executed along with eight adolescent boys whose median age was 16.

While new patterns of witch-hunting were developing in central Europe, old patterns were being repeated behind the imposing façade of Louis XIV's France, which is conventionally celebrated for its relatively early official decriminalization of witchcraft in 1682 (Mandrou 1968). However, a closer look suggests that Louis XIV and his officials did not and could not 'decriminalize' witchcraft even in the so-called age of absolutism. The famous 1682 edict was a direct consequence of the notorious 'Affair of the Poisons' which had scandalized Paris and the Court for three years (Lebigre 1989). Louis' government either hanged the venal sorcerer-priests who had performed Black Masses or left them and their principal accomplices to rot in forgotten fortresses. The resulting 1682 edict proved relatively effective in controlling the public sale of poisonous substances. But although it also spoke about the 'so-called crime of witchcraft' (*prétendu crime de sortilège*), it failed to end prosecutions for casting harmful spells.

Instead, by reviving public interest in sacrileges and dangerous magic, the 'Affair of the Poisons' sparked renewed prosecutions on such charges throughout northern France during the following decades. In the spring of 1684, the Parlement of Normandy once again sent shepherds to the galleys for 'so-called witchcraft' and poisoning livestock; they also executed three people, including another shepherd and a young boy, for magical sacrileges using consecrated Hosts. They continued to order death sentences for exactly the same crimes against another shepherd and his wife in 1692; two more shepherds were executed and another banished in 1694, officially described as 'convicted of witchcraft (*sortilège*)', this time omitting the embarrassing adjective 'so-called'. Three more Norman shepherds were sent to the galleys in 1700.

Meanwhile, trials of shepherds for illicit magic and poisoning animals seeped south from Normandy. The Parlement of Paris, which had executed no one for witchcraft or sorcery since 1625, sent a shepherd to the galleys in 1687 for 'so-called witchcraft', then three more in 1688, and finally condemned two others to death for practising illicit magic in 1691. Moreover, four shepherds, condemned to the galleys at Paris in 1693, were rearrested in Marseille and condemned to death for sacrileges performed during their journey. Ultimately, the 'Affair of the Poisons' proved more significant than the royal 'decriminalization' edict of 1682 which supposedly concluded it. More than twenty years later, three shepherds were executed at Rouen for stealing consecrated Hosts, which they intended to use to protect their flocks – a practice (and a punishment) which had not changed in Normandy since the days of Francis I. As the French like to say, 'the more things change, the more they remain the same'.

But obviously some things had changed by the 1680s. In Stockholm, appellate justice had ended a prolonged witch panic in Lutheran Sweden in 1674, and ten years later a Catholic appellate court in Vienna would depose a *Reichsgraf*, a sovereign ruler, for committing gross abuses in conducting witch trials. Around 1680, the fear of diabolical witchcraft remained very much alive in many parts of Christendom, as Salzburg's *Zauberjäckl* affair demonstrates. In Christendom's further reaches, many people would be put on trial and executed for witchcraft for a long time afterwards – in sizeable numbers both in Massachusetts and in present-day Slovenia in 1692 (Klaniczay 1994: 223); in parts of eastern Europe (a region of tardy Catholic confessionalization) far into the eighteenth century; and in the Swiss Alps a full century after the 'Affair of the Poisons'. Nevertheless, at least one major thing had changed by 1680: large numbers of old women were no longer being tried and executed as witches anywhere in western, southern and northern Europe.

NOTES

1. Information drawn from Microfilm 2 Mi 237 at the Archives Départementales of Haute-Garonne in Toulouse, a 1971 copy of an as-yet-uncatalogued *sac à procès*.
2. Recorded on this date in the unpaginated *Arrêts criminels* of this Parlement (Archives Départementales of Haute-Garonne, B 3360).
3. For example, Behringer (1994: 75) estimated 2,000 executions for witchcraft in the electorate of Mainz by taking a total of 1,778 deaths after 1600 under three archbishops (Gebhard 1989) and rounding it upwards; but Gebhard included 300 unconfirmed and probably imaginary executions from one tiny region in 1602–4, while, on the other hand, Electoral Mainz had about 80 recorded deaths for witchcraft before 1600 (Pohl 1988). Actual figures for Mainz – one of the worst-afflicted regions in Europe – therefore seem far closer to 1,500 than to 2,000 executions for witchcraft.
4. A complete microfilm copy now exists at Frankfurt, although the originals remain in Posen (Poland).
5. The original German edition is preferred; the abridged English translation (Behringer 1997) is less satisfactory.
6. Archives Départementales, Haute-Garonne, B 3439–3444 *passim*.
7. My estimate is based primarily on as yet unpublished research in financial archives at Nancy and Bar-le-Duc.
8. Scholarship on this subject is surprisingly antiquated: the last general survey (Bader 1945) remains valuable for much of German Switzerland.
9. Drawn from personal research into parliamentary criminal *arrêts* at Rouen, Dijon, Bordeaux, Grenoble, Toulouse and Aix.
10. The Inquisition's correspondence for 1525–6, which best illuminates the genesis of the famous 1526 guidelines, is in AHN Madrid, Inquisición, Libro 319.

PART 2

Witch Trials in Northern Europe
1450–1700

Bengt Ankarloo

INTRODUCTION

As we learned in Part 1 of this volume, the scope and intensity of the early modern witchcraft prosecutions are now fairly well known thanks to a number of national studies. While relying on all these studies, this second section will focus on northern Europe, in order to match the earlier concentration on western and central Europe and the Mediterranean lands. First, we will discuss witchcraft as an historical and anthropological category and make a few critical observations on matters of theory and methodology. Then we will proceed to a short description of the persecutions in the north, moving from England and Scotland in the west to Finland and Livonia in the East.

A modern observer may find it hard to understand how people in the past could hold such beliefs as those connected with witchcraft and demons. Simply to dismiss them as superstitions is not very illuminating, but to accept them as part of a different but consistent rationality may be equally difficult. Were demons and curses in those days really of the same order as horses and contracts? Even if some witchcraft actions had very practical, down-to-earth motives, such as revenge or material gain, the magic realm was to most people a region of dreams and speculation. What, after all, is the point of religious ideas and transcendental fantasies if they are merely the same thing as factual knowledge of the material world?

Physical realities impose some very definite constraints on human actions. To dreams and speculations there are, at least in theory, no limits, except those of the creative mind. Nevertheless, some fantasies are more successful than others. They manage to survive in the struggle for people's attention. It is an interesting problem why demons are so ubiquitous, and flying through the air such a pervasive dream. 'The process of cultural acquisition inevitably operates a selection in the available cultural output. The outcome of this selection is that certain features are recurrent because they are more likely to be entertained, acquired, and transmitted by human minds' (Boyer 1994: ix). Stuart Clark, taking up an idea of Clifford Geertz's, observes that seventeenth-century scholars obviously found demons 'good to think' (Clark 1997).

We are intrigued by magic and witchcraft. They are interesting representations even when we do not believe in them. We play with them and sometimes the game becomes dangerous. But in recognizing this we should not forget that they are also cognitive categories both of the witches and their accusers and also in the minds of historians looking back at them. They are elements in a classification system with several interdependent subsystems: the taxonomy of law with distinctions between the harmful and the harmless; the taxonomy of a moral order with distinctions between the intentional and the merely neglectful and between the divine and the diabolic; and the taxonomy of village life with distinctions related to reputation and social esteem, to the useful and the destructive.

These several competing classifications are associated with, and defended by, various institutions such as the Church, the judiciary, local goverment and village communities. Sometimes they overlap, as in the recognition by both secular and ecclesiastical authorities of intent (the Roman law concept of *dolus*) as a legal requisite. And there is also a powerful drive towards reconciling the different systems. The syncretism and even eclecticism of witchcraft ideologies tend to create a consensus among judges, priests, bureaucrats and the general public about the nature and seriousness of the crime. It thus becomes increasingly difficult to attack – to deconstruct, as it were – the belief-system from outside simply because as an outsider one runs the risk of being identified as a follower of the Enemy, a legitimate object of suspicion and persecution. This tendency of the belief-system to be self-perpetuating and reinforcing, together with its ability to absorb and dispose of criticism, brings to mind Thomas Kuhn's description of scientific paradigms.

The taxonomies among modern historians looking back at the persecutions are somewhat different. There is the Enlightenment classification, resting on assumptions about gross credulity and superstition and about the shame of a Church that built its power on keeping the common people in this state of ignorance. The evolutionist taxonomy looks upon witchcraft as an element of a medieval, traditional and pre-modern culture, as opposed to the more progressive civilization of Renaissance humanism, the 'Scientific Revolution' and the Enlightenment. Some areas are said to be slower to develop the modern ways of thinking, such as the northern and eastern peripheries of Europe; others, such as Holland, are thought to be advanced and seen to stop persecuting witches at an early stage. There are also some modern social science taxonomies which are inclusive; magic is said to be a universal anthropological category and witchcraft in Tudor England comparable with that in post-colonial Africa. Others are exclusive. Burr (1943) contends that diabolic witchcraft was an altogether Christian phenomenon, and Monter (1976) has declared that 'non-Western social anthropology provides keys that do not fit continental European locks'.

In one respect, popular magic is not a discontinuous category. As Stuart Clark makes clear in Part 3 of this volume, it would be wrong to think of it as a clearly delimited area removed from everyday life. Many actions are magical in the sense that they have a ritual form and rely on an esoteric causality, but they are nevertheless very practical, with aims such as securing good weather, averting sickness or preventing attacks from enemies. This feature of magic used to be misrepresented as a kind of substitute activity – an attempt to control an insecure world – but this view owed much to the now discredited functionalist assumption that every social institution serves a rational purpose. It can be found in Malinowski's compassionate and moving description of magic among 'early men':

> It enables man to carry out with confidence his important tasks, to maintain his poise and his mental integrity in fits of anger, in the throes of hate, of unrequited love, of despair and anxiety. The function of magic is to ritualize man's optimism, to enhance his faith in the victory of hope over fear. Magic expresses the greater value for man of confidence over doubt, of steadfastness over vacillation, of optimism over pessimism. (Malinowski 1954; here quoted from Marwick 1990: 331)

To Malinowski magic was an integrated and functional part of everyday life. In consequence, his view has been important in removing witchcraft from the barren fields of 'superstition' and 'ignorance'. But functionalist explanations sometimes tend to overemphasize the rational and instrumental aspects of human agency. The magical operator is not only set on achieving an end, whether good or evil. She or he also tries to understand and explain the remote and dark sides of life, to give at least some confidence and comfort in the face of adversities, the terrors of death, and the threats from unknown enemies.

But, certainly, magic is also a category of its own. There is a name for it, it has a particular technique and a cognitive scope. Some people are supposed to be good at it, others less so. It can be understood as a way of describing and understanding the world and it can be analysed as a discursive field with specific terms and definitions of what is possible and what is not.

The renewed attempts at Christianizing the European peasantry associated with the Reformations of the sixteenth century took as one of their aims the eradication of the last remains of 'pagan' or 'superstitous' beliefs and rituals. This missionary criticism by the reformers of some popular practices served to create uncertainty and doubts about the limits of the magical sphere. What was, and what was not, 'superstition'? What was strictly forbidden, and what was more or less permitted?

Things supernatural were frowned upon by the socially elevated. There was also a general feeling of an inherent danger in venturing too far into the unknown – in disturbing the powers. As a consequence, information about them was presented not as individual knowledge but as tradition: 'I have heard . . .' or 'They say . . .' There is a certain shyness in this attitude – a knowledge that phenomena and processes that transcend normal, everyday experiences are associated with several kinds of danger. Crossing the border is done with care; one does not move too far. Peasant cosmology is rarely extravagant and magic in this context is very practical, set on controlling the destructive forces threatening the health and welfare of the household. Reaching out to the other side is a careful, low-risk venture, not a bold attempt at conquering heaven or hell; not a major enterprise but a cautious exploration of the immediate transcendent neighbourhood. It is talked about, if at all, in a casual or even joking way to disclaim familiarity with it. One pretends not to know precisely how to go about it, as if the whole thing is not worth taking notice of. The other side can be dealt with only in an oblique roundabout way. This is playing it safe.

But some make a living from building up a reputation for expertise in these matters, and they clearly face a dilemma. On the one hand, they must be as careful and prudent as their fellow men; on the other, their trade depends on their vocation being commonly known. Often they are forced to take risks in order to make a living. And the others are prepared to pay them, not so much for their skills, which are common knowledge, as for their willingness to run the risks – a division of labour as good as any in the community. These practical, everyday aspects did not prevent witchcraft from being both aggressive and frightening. Among cases from Yorkshire, Sharpe (1992) found numerous instances of fits, convulsions and other painful experiences as the result of magical aggression. Witchcraft suspicions, he concludes, 'existed in a context of fear and drama'.

In the early sixteenth century, there existed a number of discursive practices and social institutions with their roots in the past which, in any description and explanation of the great witch persecutions as a historical process, may be singled out as necessary preconditions for what was to come. Their accumulation and systematic interaction were, according to this mode of explanation, instrumental in forming the judicial practices which led to the violent deaths of more than 30,000 people, mostly women, accused and convicted of witchcraft.

These basic institutions include a body of magic lore with elements from both popular culture and learned tradition. Some of these elements are similar, or even identical, to beliefs recorded in the literature of the ancient civilizations of the Near East and the Mediterranean basin. For example, the death of Germanicus in 19 BC was allegedly caused by magical operations in his own house. The exhumed remains of human corpses, together with incantations and curses, 'and other evil apparatuses, by which it is believed that souls are dedicated to the infernal powers' were found under the floor and in the walls (Tacitus *Annals*: 2.69). Sophronius (seventh century) speaks about a man who was made lame by magic. A saint appeared to him and told him to look under the threshold of his bedroom. There he found the 'wicked instrument of a sorcerer' (Ogden 1999). Instances like these were repeated in the seventeenth century. In 1654, in the province of Scania in Denmark, a miller's wife was convicted and put to death for witchcraft. She had placed a pouch containing bones, needles, finger nails and other magical paraphernalia under the threshold of the bedroom in the nearby manor house and her ladyship had become ill and eventually died (Ankarloo 1988).

To kill or injure an enemy by destroying or damaging his wax (or lead) image is a method of maleficent witchcraft so common as to be almost universal in the Old World from ancient Mesopotamia to early modern Iceland. It was also transferred to the New World in the form of 'voodoo' dolls. The idea of an immediate connection between an image and its object is straightforward enough and it can be found in many medieval texts. In the Alexander legend, Pharaoh Nectanebos is threatened by a naval attack by the Persian King Artaxerxes. When the ships approached Egyptian waters, Nectanebos ordered two wax images to be made. Placing them in a basin he read a series of incantations and a violent storm destroyed the whole fleet and all its warriors. Similarly, the *Gesta Romanorum* has a story about a nobleman going to Rome on a pilgrimage. At home his wife entered into an illicit relationship with a learned friar. Together they conspired to kill the husband by shooting an arrow at his wax image. But the knight had been warned and, looking into a magic mirror, he could see his enemies and evade their arrows. At the third attempt, the arrow turned in the air and killed the adulterous friar. In many places the wax image had to be baptized in church in order to be effective as an object of destruction. To prevent this it was prescribed in 1554 by the Bishop of Roskilde that children being baptized should be brought naked to church, 'so that people versed in magic shall not be able to hide their wax dolls with the child to have it baptized and then use it for witchcraft'. These examples indicate a complex interplay of extremely tenacious popular traditions and learned reintroductions and adaptations from the Bible and the Classics.

There was a long-standing tradition of severe sanctions against *maleficium* – physically harmful magic – both in Roman and common law areas. If anything, the harsh legal practice of the early modern monarchies served to increase the cruelty of the penal system. Legal torture and capital punishment prevailed everywhere. In many countries witches were burned alive. Occasionally, they could bribe the hangman to strangle them before delivering them to the flames. Some churchmen were concerned about the extreme cruelty of this form of punishment. It could cause, they thought, such utter despair in the Christian souls of the culprits that they would be lost for ever. For this reason, it was the official practice in some countries first to behead or strangle witches and then burn their dead bodies.

The emphasis in cases of *maleficium* is on the violent effects of the deed. It was regarded as one of the various forms of homicide, but its secret nature made it difficult to prove and it was probably regarded as a sneaky and cowardly way of getting at enemies. It was listed by learned jurists among the *crimina excepta*, where the requirements of proof could be relaxed and torture was admitted.

In addition to the prosecution of witchcraft in the secular courts, there was an ecclesiastical discipline with an emphasis on attacking forms of popular magic other than *maleficium*. Everyday practices such as folk healing, using love potions, or searching for stolen goods with the aid of a sieve (coscinomancy) were forbidden as un-Christian superstitions. The vigilance of the Church in these matters was bolstered by the Reformations and Counter-Reformations of the sixteenth century. In fact, the suppression of popular magic has been interpreted as part of a more general campaign lauched by the militant Church to Christianize, at long last, the European peasantry (Delumeau 1978). The battle against paganism in remote areas could take the form of witch persecutions, as in Estonia, where they were introduced not by the crusading Teutonic Knights of the late Middle Ages, but as a result of the conquest of Lutheran Sweden in the early seventeenth century. A series of episcopal visitations to the outlying parishes resulted in outraged reports about the heathen worship of sacred groves and in the denunciation of several witches (Kahk 1990). But this confusion of witchcraft and peasant paganism did not prevail everywhere. The Protestant clergy of Denmark were little inclined to participate in the persecution of witchcraft proper, focusing their missionary zeal instead on healing and protective magic (Sejr Jensen 1982; Johansen 1990: 362).

Finally, there was the idea of the diabolical pact and the emerging notion of diabolism. As witnessed by the iconography of the later Middle Ages there was an increasing obsession with the Devil and the demonic realm. The systematic association of popular superstitions with demonic magic became part of the missionary campaigns of the Reformed Churches, both Protestant and Catholic, in the early modern period. This was a dangerous step because the diabolical pact was looked upon as an organized conspiracy on a par with other heretical movements. This idea was, on the whole, an extension of medieval Christian traditions even if some of its components may have had their origins in ancient times. It led to conceptions of a struggle for each individual soul between good and evil as represented by God and Satan, the dreaded outcome of the pact being the ultimate sin of apostasy.

Even if we know much about when and where the persecutions took place and how many people were affected, we know much less about the more difficult questions of 'how' and 'why'. Fortunately, the step from documentation and description to interpretation and explanation is not too great. In fact, a careful and judicious description takes us a long way towards understanding. When it comes to discussing causes it is best to avoid two dangers: on the one hand, reductionism, and on the other, the indiscriminate and incoherent heaping of too many explanations together. Quaife (1987) has found no less than 66 different causes of the witch craze presented in modern scholarship. His slightly ironic enumeration includes simplistic explanations, such as the backlash of a frightened patriarchy or the introduction, in the late Middle Ages, of hallucinogenic drugs (e.g. henbane), but also a bewildering plethora of sophisticated sociological observations about village life, class differentiation, economic stagnation, wars and famine, and their supposed connection with the witch craze (cf. Clark 2001: 3–6).

The explanations are not always mutually exclusive. Some can be combined in models of multicausal processes. They can also be applied at different levels of abstraction and generality. It is one thing to explain the excessive persecutions in some of the Rhineland provinces of Imperial Germany, and another to understand the background factors which gave rise to the witch beliefs prevalent all over Europe. The former problem may be solved within the framework of the legal and political instititutions of Germany in the era of the Thirty Years War; the latter is primarily associated with popular culture and élite mobilization during the transformation of the Western Monarchies.

Thus, it is not possible to offer a single covering explanation for such a large and complex phenomenon as witch beliefs and witch-hunts. In the trials of the sixteenth century we are confronted with a number of narratives gradually converging into a single discourse with recurrent stereotypes and a few basic propositions. It is a common opinion in recent scholarship that popular magical beliefs were restructured when subjected to élite interpretations. This may be true in the sense that ordinary people were not left alone in their villages. They were taxed and exploited by their lords, they were educated and controlled by the Church and their crimes were punished by the judicial system. In line with this general penetration of the countryside, the dramatic rise in witch persecutions has been explained as the result of a fundamental reinterpretation and demonization of popular magic by interventionist governments and zealous religious reformers. Robert Muchembled (1978a) has described the relation between élite and popular culture in early modern France as one of interference and subordination. Carlo Ginzburg, in his influential book *I Benandanti (The Night Battles)* (1966/1983), was able to demonstrate that the Roman inquisitors, when confronted with a local fertility cult in Friuli, immediately interpreted it in demonological terms; and that the peasants were gradually persuaded to accept this new interpretation.

One should be careful not to overstate this process of acculturation. The ruling classes did not just apply a ready-made demonological interpretation of the superstitions of the peasantry. Rather, it was a gradual and dynamic process. Everybody was learning a new way of looking at these things. Leading churchmen and judges were for a long time reluctant to accept the change of emphasis from *maleficium* to devil's pact offered in prominent demonologies such as Francesco Maria Guazzo's *Compendium Maleficarum* (*A Summary of Witches*) (1608) or Jean Bodin's *De la Démonomanie des Sorciers* (*On the Demon-Mania of Witches*) (1580). A certain scepticism was still common up to the early 1600s. At a Stockholm trial in 1596, a woman confessed to be 'of the bad sort riding to Blåkulla [the devil's sabbat]. Not long ago she had intercourse with the devil. But she was admonished to tell the truth and to refrain from lies and deceptions' (Ankarloo 1990: 289). And when consulted in 1619 by the High Court in a witchcraft case, the bishops of the realm stated as their opinion that a compact and participation in the sabbat was not enough for capital punishment to be invoked; *maleficium* had to be proved as well. This conservative stand was only gradually abandoned for the more advanced view that all magical practices were, explicitly or implicitly, proof of a compact with the devil and therefore a capital crime.

It would also be wrong to think of the witch persecutions only as waves of enforcement, as the result of pressures from above on a sullen or indifferent peasantry – especially in the light of what William Monter has already said in Part 1 of this volume about the initial pressure to arrest witches coming from the communities to which they belonged. Often the court audience was clearly hostile to the suspected witches. In a typical case, a peasant, or his wife, was accused by neighbours of having made their cows run dry. These allegations were supported by others with similar experiences. If the suspect could persuade eleven villagers to join him or her in an oath of purification s/he might be acquitted. But if this legal help, as often happens, was withdrawn s/he would be convicted. The outcome in such cases was almost entirely dependent on local opinion about the suspect. A further step in cases of this type was when the accused was deprived of all support from relatives and neighbours, and when the majority took an active part in demanding strong legal actions. Sometimes the records contain clear traces of such pressures. A witch was executed in 1610 'after the unison cry from the clergy, the jury and the

whole county demanding that such a vile body should be removed'
(Ankarloo 1971: 69).

Popular beliefs were probably restructured when subjected to learned
interpretations. But the distinction between learned and popular concepts
is not a very clear one. Certainly there was a constant interaction between
the two. We begin to find in the judicial records from all over western
and central Europe a fairly uniform body of witch lore. The very same
detailed questions were asked everywhere in prisons and courts of law.
Gradually they tended to imply diabolism and other ideologically damaging aspects of the alleged acts. Often the suspects were very clear about
these implications and they tried to offer less harmful interpretations of the
legal testimonies and the *corpus delicti*. A salve found in the house of one
suspect was not, she claimed, for flying through the air, but simply a
cosmetic. The accused were rarely surprised at the accusations as such.
They recognized the acts implied by the questions; they knew what the
game was all about. This was common knowledge.

A discursive wave is rolling over western Europe in the late sixteenth
and early seventeenth centuries. The number of books on witchcraft
published and republished in the years 1575–1625 by far exceeds that of
any other half century. And the number of trials reached its peak in the
same period. Any explanation – or better, any set of interrelated and
mutually consistent explanations – must take account of the regional and
temporal variations, the rise of government and post-Reformation religious activism, the social dynamics of village life, the role of both popular
and élite culture and, not least, gender relations. Let us briefly discuss
some of these factors.

THE RISE OF GOVERNMENT AND THE JUDICIAL REVOLUTION: ACCUSATORIAL VERSUS INQUISITORIAL REGIMES

The governments of many countries in the early sixteenth century were
once called 'new monarchies'. And indeed, the reigns of such kings as
Henry VIII in England, Francis I in France or Gustav Vasa in Sweden
represented something qualitatively new, a vigorous and self-asserting style
of rule. The control of the Church and the militia, and of taxation and
local administration, was gradually taken over by the king and his servants
at the expense of both the nobility and the local communities. As an
integral part of this political transformation of early modern western
Europe, the judicial system and the courts of law were subordinated under
a bureaucracy of professional lawyers and literate judges appointed by the
king. Procedures changed from the oral to the written.

Extended in time and scope into the seventeenth century and most of

Europe, this process has been labelled 'the judicial revolution' (Lenman and Parker 1980). It has also been associated with a change of legal ideology. The local courts of the Middle Ages have been described as part of a decentralized communal system where people could settle their disputes among and by themselves. Justice was restitutive, with the purpose of restoring peace and order by forcing the defendant to compensate the plaintiff for the damage done. Fines and public excuses were the typical restitutive elements of such settlements. The new centralized court system, on the other hand, was more likely to exercise a punitive justice set on deterring from crime by meting out cruel and frightening punishments.

It is easy to see how this ideal–typical dichotomy could be construed as an opposition between the benevolent neighbourly justice of old and the insensitive, bureaucratic justice of big government. We should beware of such a romantic view of the 'good old days'. Central control and local freedom could have very different effects. It is not necessarily true that the high royal courts were more reckless than petty princes or city oligarchies in implementing the new punitive system. The bureaucratic and professional system of rule in the new monarchies was also more formal and legalistic. The supervision by royal courts of local jurisdictions often served to protect the accused from the wanton vindictiveness of provincial judges and juries or the indiscriminate use of torture by zealous bailiffs and prosecutors.

A case in point is a Danish witchcraft statute of 1576. It provided protection for those who were convicted of witchcraft in the local courts. The widespread practice of burning them at once had made their right of appeal to higher courts illusory. From now on, all such sentences had to be confirmed by the provincial court of appeal (*landstinget*), before the execution could take place. In England, after a judicial decision in 1590, all 'difficult' cases were removed from the lower quarter session courts to the higher assize judges, a reform which helps to explain the relative restraint of English courts in witchcraft cases. Similarly, the role of the Parlement of Paris in curtailing the vicious practice of French local courts in witchcraft cases has been demonstrated by Alfred Soman (1978, 1981). In the Dutch province of Groningen, 57 people were executed for witchcraft in the late sixteenth century. All these executions took place in the countryside, 'especially in areas where the political and judicial authority of the city was limited' (Priester and Barske 1986: 76).

The participation of the general public in the suppression of magical evil-doing was common and understandable enough in cases of *maleficium* – material harm perpetrated by the alleged witches. We can discern a long medieval tradition both in law and in legal practice of local courts passing death sentences on people who had secretly and maliciously destroyed the crops or killed cattle. Justice in such cases was often swift and without mercy.

Juries or other forms of lay participation in the courts were used both in England and Scandinavia. This did not always prevent the outbreak of violent hunts. In fact, many local juries were more inclined to convict than the professional judges in the high courts. In 1673, when the conviction of ten witches in Bollnas in central Sweden was contested by two legal experts commissioned by the government, the peasant jury angrily rejoined that 'if these old hags are not removed, then we will give the first one of those who transvect our children a lead bullet to let them go' (Ankarloo 1971: 139).

In Germany, common law was rapidly giving way to Imperial law which included several Roman law institutions. Inquisitorial procedures and a repressive penal law were substituted for medieval customs, first in the cities, then gradually throughout the Empire. In the Imperial code, known as the *Carolina*, of 1532, harmful witchcraft was punished with death and torture was admitted.

Witchcraft statutes were enacted in 1563 in both England and Scotland. In spite of the close timing of these laws, and their attribution by many scholars to the militancy of the Reforming Churches, they were in fact quite different. The English statute was merely a revival of an act from the time of Henry VIII, which had been repealed by Edward VI in 1547. It was aimed at maleficent sorcery only, making death the penalty for those actions 'whereby any person shall happen to be killed or destroyed' (full text in Rosen 1969: 54–6). There is no indication that the Protestant ministers returning from their exile during the reign of Mary were instrumental in reviving this legislation. In Scotland, on the other hand, the witchcraft act was part of a larger moral crusade aimed at the enemies of God: witchcraft, adultery and sodomy were all made capital offences and the definition of the crime of magic was much wider than in the English case, including any 'practising of witchcraft, sorcery or necromancy, or for pretending to any knowledge of such arts, or for consulting any person who thus pretends' (full original text in Normand and Roberts 2000: 89).

The medieval Nordic laws, in line with comparable codes on the Continent, originally appear to have penalized only witchcraft that was physically injurious to men and women (and in some cases animals). This was called *förgörning* (to destroy), a term roughly equivalent to the *maleficium* of Roman and Canon tradition. It was treated with outlawing just as other kinds of manslaughter: the victim's kinsmen were free to take revenge and kill the witch. Gradually, this very old form of reprisal was replaced throughout the system by a formal death penalty, and at the same time the crime was extended so that the killing of cattle by magic was also deemed to be a capital offence. From the twelfth century onwards, statutes were adopted against superstitious practices of a less harmful nature. This was obviously spurred on by the Church. Cases of this type were to be brought before a bishop's court.

The most explicit criminalization of magic during the Middle Ages was to be found in the Swedish and Norwegian codes. In Denmark, processual rules regarding the treatment of *maleficium* (*förgörning*) were probably received in the secular Jutland code only in the late Middle Ages from the ecclesiastical statutes of Scania and Sealand. Characteristically, only harmful acts directed against persons were penalized. The superstitions and pagan practices of the common people were still the concern of the Church discipline.

In Sweden and Norway, church law was adopted from the ecclesiastical sections of the old provincial codes, mostly the Uppland and the Eidsiva codes, respectively. They contained regulations against superstitions. Eventually most non-harmful magical practices came to be dealt with chiefly under purely ecclesiastical law, usually in close connection with Canon law (I, lib.v, tit. x–xxi). Breaking the law led to being debarred from the Church and denied the sacraments. Atonement was achieved through penance and fines. Towards the end of the fourteenth century, these fines are prescribed in more detail, particularly in the Swedish sources. The forbidden practices are clearly defined as the devil's art (*ars dyabolica*). In devotional and homiletic literature, such as the collection of tales for preachers (*exempla*), compacts, exorcism, defilement of the host and other heretical acts are described in accordance with similar phenomena in western Europe. The sparse material from the court records of the later Middle Ages contains examples of people being condemned to death in secular courts who had obviously offended against God, for instance by making a compact with the devil. The Church also explicitly branded magical activities (*incantationes, sortilegia*) as crimes against the faith in line with heresy and usury. As a rule, ecclesiastical discipline set its sights on exorcising and healing magic – the simple popular customs associated with everyday problems and conflicts – leaving harmful witchcraft to be dealt with by the secular courts.

Both in England and Scandinavia, the accusatorial, as opposed to the inquisitorial, procedure was still in general use. In order to prosecute a crime one had to find a plaintiff willing to make the charge, accusing the culprit of the evil deed. But at least in Sweden, inquisitorial procedures *ex officio* from the bench and with a government servant or a clergyman as public prosecutor were coming into practice in witchcraft cases towards the end of the sixteenth century.

Such changes are clearly associated with the judicial revolution – the gradual emergence of the modern state with a strong bureaucratic organization. They were given support by the Reformed Churches. In the opinion of the Protestant teachers, the king was responsible for the well-being, both spiritual and corporal, of his subjects. He was, in Melanchthon's words, the custodian of the two tablets of law (*custos utriusque tabulae*). It was the duty of the state to avert the wrath of God by punishing all the sins within the realm. Consequently, when village people quarrelled and hurt each other it was not simply a private feud which they possibly could solve by seeking the aid of the law courts. Instead, the opinion began to prevail that crimes, all crimes, were a threat to the divine and secular order as embodied by the state. In the course of the late sixteenth and early seventeenth centuries this view was gradually accepted by all public servants down to the local bailiffs and clergymen.

First, there was a benevolent, paternalistic element in this royal interference with local justice. In 1550, the Swedish King Gustav Vasa was worried by the numerous cases of witchcraft in the province of Dalarna:

> Some witches among you entertain various superstitions and thereby effect much evil, distracting with their witchcraft good people from God and everything Christian. We are sure, that you have heard from your preachers about the damages and disasters emerging from witchcraft (which is nothing but manifest idolatry), so that God Almighty punishes such sin both here on earth and then in eternity. Therefore, beloved subjects, we advise and admonish you not to suffer such improprieties among you, but where you know that there are such men and women who use witchcraft and magic, then you shall apprehend them and bring them to our Bishop, and what he may decide to do with them, you shall help to uphold and not oppose. (Ankarloo 1991: 293)

Soon, the supervision of justice was left to a whole body of professional judges and court servants, many of whom had a university training. They were instrumental in introducing the new interventionist ideology, Roman law procedure and the modern demonology. All these three elements were combined in printed and widely read works such as Jean Bodin's *De la Démonomanie des Sorciers*.

The basic difference between accusatorial and inquisitorial regimes was blurred in some countries by the introduction of the concept of *crimen exceptum* – extraordinary crimes so disgusting, secret and generally harmful that they outraged the whole community. They might be prosecuted without regard for the ordinary procedures. In other countries, such as England and Denmark, the basic accusatorial system remained in force throughout the period and probably served to limit the extent of persecutions. The allegations of plaintiffs acting on their own initiative have been thought to give a more genuine reflection of popular beliefs (Kieck-hefer 1976). Inquisitorial proceedings, on the other hand, might be expected to contain more learned elements, opinions held by the inquisi-tor or the state prosecutor and based on legal and theological doctrines set down in the famous demonologies from *Malleus Maleficarum* (*Hammer of Witches*) to Benedict Carpzov's *Practicae Novae Imperialis Saxonicae Rerum Criminalium* (*New Rules in Criminal Cases for Imperial Saxony*). Taking these procedural differences into account, there seems to be a certain correlation between accusatorial popular trials and the victimization of old women and village healers. The learned inquisitorial persecutions associated with the systematic purges during the great witch crazes in Germany and elsewhere tend, on the other hand, to strike blindly among high and low alike. Eventually, the very fact that members of the local élites ran the risk of being accused of witchcraft became a major factor in curtailing the whole business.

But *maleficium* cases long remained the most frequent. The magical techniques of the early modern period were similar to those of the Middle Ages: hair, bones, nails, and other simple paraphernalia had devastating effects when placed on a neighbour's property, in the stables or under the threshold. Court audiences were sometimes quite vocal in their condem-nation of such activities and in many cases there was active peasant participation in the accusations. On the other hand, the defendant often had social and legal resources to protect himself or herself against such attacks. In the Swedish material up to the early seventeenth century, about 170 trials have been found in the court rolls. In these cases more than half of the accused were able to free themselves; another 23 per cent of cases were never brought to a recorded end and were probably settled out of court. Less than a quarter led to convictions. Much the same proportions were also found in the witch trials of the Österbotten province of Finland in 1665–85 (Heikkinen and Kervinen 1990). An estimate of the convic-tion rates in Estonia indicates that 65 (or 32 per cent) out of 205 accused witches were put to death, most of them in the period 1610–50 (Madar 1990).

This is a far cry from the rates found in continental trials in general, but also those in the other Nordic countries. In Denmark, convictions declined from 70 per cent in the early seventeenth century to 37 per cent in 1656–97 (Johansen 1990; 1991). In Norway, the statistics covering the period 1580–1660 worked out by Hans Eyvind Naess (1982; 1990) indicate that conviction rates varied from 55 per cent for superstition to 66 per cent in *maleficium* cases, to 82 per cent when diabolism was the main charge. It should be pointed out, however, that the foundations for these figures are sometimes very shaky. Short of systematic surveys of the court rolls, one runs the risk of overestimating the convictions, since for obvious reasons they are recorded at length more often than the acquittals, both in the judicial and fiscal source material.

In Denmark the legal foundations of the persecutions underwent repeated and substantial revisions in the early modern period. The witchcraft statutes of the medieval Jutland code only had the vague and inconclusive provision that *maleficium* cases should be sworn before the bishop. Nothing was said about the penalty, but in practice, as becomes clear in the sixteenth century, burning at the stake was freely used. In the 1520s, King Christian II tried to introduce torture and a more inclusive definition of witchcraft in line with that of continental law. A threat followed by damage of any sort (the *damnum minatum* of Roman law) was to be punished 'according to practice', i.e. with the death penalty. But Christian was soon deposed and his law was repealed. A provision in favour of a more cautious practice was introduced in 1547, when torture was to be resorted to only against convicted criminals to make them denounce accomplices. Judicial torture with the aim of forcing suspects to confess was explicitly prohibited. Finally, in 1617, a statute specifically singled out those who had made a compact with the devil. They should be burned as witches proper.

The Danish legislation was also applied in Norway. In addition, the Norwegian clergy managed in 1584 to get the king's approval of a statute which imposed the death penalty for superstition, a radical and rather surprising extension of the law. The witchcraft statute of 1617 was milder – the penalty for superstition became exile rather than death. What these differences in law actually meant in practice is hard to tell, since in Norway court rolls are preserved only from the seventeenth century onwards.

In Sweden–Finland the medieval national code was still in use penalizing only *maleficium*. Torture was prohibited. In the semi-official and widespread judicial rules of the sixteenth century it was stated that confessions made under torture were not to be admitted in court. It appears, however, that witchcraft cases were excepted from this rule. Several instances indicate that coercive methods were regularly and openly used, at times by direct royal decree. In 1614, a bailiff in southern Sweden who had used torture was brought before the royal court of appeal. The local judge in a defence petition pointed out that torture had been used in a witchcraft interrogation. The suspect had been questioned about *maleficium* 'and nothing else'. The bailiff was accordingly released.

In the Baltic provinces of Estonia and Livonia under Swedish rule the reception of German law (via the *Carolina* and Carpzov) was strong and torture was in common use. It was expressly legalized in a statute of 1632. The Swedes repealed it at the end of the seventeenth century but it was still resorted to by the courts well into the eighteenth.

CONSOLIDATION OF PATRIARCHAL SOCIAL RELATIONS

The overwhelming majority of those convicted and punished for witch-craft were women. Most estimates give 80 per cent as the average proportion. In the medieval laws, in the theological tracts and in popular lore, the stereotype witch was already a woman. The gender aspect is crucial for the understanding of early modern European witchcraft. For some time this obvious fact was used to paint a more pronounced feminist picture – witch persecution was the vicious response of a patriarchy[1] in crisis. This interpretation required another witch image; not the poor old crone of the Grimm *Märchen* and modern class-oriented sociology, but a young, talented and vigorous woman, a real threat against male supremacy in the rural community. No serious attempt has been made so far to find support for such an image in the historical sources.

With these critical observations in mind, it is still important to specify the ways in which the gender aspect of the witch persecutions can be related to structural conditions and processes of change in the fifteenth and sixteenth centuries. Was male dominance and gynophobia part of the medieval tradition or did gender relations change in such a way that this can serve as an explanation for the persecutions? Can regional and temporal variations tell us anything about the dynamics of this alleged battle between the sexes? Did the status and social role of women change in any crucial way in the period of witch beliefs?

Christina Larner (1984) has pointed to a series of developments which combined to create a view of woman as irregular and a threat to order. In penal law she was gradually recognized as responsible for her own acts. At the same time, a number of female deviations such as adultery, prostitution and infanticide were criminalized. As a result, women's behaviour in situations of conflict was perceived as a public concern. Cursing and bewitching were identified as the female counterpart to the physical violence of the male world. In addition, gender division and sexual tensions were pronounced as a result of excessive male mortality in a period of major wars. The sex ratio was highly unbalanced in many local communities.

Others have made similar observations. In his study of witchcraft in south-western Germany, Erik Midelfort (1972) was struck by the high number of unmarried women in his area of research. This was, he claimed, an expression of a general 'European marriage pattern' as described by John Hajnal (1965). As opposed to the customs of eastern European and non-European cultures, in western Europe people married very late. The shortage of land and other economic constraints served to postpone family formation. As a result, many young men and women had to wait until their late twenties or even early thirties before they could marry. Young bachelors were absorbed by the military system and other male institutions, while the girls stayed in the villages and formed a substantial group of 'spinsters', the object of ridicule, parental concern and sexual suspicion.

In Sweden, Ankarloo (1971) found an expression of the moral independence of women in the fact that in many places they were entrusted with the task of transmitting the cosmological and transcendent folk tradition to new generations. During the witch persecutions in the province of Dalarna, this cultural role of women was seen as a danger by some priests, who proposed that church schools should be founded so as to save children from the evil influence of women. In these parishes the sex ratio was also extremely unbalanced. The continental wars had reduced the number of adult males so drastically that, at the time of the witch persecutions, there were more than 200 women for every 100 men aged between 14 and 45. More than half of the girls had no prospect of finding a husband in the near vicinity. The world of God and men was thus set in opposition to another where Satan and women ruled. Some of the older witches who confessed, when asked if they did not see the enormity of their crimes, responded that they had not given much thought to it. And the men were not quite sure how to react. Many did not even try to defend their own wives and daughters. They seem to have been put off by the demonic fantasies about free celebrations, a free sexuality and the supernatural freedom of flying through the air. Their concern was for the children. Should they be brought up according to the rule of God and the law or by Satan and flying women? When freedom and social control were perceived in such terms, the men sided with the 'patriarchal' establishment. The women were the rivals of each other.

But it should be noted that in some northern regions magic seems to have been a male specialty at least as much as a female one. For a long time, a majority of those suspected of witchcraft in Finland were men. In the sixteenth century they constituted 60 per cent of the accused and as much as 75 per cent of those convicted. From the middle of the seventeenth century, when diabolism and other learned notions were introduced, these proportions were reversed. In the 1660s almost 60 per cent of the condemned were women, and, when persecutions reached their peak in the following decade, two-thirds were female. As soon as the witch-hunt began to subside in the 1690s, men again dominated. It seems possible to conclude that malevolent witchcraft, as well as the beneficial magic in the old tradition as defined by the Finnish peasantry, were not strongly gendered categories.

Just as in Finland, magic in Iceland was a male trade. Of the 120 suspects brought to court, only ten were women, and among 22 burned for witchcraft, only one was a female (Hastrup 1990).

DEVELOPMENT OF THEOLOGY AND DEMONOLOGY

The Protestant Reformations did change some of the legal practices. The persecution of superstitions other than *maleficium*, which had been the concern of the Church in the medieval period, was taken over by the state and was henceforth handled in the secular courts. The Protestant clergy took an active part in finding and accusing the magical operators, and also in submitting to Church discipline those who were ignored by the civil courts. As a result, there emerged a system in which the clergy assisted the secular arm in persecuting sorcery and witchcraft, but where the main responsibility lay with the regular courts.

During the seventeenth century the Church set its stamp on development more through influencing the authorities and public opinion than through direct measures of its own. The bishops and their chapters still had important duties on the regional level. Witches that the courts for one reason or another felt could be spared the death penalty were usually condemned, in addition to the lower civil punishment, to church penitence (*publica poenitentia*). It was the duty of the Church, after receiving a report from the local court, to effect this punishment. In addition, the clergy continued, by visitations and interrogations, to keep check in the villages. Serious cases of witchcraft were remitted to the civil court, sometimes with the priest acting as a public prosecutor. The less serious cases were punished directly by penitence, often combined with fines or whipping. Thus in many Protestant countries clerical justice came to complement the secular.

Since the Church had played an important role in defining the new, religiously shaded forms of crime, it was natural that its co-operation was requested in recognizing them in practice. In a number of witchcraft cases during the seventeenth century, the Swedish Royal Court of Appeal requested expert opinions from the chapters. The earliest of these pronouncements were, as we have seen, still carefully restrained. Proven *maleficium* or explicit rejection of God was required for the death penalty. But from the middle of the century a change of attitude can be discerned. In a number of church rescripts several offences against the Ten Commandments of God, each of which is worthy of death, are grouped together under the heading of witchcraft. In accordance with the current theocratic doctrine of punishment, the Old Testament (Exodus 22) is now cited as the primary legal source. Contemporary theological and scholarly dissertations at the universities dealing with magic and witchcraft are heavily reliant on continental models. They deal at special length with the problem of delimiting the power of the devil from that of man and God. The flight to Blåkulla and the witches' sabbat are described in much the same way as in the great craze of the 1670s. The aspect of witchcraft as religious transgression rather than *maleficium* is given prominence to justify demands for a stricter application of the law.

In Denmark the professors of theology at the University of Copenhagen were giving advice to the authorities in 1617 when the new statute on witchcraft was enacted. A few decades later, the Bishop of Sealand, Jesper Brochmand, in his handbook *Universae Theologiae Systema* (*System of Universal Theology*), tried to introduce the more advanced and repressive ideas on witchcraft expressed by authors such as Bodin, Binsfeld, Carpzov and Del Río, seemingly with very little success. On the whole, the influence of the churchmen in Denmark appears to have been more limited than elsewhere in the North.

SOCIAL TENSIONS ON THE LOCAL LEVEL

Who were the witches? In recent scholarship there have been numerous candidates – poor widows, women healers, feminists, migrants, to name but a few. Is it possible to test with any reasonably rigorous method these various hypotheses about the social and cultural profile of the people convicted of witchcraft? Unfortunately, in the great majority of cases the necessary information about age, marital status and other social indices of the accused is simply not to be found. Alan Macfarlane's study of English witch persecutions (Macfarlane 1970) is a case in point. It suggested that the accusations were primarily directed at elderly people who were perceived as a growing social burden at a time of rapid change in village life. But Macfarlane was unable to test this hypothesis, since out of about 300 registered suspects the age was given for fifteen only.

In some local studies the court records have been linked with other sources produced by the ever-growing state bureaucracies – census and tax lists, prison accounts, birth and death records. Studying witchcraft in Denmark, J. C. V. Johansen nevertheless had to resign himself to the fact that the government sources were simply insufficient for any reasonably safe assessment of the economic status of the convicted witches, but that, possibly, the accusations tended to be directed from the tenant farmers against women among the cottagers. In two urban areas the moderately poor turned against the destitute (Johansen 1990: 351–2). In another study (1991: 98) he was able to assess the fortunes of only 23 out of more than 400 witches. The value of their estates ranged from 1 to 567 dollars (median 19, average 73). Again, he concludes that in the great majority of cases no reliable estimates can be made of the socio-economic status of the accused.

In seventeenth-century Norway, according to Naess (1982), poverty and social disruption resulted in a deep structural crisis. Conflicts in the peasant community about the bare necessities of life gave rise to rumours, threats and open accusations of witchcraft. Most of them were directed against the very poor. His conclusion is based on indications of poverty in the records of slightly above 20 per cent of 877 registered cases. It is a bit risky to generalize this tendency to the remaining majority. The cost of the trials and the executions was supposed to be paid from the confiscated estates of the convicted. Perhaps one should ask why a court clerk in some cases chose to make a note of the poverty of the witch. A detailed study of the parish of Mora in Sweden based on tax material (Ankarloo 1971) indicates that most of the 60 women accused of witchcraft belonged to indigenous middle- and upper-level farm families. None of them were poor migrants.

To conclude, the a priori assumption that the witches on the whole were poorer than their accusers is not strikingly improbable, but the empirical support for such a simple socio-economic explanation in not very impressive. Altogether, these and other careful studies include fewer than a thousand suspects and they fail, both jointly and separately, to give any clear-cut picture of the social position of the 30,000 or more who were executed as witches. There is no justification for Horsley's categorical statement (1979: 689) that recent studies, 'including some basic and largely quantitative sociological analyses', all confirm 'the now familiar generalization that the vast majority of witches were poor, elderly women'. There is no such confirmation and no such consensus in recent studies, and it is doubtful if we will ever be able to give a reliable and sufficiently elaborate account of the complex social dynamics of the witch persecutions.

It is also necessary to criticize the reductionist methodologies of many explanations contending that the attack on magical beliefs and the onset of witch persecutions in early modern Europe can be fully understood as caused either by the rise of government, the militancy of churches, patriarchal gender relations or social tensions among the peasantry. It is not in itself unreasonable to think that the poor sometimes tried to use magic or threats of witchcraft to gain some resources and exert a little power. Women may have resorted to witchcraft fantasies to express their anxieties and frustration in the face of an oppressive patriarchy. The churchmen and the royal bureaucrats may have found it proper and necessary to mount an attack against popular beliefs in their endeavour to organize the peasant world into a uniform and transparent commonwealth. All these processes are certainly there, often in a multi-layered interaction, but only fragments of them are visible in the sources. When trying to reconstruct the rich and complex realities of past witchcraft beliefs and practices we must do this with proper respect as to what can be ascertained and supported with evidence, as opposed to what are merely our own beliefs and practices. Creative theorizing must be combined with methodological rigour.

THE SIXTEENTH CENTURY: FROM SORCERY TO WITCHCRAFT

The Protestant Reformations which affected all the countries of north-western Europe did not succeed in changing the old beliefs in magic and sorcery. It is particularly interesting to note that the most peripheral areas, Iceland and Finland, seem to preserve in virtually unchanged form the ancient verbal and shamanistic magic associated with the runes and the *utiseta*. These were, as we observed earlier, male activities. In sixteenth-century Finland more than half of those accused of witchcraft were men. Only with the shift to demonic magic and the sabbat did the percentage of women start to increase, surpassing that of men in the 1650s. However, with the return of traditional magic, after the exhaustion of the violent witch panic in the 1670s, men again became the dominant group. In Iceland, magic remained an exclusively male activity throughout the period.

During the last decades of the sixteenth century these new demonic elements of the witchcraft trials begin to appear in the court records. An inquisitorial judge or a public prosecutor would accuse the defendant of being in compact with the devil. The witches' sabbat is then described in detail – numerous women fly through the air to celebrate the blasphemous orgies at the devil's meeting. In the Swedish (and to some extent Norwegian) tradition this meeting place was called 'Blåkulla', i.e. the blue (or black) hill. The name had already occurred in the fifteenth century, but an explicit connection with the witches' sabbat is first made a century later. Olaus Magnus in his *Historia de Gentibus Septentrionalibus* (*History of the Northern Peoples*) (1555) offers the information that, at certain times of the year, the Nordic witches gather at Blåkulla to try their arts and sorceries. Those who are late for this devilish meeting are punished cruelly. But on this issue everyone should follow his own conscience rather than trusting others – it appears that the learned bishop had his doubts. The writings of Olaus Magnus were widely read in Europe, and they rendered the North the somewhat exaggerated reputation of being the homestead *par préférence* of witches and wizards. Jean Bodin, in his *De la Démonomanie des Sorciers* remarks that 'there are more witches in Norway and Livonia and the other Northern regions, than there are in the rest of the world, as Olaus the Great says'.

The change of emphasis in the view of witchcraft from physical harm to spiritual transgression, from *maleficium* to devil's cult, was in fact more pronounced in Sweden than in Norway or Denmark. It was directly connected with the Blåkulla myth and with the idea of a witches' sabbat, an important precondition for the great witch panic of the 1670s, which only affected Sweden and Finland. In Denmark, particularly, the crime of witchcraft, although common enough, never went through the full transformation from *maleficium* to sabbat. Neither did the legal procedure adopt the inquisitorial elements of the continental witch trials, retaining, instead, strong accusatorial traits throughout the period. This may help to explain why the rate of persecutions in Denmark, after a strong upsurge in the years 1615–25, gradually went down to almost insignificant levels in the following decades.

Later on, other methods became more common against suspects who refused to confess to their crime. They were sentenced to death and led out to the place of execution in the firm belief that they were about to die. A priest was present to remind them of the conditions for the salvation of the soul and he urged them finally to confess. Those who then submitted were executed on the spot, while those who refused to comply were returned to prison. Water ordeals, shaving and the needle test were also to be found in the local courts right up to the great craze of the 1670s. The evidence of accomplices was sometimes admitted and the advent of such terms as *crimen exceptum et occultum* and *crimen laesae Divinae Maiestatis* applied to witchcraft indicates the influence of continental legal doctrines.

Summing up the lines of development of the sixteenth and early seventeenth centuries we find three sorts of magic being the object of intervention by the authorities and the courts of law: the two old categories of superstition and *maleficium* and the new syndrome of apostasy, compact and witches' sabbat. The number of cases is hard to ascertain since court records were not universally kept before the end of the sixteenth century. But the activity was probably fairly low, with scattered and isolated cases of *maleficium*. However, with the advent of modern demonological ideas and with the penetration of the countryside by government officials and clergymen supporting the interventionist policy of the Protestant kings, the stage was set for more extensive persecutions.

WITCHCRAFT BY REGIONS

In the early modern period the British Isles, the Netherlands, Scandinavia and the Baltic area was a region with certain traits in common. It was held together by the important Baltic trade, it had a common law tradition and it was the main location of the Protestant Reformations.

As we saw in Part 1 of this volume, the German Empire, and in particular its Western principalities, stand out as the central area both of witch persecutions and of ideological development. Here most of the executions took place, and here the bulk of demonological literature was produced, distributed and incorporated into the learned tradition in both law and theology. A striking feature is the detailed conformity of witch accusations all over Europe. While many contemporaries regarded this as proof of the omnipresence of the devil, we are more inclined to see it as the result of a process of ideological diffusion accelerated by the printing press. Some areas were quicker than others to adopt the modern learned idea of witchcraft as a conspiracy of demons and evil women directed at the social order of the Christian community. But in most places these new and frightening features were developed against a backdrop of old-fashioned sorcery associated with perennial local conflicts between neighbours accusing each other of magic evil-doing. So while converging towards a new, strongly transcendent concept of witchcraft as a spiritual transgression, many areas still retained the popular and less extravagant image of the village witch.

If we look at northern Europe as a whole, a fairly uniform pattern can be discerned. The transition from maleficent sorcery to demonic witchcraft was a necessary precondition for the extensive persecutions and the numerous burnings in the Rhine valley area. In many other parts of the West and North this transition never fully took place. In England, the United Netherlands and southern Scandinavia executions of convicted witches were few and scattered. After a period of climactic persecutions in the decades around 1600, witchcraft cases tended to disappear from the courts all over the region. In comparison with other crimes, witchcraft cannot have been perceived as a major problem. George Kittredge (1929: 328) has observed that, in the reign of James I (1603–25), the county of Middlesex executed 40 witches, but more than 700 persons for other crimes. In Essex between 1560 and 1680, 5 per cent of all criminal indictments were for witchcraft (Macfarlane 1970: 30) and, in seventeenth-century Norway, the proportions were about the same (Naess 1982: 88). It may also help to put things in perspective to note that, in early modern Sweden, in spite of the great Blåkulla panic of the 1670s, more men were put to death for bestiality than were women for witchcraft (Liljequist 1992).

To make systematic regional and temporal comparisons of the differential rates and the relative intensity of witch persecutions is very difficult, in many cases almost impossible, since court records have been preserved in a very uneven, haphazard way. There are some difficult and time-consuming methods of compensating for this lack of court rolls. Local government accounts may include lists of fines and confiscations in criminal cases, or the expenditures for witch burnings and other executions. A few historians, notably Hans Eyvind Naess in Norway, have successfully used these indirect and scattered sources. But it should be kept in mind that their conclusions are sometimes based, as are those of English or Scottish historians of witchcraft in their respective countries, on imperfect and circumstantial evidence. For sixteenth-century England our knowledge is mostly confined to conditions in the south-east, the wider London area. Only from about 1650 are sources available from the West and North. Similarly, in Denmark continuous series of court books from the early seventeenth century exist only from the Viborg jurisdiction of northern Jutland, the material used by Johansen (1991) in his monograph.

England

In late medieval England accusations of witchcraft and magic evil-doing were part and parcel of the intense rivalries between the great noble houses. Lady Alice Kyteler was tried in 1324 by both ecclesiastical and civil authorities for compact with the devil. She was also charged with having killed three husbands and made a fourth mad with sorcery. A century later, Eleanor Cobham, Duchess of Gloucester, was involved in a sorcery case in London. Two of her accomplices were convicted and executed. Even later on, witchcraft retained some of this aristocratic flavour. Jane Shire, mistress of Richard III, was jailed for sorcery. In one of the alleged conspiracies against Queen Elizabeth I, the time-honoured method of piercing a wax doll with needles was resorted to. As late as 1622, the widow of Francis Shute was charged with having used sorcery to retain the affections of her lover, the Earl of Sussex.

But, otherwise, witchcraft in Britain has been seen as prominent among the general population rather than in high places. The two modern classics in English witchcraft studies, by Alan Macfarlane (1970) and Keith Thomas (1971), both focus on malevolent sorcery in the village communities of a period – the late Tudor and early Stuart ages – when social relations were strained by processes of rapid social differentiation between affluent and poor. The circumstances surrounding the witchcraft suspicions which they encountered in the court records were so often linked to classical *malefi-cium*, magical evil-doing, that they were led to build their whole explana-tory model around them: an angry encounter between a poor woman begging at the door of a more affluent neighbour, a refusal, a dark threat as the supplicant goes away and, a few days later, an illness or other misfortune occurs in the house of the uncharitable villager. In the course of everyday life situations of this kind could easily arise. They were in fact so common and ubiquitous that they had a section of their own in Roman law – *damnum minatum, malum secutum* (meaning 'a threat and a subsequent harm'). Such a sequence of events often led to accusations of, and also convictions for, witchcraft. Sometimes a member or two of the witch's family could be brought in as well. But most of these cases were individual and did not lead to mass persecutions. Full-scale panics with the devil's pact and witches' sabbat were in fact so rare in England that they were widely publicized when they occurred. One such sensational mass trial took place in Lancashire in 1633. Edmund Robinson, a 6-year-old boy, accused several women of witchcraft and of being in league with the Devil. Edmund was sent with his father to London, where he was submitted to closer legal investigation and eventually he retracted. This and other cases indicate that the higher courts did not allow things to get out of hand so as to produce mass accusations of this kind. But in 1645–7, during the turmoils of the Civil War, a certain Matthew Hopkins, styling himself as 'witch-finder general', created the last major witchcraft panic in the south-east. Almost 250 people were accused and submitted to unusual and aggressive methods of interrogation. They were kept awake for days on end and they were pricked with sharp needles in search of insensitive spots believed to be the devil's mark. As a consequence, several of them made elaborate confessions about being at the witches' sabbat, having sexual intercourse with demons and signing a devil's pact in their own blood. Even though the Hopkins affair seems to indicate that well into the seventeenth century the outbreak of witch panics on a continental scale was a possibility, available statistics from the south-eastern counties show that the number of accusations and the long-term rates of conviction for witchcraft were steadily declining. Magic and witchcraft were never fully demonized in England. The many scattered individual cases of maleficent sorcery that were brought to court rarely developed into systematic purges. A judicial system with an accusatory rather than an inquisitorial procedure, the absence of legal torture and the critical supervision of the higher courts combined to make witch hunts a marginal phenomenon in English history.

Scotland
Scotland was different. Several witch panics occurred in the 1590s, in 1629, 1649 and, largest of all, in 1661–2. The first major persecution was connected with a sensational witchcraft case involving both the royal houses of Denmark and Scotland. In 1589, King James VI sailed to Copenhagen to marry Princess Anna, sister of Christian IV, the King of Denmark. When bringing his bride back to Scotland he ran into terrible storms. The ship had to seek shelter in Norway for several weeks before being able to continue. The admiral of the escorting Danish fleet blamed the whole incident on witchcraft brought about by the wife of a high official in Copenhagen whom he had insulted. Several noble members of the Scottish court were implicated, and witch trials were held in both countries. The incident soon developed into a large scale witch-hunt. More than a hundred suspected witches in North Berwick were arrested. Under torture many of them confessed to having had nocturnal meetings

with the devil in the church. There they had danced, given their master the obscene kiss and promised him to do all kinds of evil. Subsequently, to fulfil their promise they had conspired to poison the king and members of his household and they were also implicated in the disastrous royal sea voyage from Copenhagen.

Later on in the 1590s, numerous trials seemed to indicate that Scotland was on its way to adopting the fully demonized witchcraft concept from continental Europe, and the Reformed Church criticized the secular authorities for being too lenient in their struggle against the enemies of God. As a consequence, the government took measures aimed at getting some sort of general control over persecutions that threatened to get out of hand. In 1597, it was ordained that all witchcraft cases were to be removed from the local courts to special commissions set up by the Privy Council. Such judicial supervision from higher authorities was at this time also exerted in England, Denmark and Sweden and probably served to make the legal treatment of witchcraft in these countries a bit more cautious. Not so in Scotland. The commissioners did not show much restraint in their work. Most of them were recruited among the gentry and they were prone to give in to local pressures from a frightened peasantry and a militant Church. Torture was freely used and professional witch-finders, using pricking needles to find the devil's mark, were very active, particularly during the last big persecution waves of 1649 and 1662.

Nearly two thousand recorded witch trials have been found in the Scottish archives. The great majority of these trials, 1,631 cases, fall in the period 1620–80. After that the incidence declines rapidly, and by the beginning of the eighteenth century persecutions stop altogether.

The Netherlands
In those parts of the Netherlands that were breaking loose from Spain, eventually to become the United Provinces, the intensity of witch persecutions in the later Middle Ages was as low as in other parts of northern Europe. There were a few executions in Maastricht in 1413 and in Nijmegen around 1470. In the sixteenth century scattered incidents of witchcraft occurred in Utrecht (1530), Groningen (1547) and Gueldern (1550). From the mid-1560s there was an increasing number of cases in the western provinces. During the century as a whole, there were 54 capital convictions in Groningen and about twenty in all in the provinces of Utrecht and Holland. Altogether, fewer than 150 executions took place. In addition to this number there were about 40 burnings in the Limburg area where violent hunts occurred up to the late 1620s. But Limburg was then still under Spanish rule, and most historians, therefore, do not include these cases among the persecutions in the United Netherlands.

From the beginning of the seventeenth century, Dutch magistrates ceased completely to impose the death penalty for witchcraft or maleficent sorcery. In later nationalist historiography, the Netherlands has therefore been eulogized as the first European country to put an end to the witch persecutions. It was the honour of the Fatherland (*de Roem des Vaderlandes*, Scheltema, 1828) to have abandoned medieval superstition at such an early time. Accepting this general view, many later historians have tried to find the explanations for this precocious enlightenment among the Dutch. One such explanation has focused on the intellectual development of the region. The influence of Erasmian philosophy and the critical role of Leiden University induced a healthy scepticism among the secular élites, making them increasingly reluctant to accept the demonological cosmology and the legal doctrines behind the violent witch-hunts endemic in nearby regions. Furthermore, the clergy of the Reformed Church was not allowed to exert any considerable influence on legal practices and other secular matters, as they did for instance in Geneva and in Scotland. When the Calvinist preacher and demonologist Lambert Daneau was called to a chair at the University of Leiden, his theocratic pretensions soon led to open conflict. The council of Leiden declared its will to 'resist the inquisition of Geneva no less than that of Spain' and Daneau had to leave (Trevor-Roper 1967: 170). A more structural explanation contrasts the urban, cosmopolitan Netherlands to more backward, rural areas of Europe. The 'openness' of urban culture made way for more tolerant attitudes than did the 'closed' rural communities (Schöffer 1973).

This broad interpretation has recently been challenged by Dutch historians as, on the one hand, too vague and general, and, on the other, too provincial, neglecting similar trends in nearby England and Scandinavia. First and foremost, as in other countries in the north-west, the demonological interpretation of magic was never firmly established in the United Netherlands. In addition, the crucial causes behind the decline of witch persecutions are to be found within the legal system and the Reformed Church. Progressively, the judiciary was staffed by men with a formal and uniform legal education. The differences between the various local jurisdictions were overcome and the control of the inquisitorial process used in capital cases was increased. There is a visible tendency among judges in the late sixteenth century to ask for solid empirical proof in all criminal cases, including those dealing with witchcraft. As for the Church, its emphasis was on suppressing popular magic such as that found in healing, prophecy and exorcisms. For that purpose the death penalty was not appropriate (Blécourt 1986).

Denmark

In Denmark and the two other countries under its rule, the evidence of witch burnings in the sixteenth century is not very extensive and dates mostly from the end of the century. In Denmark proper, several of the most widely known cases were associated with royal and noble circles. In 1543–4, witch trials were conducted on both sides of the Öresund (the straits between Sealand and Scania). They revealed evil deeds and the use of magic against the king's navy and against the king himself. A woman was accused of having made a wax figure in the king's image, but she denied this. True, she had made the puppet, but it was made to resemble a stonecutter in the city of Malmoe, and she had it christened by the Reverend Jochim, vicar in a neighbouring parish.

A wax image also plays a central role in the case against the noble Lady Christence Kruckow. In the 1580s she was a young girl living in the house of Sir Eiler Brockenhuus. He married Anna Bille, but it appears that Christence had ambitions to take her place. Lady Anna gave birth to fifteen children. Unfortunately, they were all stillborn or died at a very tender age. Finally, one of the servant girls was arrested, and she confessed that she and another servant had assisted Lady Christence in magical assaults against Lady Anna at the time of her marriage. The two servants were burned as witches in 1597, but the noble relatives of Christence managed to save her life. She moved to the city of Aalborg. There it was soon revealed that she and her sister had been present at a secret meeting where a woman gave birth to a wax child. It was christened and given the name Maren in order to harm a neighbouring woman with that name. Two of the accused were burned but the Kruckow sisters managed to escape again. Later, the bad reputation of Christence got her into new trouble. In 1618, she and four other women were accused of having bewitched a vicar's wife, driving her mad with the familiar wax image. The four commoners were burned after having confessed. Under torture they also implicated Christence, who was arrested and brought to Copenhagen. There she was tried by the House of Lords, deprived of her noble status and condemned to death. Her fortune was confiscated and handed over to the University of Copenhagen, where it still exists as 'The legacy of the beheaded Lady'. The general outrage caused by these and other prominent cases helps to explain the promulgation in 1617 of the new statute against witchcraft. For the first time the crime was defined in detail and the different punishments listed. Those who entered into a pact with the devil should be burned; those guilty of other kinds of witchcraft, including healing practices, were to be fined and exiled.

In practice, however, *maleficium* of the traditional kind continued to be punished by death in the local courts, and about half of these verdicts were also upheld by the *landsting*, the regional courts of appeal (roughly equivalent to the French *parlements*). They insisted on more careful procedures, demanding full proof with at least two independent witnesses, and rejecting hearsay evidence.

From the *landsting* of Viborg, with jurisdiction over the northern part of Jutland, the sources are well preserved and have been investigated by Jens Christian V. Johansen. They indicate a strong upsurge of trials, a veritable witch craze, in the 1610s and 1620s. The explanation offered by Johansen takes into account several contributing factors. Before the promulgation of the new witchcraft statute in 1617, the Danish peasants were more inclined to settle minor cases of *maleficium* out of court. The new law was introduced at a moment of economic crisis with declining export prices. This made people focus their grievances on witches. During the eight years of 1617–25, a veritable purge took place with hundreds of trials. When all these witches had been tried in due order, the supply of suspects was exhausted for a long time. When conditions favouring a new purge returned several years later, the legal opinion concerning witchcraft had changed so as to prevent further persecutions. From 1656 to 1686 only one single death sentence for witchcraft is known to have been pronounced in Jutland, and at the time there were complaints in Copenhagen that the county court judges sided with the witches.

In spite of the general excitement around 1620, the content of the accusations remained the traditional ones, mostly *maleficium* causing the death or sickness of men and animals. For this reason the wave of persecutions, although on a continental scale, cannot be compared to the craze of the 1670s in Sweden and Finland. Compact and sabbat never became important ingredients of the witchcraft lore of the Danish peasantry. The courts and the clergy did not do much to introduce, as in Sweden, the modern learned concepts of diabolic assistance in all cases of magic.

Nevertheless, just as in Sweden, traces of a popular concept of demonological witchcraft, although in a less developed form, are to be found in the trial records. The devil's mark is one such notion. Initiation rituals including apostasy are referred to. Occasionally the witches gathered in groups of twelve, and familiars in the shape of beautiful young men took part in these meetings. It seems that the popular mentality, partly of course under the influence of learned concepts from above, was on the verge of creating a complete demonological discourse. It happened in Sweden – why this development was arrested in Denmark is an interesting question.

Norway
In Norway the persecution of witchcraft was conducted in a way similar to that in Denmark. Altogether, less than a thousand trials have been recorded in the source material, 280 of which ended with capital convictions. *Maleficium* remained the single most important charge until the 1660s, when diabolism was introduced on a large scale. From 1617, the same witchcraft statute as that in Denmark was in force in Norway. It

required that at least two independent accusers took full responsibility for the indictment. It also invalidated the testimony of any witch or sorcerer or any other criminal to be used as evidence in court. These rules were frequently ignored. Death sentences were passed in cases of white magic, despite this also being forbidden according to the law modified in 1617.

Just as in Denmark, torture was legally permitted only against convicted witches, but it was nevertheless also freely used against suspects. Only towards the end of persecutions in the second half of the seventeenth century did the justices of the district courts intervene against these illegal procedures. Until then the convicted witches were forced under torture to denounce accomplices. These were promptly indicted and in many cases sentenced to death without any further proof. In his study of the Norwegian witch persecutions, Hans Eyvind Naess found 90 well-documented trials in which 353 suspects were denounced by convicted witches. In fact, the majority of death sentences for witchcraft in Norway were passed in this way. These harsh and illegal actions taken by the local officers responsible for the administration of justice had the support of popular opinion. In addition, the clergy warned their congregations against the servants of the devil. The procedures in common use on the Continent in such trials were brought to Norway by clergymen, judges and bailiffs born or educated in Denmark and Germany.

There were two periods of particularly intense persecutions, the first in the 1620s, coinciding with the upsurge in Denmark and with 69 capital convictions; the second in the 1660s, with ingredients of diabolism and the sabbat similar to the great Swedish craze and with 47 death sentences.

Naess is inclined to explain the Norwegian persecutions in social terms: a sharp increase in population up to the middle of the seventeenth century created a rural proletariat of beggars and vagrants, from which the suspects were recruited. These conclusions are based on the fact that, in about 80 per cent of the 200 trials containing information about the economic situation of those accused, they were characterized as extremely poor.

Iceland

In Iceland, 120 witch trials took place in the period 1604 to 1720. The population of about 50,000 lived in scattered farmsteads. Towns or even villages were entirely absent. In the second half of the seventeenth century, the average temperature declined, hitting the rock bottom of the Little Ice Age in the 1690s and leading to a general impoverishment of the Icelanders with recurrent famines and deaths from starvation.

The Danish witchcraft statute of 1617 was introduced in the 1630s, setting a new standard for the persecutions. Just as in Finland and Livonia, magic in Iceland was a male preoccupation. Of the 120 trials, only ten concerned women, and, among 22 burned witches, only one was female.

Like most persecutions where *maleficium* is the dominant charge, the Icelandic cases demonstrate a 'solitary pattern'. The witches are lone figures caught in a web of suspicion. The common people were concerned about individual damage or misfortune, while the priests and the officials waged war against Evil on a much more abstract level.

Into the seventeenth century the magic of the Icelandic witches still had many archaic traits. Runes were used to conceal curses which could not be spoken openly. The first wizard to be burned (in 1625) was caught with a sheet full of runes in his house. They were seen as proof of devilish undertakings. In addition to runes, *galdrastafir* (magic wands) were used in combination with incantations. As elements in a largely oral tradition, the formulas were normally transmitted from father to son, but some of them were collected in 'black books' (*Galdrabækur*) used by learned magicians. The old Nordic beliefs in the ability of some wizards to change shape (*hamr*) or to fall into trances using the shamanistic technique of *utiseta* were still part of a living tradition in seventeenth-century Iceland.

Sweden

In Sweden, the legal tradition handed down from the Middle Ages to some extent prevented the outbreak of an epidemic of witch persecutions. A plaintiff was required in the accusatorial process, while torture was in principle forbidden and only reluctantly resorted to. Convicted witches were not admitted as witnesses and the law itself only treated *maleficium*; nothing was said about compact and the witches' Sabbat. Most of these obstacles were overcome in the course of the seventeenth century. The legal procedure became more and more inquisitorial, and witchcraft was looked upon as an exceptional crime (*crimen exceptum*) justifying deviation from the ordinary rules of law. But one difficulty remained. In cases where the witches' sabbat was the main charge it was dangerous to give evidence. Who could tell about Blåkulla, intercourse with the devil and the celebration of the Black Mass except those who took part themselves? Who would want to step forward and testify about witchcraft if she ran the risk of being convicted herself of the same crime?

Beginning in the early 1660s, several witch trials were conducted where these difficulties were overcome. The main witnesses were children, innocent creatures who were taken against their will to Blåkulla by the old witches. They were victims rather than accomplices. Such charges were made in many places in the far north, in Vardöhus in Norway, in Angermanland on the Swedish east coast and, most importantly, in the parishes around the lake Siljan in the province of Dalarna. In December 1664, a 5-year-old boy from Älvdalen was bribed with food by the villagers to testify against his own family. He accused his grandmother and his mother of having a horn with grease, which they used to anoint a calf, and then father and mother rode with the boy to Blåkulla, and he sat on his mother's lap. In Blåkulla they were generously fed with fish, butter, porridge and sweet milk. After dinner they beat each other with the furniture. The boy had also seen a black crone and an ugly man boiling tar in a large cauldron.

The great persecutions were not primarily the result of an enforcement wave started from above and imposed on an indifferent or even hostile peasantry. On the contrary – the vindictiveness of the neighbours and their active participation in the inquisition are remarkable. Conversely, the authorities were very reluctant to start with. Only later did the clergy and the provincial governor step in to organize the hunt. It is also worth noting that, from the very beginning, hungry dreams of rich food were powerful ingredients of the stories.

On this occasion, the court dismissed it all as mere childish fantasies or dreams induced by the devil, but only a few years later similar things were told by other children in the parish, and now the game began in deadly earnest. In 1668, a great number of people, mostly women, were charged with riding and taking children to Blåkulla. The local court delivered the death sentence against eighteen women, among them four minors. Some had confessed under torture, while others were convicted on the evidence of the children and the accomplices. The verdicts were as usual sent to Stockholm for the scrutiny of the Royal Court of Appeal. It repealed the convictions of the young girls, and among the others the death sentences were confirmed only against the seven women who had confessed. The executions took place in the following summer. The witches were beheaded on top of the pyre and then it was set on fire to burn the dead bodies. This was the prescribed mode of execution everywhere in the Swedish-Finnish realm during the great persecutions. The philosophy behind it was that too cruel a death, such as burning alive, would bring the victim to desperation and consequently her eternal soul to damnation.

At the time of the first executions new investigations showed that the panic was far more widespread than had been feared. The centre of it was the parish of Mora. The peasants there had even sent a delegate to Stockholm to ask for more energetic measures to protect their children against the witches. To speed things up, the regency government appointed a royal commission empowered to carry out at once the death sentences decreed by its own judgements. It completed its assignment in Mora in two weeks in August 1669. Sixty suspects were interrogated and hundreds of children came forward with charges and tales of journeys to Blåkulla. Twenty-three persons, again mostly women, were sentenced to death. Of these, fifteen who had confessed were executed immediately. The parish priest, Elaus Skragge, who wrote a widely publicized account of the Mora persecutions, relates the outcome, obviously unaware of the murderous antecedents of the day of execution: 'They went on Bartholmew's Day, seven on the first pyre, five on the second and three on the third, a horrible spectacle. The pyres were built on a clean and sandy point by the river with water on both sides and in clear and beautiful weather. Several thousand people from all the surrounding parishes were present.'

But even these severe measures did not help. In the following year the craze spread through all the villages around the lake. Reports of at least 300 suspected witches and literally thousands of possessed children poured in to the government. New delegations from the stricken parishes went to Stockholm to demand that new measures be taken. The government was still reluctant. Some of the regents advocated a policy of silence. Their experience from the war in Germany indicated that the more one meddled with these things, the worse they got. But in the name of justice they had to yield to the insistent public opinion. Mora had been granted a royal commission: the other parishes were entitled to the same favours. A new royal court was sent out at New Year 1671 and soon other provinces were in turmoil as well.

The craze spread along the coast to the north and several new commissions had to be set up. One in Hälsingland was in session during the first months of 1673. Its president was Gustaf Rosenhane, a widely educated civil servant. In addition to the priests and the local judges, he had at his side two legal experts, Anders Stiernhöök, justice of the Court of Appeal, and Carolus Lundius, professor of Laws at Uppsala. From the very start the three gentlemen objected strongly to the irresponsible way the trials were conducted. Their criticism was both formal and rational. To base judgement, particularly when it concerned the death penalty, on evidence from accomplices and small children was utterly illegal. Moreover, the factual content of the stories about Blåkulla was of such a nature that it left grave doubts as to their verity and substance.

The majority of the court held a different opinion. It was necessary to rely on the only evidence available. 'Where do you find bread in the desert?', they argued, demanding harsh and effective legal measures. A number of death sentences were pushed through by the priests and the local representatives against the opinion of the president and his adherents.

Still there was no end in sight. An unknown number of children were affected and more than a thousand suspected witches were arrested and interrogated. During the first years, the distribution of this moral panic can be followed fairly well from village to village, almost from farm to farm. Judging from the speed and direction of the spread it seems likely that the close communications between neighbours and villages played a decisive role. This is also corroborated by the conformity of the accusations within and between local groups down to the individual families.

Rumours and stories circulated, influencing young and old. There were also professional witch-finders, mostly young boys who could 'see' who travelled to Blåkulla and were paid for their services out of the parish coffers. Some of the bolder ones exacted food and drink from people in return for not defaming them. This combination of begging and blackmail was often carried out by poor orphans. The authorities tried to stop the traffic but it was kept going by priests and parish elders.

The Blåkulla mythology was from the very beginning familiar to most people. Over the years there were minor additions and a visible shift of emphasis, but, on the whole, the stories are the same in all the thick volumes of witchcraft records (a conservative estimate comes close to 10,000 pages). Blåkulla is a naïve reflection of the peasant world. Most of the features are really mirror images, dichotomously transformed. One eats with the back of the neck, holds things with the left hand, copulates back to back and gives birth from the anus, 'but it does not hurt'. The meaning of these everyday but back-to-front activities is scarcely evil. On the contrary, Blåkulla is depicted at this stage as pleasant. It is a light, decorated dining hall, a wedding feast with lots of food, milk, porridge and bread 'sweet as figs'. It is the religious customs which, when transformed, acquire sinister implications. The dichotomy becomes perversion – rejection of God, compact with Satan, rebaptism, being entered in the black book and prayers of damnation ('Our Father which art in Hell').

Thus, left to itself Blåkulla functions in a chiefly pleasant manner. However, he who breaks the agreement with the devil is subjected to mistreatment. The food is turned into frogs and mire and the dining hall becomes cold, dark and painful. Satan, who first appeared as a friendly bearded man, suddenly becomes hairy, with horns and tail, and nakedly diabolical. Snakes are woven into lashes in a way reminiscent of the Viking witch on the Hunnestad monument. Some witches assume the guise of crows, ravens or other black birds. The renegades are flayed alive and their skins are put on spikes on the wall or pumped up with air and light, so that they seem to occupy their high seat at the table like empty ghosts, 'luminescent'.

But horror, too, has its bounds. Blåkulla is not Hell, which lies below in the nether regions. The devil is chained under the table. White angels step in to protect the tormented children. Good and Evil are mixed together, competing for the souls of the young and experienced differently by different children. In this unstable, chaotic environment, white angels appear to defend the children, the innocent, against the forces of Darkness. Clearly, chiliastic elements are connected with this graphic confrontation between Heaven and Hell.

Almost everywhere the local population actively participated in the trials. The authorities were influenced by insistent demands from the parish delegations sent to Stockholm. There is also a great deal of evidence that parents and relatives used bribes and other pressures to make children and suspects confess and tell about the journeys to Blåkulla. Private assaults and direct lynchings on declared witches also occurred.

Some families ran greater risk of being accused than others. More than half of the interrogated or condemned witches belonged to families with two or more accused members. Family feuds may naturally have contributed to this but accusations within the family were just as common as between different kin groups. The current hypothesis in witchcraft research that accusations were primarily directed against the very poor cannot be verified in the Swedish material. A survey of the economic situation in Mora, based on details of sowing and harvesting from the tithe lists, seems to indicate that relatively more of the suspects belonged to the middle and upper levels of the community.

The transvected children who gave evidence against the accused played a decisive role in establishing proof. During the whole period, several thousand must have appeared in court. In the early trials each child accused only one witch, but, later on, above all in the north, they said that they were transvected by two or more in turns. Moreover, they saw others at the feast in Blåkulla. Thus the number of accusations varies, while showing an upward trend. The children's participation also varied. In the North about a fifth of the young witnesses provided more than half of the evidence. These energetic and vindictive children also displayed a marked conformity in their accusations, often directing them at local family groups.

The pressure brought to bear on the accused varied in different ways. Torture was sometimes used. The priests who collected the preliminary material and the court itself were able to regulate the number of witnesses at will. As a consequence, there were many witnesses especially against those who denied the charges. The supply of accomplices ready to give evidence was also clearly related to the needs. In those districts where many suspects confessed, the children played a minor role, and vice versa.

As a result of all these irregularities the governor of the northern province felt uneasy about the continuation of the legal proceedings. It was to be feared, he reported to Stockholm, that the number of executions would be intolerable. But the goverment responded this time with an even more repressive policy. 'One cannot relax a rule in the face of mere quantity. The honour of God and the purging of the country from such a grave sin must be our prime consideration.' The use of torture against strongly suspected but stubborn witches was officially sanctioned.

The year 1675 was to mark the zenith of the trials. The exact number of executions is not known but everything points to there being at least

100 victims. Again the governor expressed his distaste concerning the turn which the trials had taken. The evidence of the children, the most important proof against those who refused to confess, was conflicting and uncertain. Before this and other legal and practical problems had been solved he refused to sanction further executions. With the approval of King Karl XI, who by now had come of age, the great commission of the north was terminated. After four years in the north the craze was now on its way south. In the province of Uppland near Stockholm, isolated cases had occurred by the beginning of 1675. In the following year, when Stockholm was also involved, two new commissions were set up. And it was in the capital that the end was to come. For the first time the justices of the royal court and the members of the government were able to see the craze at close quarters. Gradually they were able to assess the criticism which for a long time had been voiced by some of the commissioners in the provinces. But it took a long while, almost two years, before the change definitely took place. In the beginning the matter was given little attention. In the summer of 1675 it was an upper-class entertainment to visit the nursing homes set up to protect the possessed children. The Count de la Gardie invited the French ambassador Jean de Feuquières to see the spectacle of the raving children. In a letter to his king the sceptical Frenchman comments: 'I sometimes went to see this little comedy, which at least I found to be well acted' (Ankarloo 1971: 195, note 11).

To begin with, the Stockholm commission conducted its investigations along the old lines. Several death sentences were passed. One woman was burned alive – the only instance during the great trials. And then, all of a sudden, the child witnesses began to confess that their stories were pure make-believe and that the accused witches were innocent. The court thereupon sifted all the evidence with the same result, and all the condemned women were set free.

And so, in 1676, the witch trials came to an end after almost ten years of turmoil involving thousands of people as witnesses and suspects and with more than 300 executions. Instead, official proceedings were launched against a handful of the most active witnesses, four of whom were sentenced to death for making false accusations. A prayer of thanksgiving was printed and distributed throughout the country: God had finally subdued the ragings of Satan.

Finland

Finland went through roughly the same development as Sweden. Up to the middle of the seventeenth century *maleficium* cases were dominant. A remarkable trait is that for a long time a majority of those accused of witchcraft were men. In the sixteenth century they constituted 60 per cent of the accused and as much as 75 per cent of those convicted for witchcraft. From the middle of the seventeenth century when diabolism was introduced, these proportions were, however, reversed. In the 1660s almost 60 per cent of the condemned were women, and, when persecutions reached their peak in the following decade, two-thirds of the convicted were female. As soon as the witch-hunt began to subside in the 1690s, men again dominated in both categories. We can conclude that malevolent as well as beneficial magic as defined by the Finnish peasantry was a male preoccupation.

A closer study of the early trials indicates that most accusations for witchcraft were associated with foodstuffs and cattle, sickness and health being the second largest group. A victim of witchcraft or his or her relative accused the witch of having caused an illness. If the conflicting parties did not have the powers to bewitch the enemy, these services were readily purveyed by travelling professionals. Sorcerers were also consulted to find stolen goods (coscinomancy) and to take revenge on the thief. The great persecutions roughly coincided with those in Sweden, culminating in the 1670s. Witch-hunts took place in the archipelago of Åland in the Baltic and in the province of Österbotten along the west coast facing Sweden. In Åland the local judge introduced the contemporary demonological concepts as set down by authors such as Benedict Carpzov and Michael Freude. The most important charge was that of having a pact with the devil. The suspects were interrogated after conviction in order to obtain denunciations, and torture was used. The devil's mark and witch ointment were searched for. In short, most of the elements of a witch craze were present. Eight or nine women were condemned to death. But in 1670 it was revealed that much of the evidence had been fabricated by the suspects in the face of threats and torture, and so the persecutions came to an abrupt end.

In Österbotten, twenty women and two men were sentenced to death between 1674 and 1678. It should be noted that these trials, as well as those in Åland, took place in areas on the Baltic, where the population was of Swedish origin, speaking Swedish rather than Finnish. The connection with the trials in Sweden proper was also clear almost everywhere, children and young people playing an important role as witnesses and testifying about visits to Blåkulla. There are, however, specific traits in the Österbotten trials worth noticing. The towns in the area were small, with only a few hundred inhabitants, but their business life was lively because of the important tar trade. As compared to the rest of the country, the province was wealthy. Suspicions voiced in the trials were partly connected with misfortune in business, reasons for which were sought in witchcraft. The rumours also brought to light many long-standing conflicts between families.

Estonia and Livonia

In Estonia and Livonia, the Baltic provinces under Swedish rule in the seventeenth century, the authorities, among them Hermann Samsonius, the Bishop of Riga, took a rather conservative and careful stand in cases of witchcraft. In 1626, Samsonius published his *Neun ausserlesen und wohl-begründete Hexenpredigt* (*Nine Selected and Well-Founded Witch Sermons*). There he recognized three kinds of witches: (1) the melancholiacs who were blinded by the devil, imagining that they had signed a pact with him, without actually doing so. They were sick, and should not be punished. (2) Those who in fact had made a compact with the devil, but who had brought no harm. They were to be expelled from the parish. (This was also the position taken by the Swedish bishops at about the same time.) (3) Those who had a pact with the devil, served him of their own free will and had brought harm to man, beast or harvest. Both God's word and the German Imperial code, the *Carolina*, ordered this category to be burned alive. In spite of their relative restraint, these arguments had very little to do with the popular witch figure in Livonia, which never developed demonological traits. As in Finland, the magical operators were often males and their concern was the death or sickness of men and cattle, werewolves and, as a special and somewhat curious trait, magic associated with the fermentation and serving of beer. In fact, the most common accusation was poisoning with 'hexed' beer, whereby the victim's body was infested with worms, toads or vermin. For instance, a peasant's wife was charged with having placed the curse of snakes on the beer at a wedding. She had blown into the jug of beer and then given it to the groom to drink.

Belief in werewolves was widespread. At numerous trials people of both sexes were accused of doing harm while werewolves. A woman confessed that she had been a werewolf for four years, and had killed a horse and some small animals. Then she had hidden the wolf skin under a stone in the fields. Another woman confessed that an old hag had led her into the woods and fed her sweet roots – then they began hunting together as werewolves. When asked by the judges if his body took part in the hunt, a male werewolf confirmed that he had found a dog's teeth-marks on his own leg, which he had received while a werewolf.

In the preserved court records of the sixteenth and seventeenth centuries from Estonia and Livonia, no more than about two hundred cases have been found, and only 65 of those resulted in a death sentence. The virtual absence of diabolism in the Baltic trials helps to explain why no large-scale witch craze broke out in the area. If the persecutions, as some scholars believe, were part of an educational programme to Christianize and advance the common people, Livonia may be considered a negative case in point. The cultural and social distance between the indigenous peasantry on one hand, and the German landowners and the Swedish rulers on the other, delayed the implementation of such a programme until the end of the seventeenth century, when witchcraft was becoming outmoded.

CONCLUSION

The various parts of north-western Europe exhibit great similarities in the field of magic and witchcraft. The legislation was basically the same everywhere, directed almost exclusively against *maleficium*. The legal procedure gave much room for the contending parties, the accusatory process being predominant at least up to the end of the sixteenth century. In the more peripheral areas of Iceland, Finland and Livonia, the typical magical operator was a man, probably a trait going back to pre-Christian times. But there are also some interesting differences. The fully demonized witchlore, in Sweden and Finland associated with the sabbatical Blåkulla, was never incorporated into the cosmology of the Danish or Livonian peasantry.

The discourse of witchcraft was the result of a constant merging and restructuring of heterogeneous elements such as the ancient idea of flying and dreaming, the *gandreið* and the *utiseta*, the popular etiology of sickness and misfortune and the learned demonization of nature. The pace and extent of this process was somewhat different in the various Nordic countries. It went further in Sweden and Finland, contributing to the great witch panic of the 1670s.

Perhaps the militarization of society and the constant fiscal demands associated with Sweden's long wars in Livonia, Poland and Germany created a more ambitious and interventionist style of government – an active concern on the part of the clergy and the local civil servants with conditions among the peasantry, which furnished the soldiers and paid the taxes. In Livonia and Denmark, the land-owning aristocracy in control of local government was less inclined to see witchcraft as an ideological problem, intervening only when it was perceived as a direct physical threat.

In Sweden, the spectacular revelations in Stockholm in 1676 put an end to the great witch craze. After that only scattered cases occurred. The last execution for witchcraft took place in the 1710s. In the new National Code of 1734 maleficent witchcraft and compact with the devil were still capital offences. However, the statute was never used and it was finally removed in 1779.

Around the end of the seventeenth century the witch persecutions came to an end almost everywhere in the north. Occasional outbreaks in the countryside were suppressed when brought before the higher courts. In

1686 Denmark carried through its final witchcraft legislation (later also applied to Norway and Iceland), an ordinance which stipulated that all death sentences pronounced by the county courts had to be appealed to the supreme court. After 1650, persecutions were in fact so rare in most of western Europe that, when they occasionally occurred in distant and exotic provinces such as Scotland or northern Scandinavia, they created a genuine sensation.

In the 1670s, for instance, leaflets and popular prints were spread by hawkers and sold at the great fairs describing in vivid detail the witches of Dalarne in Sweden and their transvection of numerous innocent children to the devil's sabbat. This baroque *reportage* was originally written by an eye-witness, Elaus Skragge, vicar of Mora. It was immediately printed in both Dutch (*Translaet uyt het Sweets: Zijnde getrocken uyt het Prothocol over de examinatie de ontdeckte Toverey in het Dorp Mohra*, s'Gravehage, 1670) and German (*Ausführliche Bericht von dem entdeckten grausamen Zauberei in dem Dorffe Mohra und ombliegenden Plätzen in Schweden*, 1670). It was reprinted in *Diarium Europaeum* (Vol. 20, Frankfurt/Main, 1670), *Theatrum Europaeum* (Vol. 10, 1677) and in Heppel's *Relationes Curiosae* (Vol. 5, Hamburg, 1691). An English translation, also from the Dutch version, was made by E. Horneck, *An Account of what happened in Sweden*. It was printed with the 1683 and numerous later editions of Glanvill's famous *Sadducismus Triumphatus*. In Scotland, George Sinclair used it in *Satan's Invisible World Discovered* (Edinburgh, 1685) and, in America, Cotton Mather included it in *Memorable Providences Related to Witchcraft and Possessions* (Boston, 1689). The English version was used by Balthazar Bekker in his celebrated *De Betoverde Weereld* (Amsterdam, 1691 – the *Account* is in Part IV, Ch. 39). With Bekker's book it was again translated into several languages – German in 1693, French in 1694, and English in 1695. Already in the first Dutch edition the facts about the Mora trials in particular were distorted and grossly exaggerated. The number of those burned alive was said to be 84 adults and fifteen children (rather than in fact seventeen adults beheaded and then burned). Even in modern 'scholarly' works, the *Account* is quoted as the plain truth (e.g. Robbins, 1959). The sensationalisms of now and then are not very different.

NOTE

1. In both ancient and early modern times 'patriarchy' was understood as the rule of fathers over sons and of parents over children. Sir Robert Filmer's *Patriarcha* (1680) takes its arguments from the differential succession of Adam's and Noah's sons in the Old Testament. In his devastating critique of Filmer, John Locke treated the relevant biblical texts as ethnographic evidence, thus laying the ground for a

modern social interpretation. Luther was also careful to stress the supplementary family authority of mothers. The dominant connotation of 'patriarchy' today seems to be the rule of men over women. This was essentially the creation of nineteenth-century anthropologists such as Bachofen, Morgan and Engels. From them it was adopted by the gender theory of the late twentieth century.

PART 3

Witchcraft and Magic in Early Modern Culture

Stuart Clark

The first two contributions to this volume have concentrated on the legal prosecution of witches in, first, the central, western and southern areas of Europe, and, then, in what at the time would have been called the 'septentrional' lands. This will have given a good impression of the various ingredients that went to make up the trials themselves and the immediate circumstances in which they took place. But witchcraft and magic reached much further into early modern life and thought than this. Legal prosecution itself would have been impossible without more widely shared assumptions about their importance and relevance in other contexts. This final essay looks at manifestations of witchcraft and magic in the broader culture of the period by considering three of these contexts. The first concerns the beliefs and practices associated with magic and fear of *maleficium* among the broad mass of the European population, which are very much continuous with those described in earlier and later volumes in this series. The last concerns a kind of magic far more restricted both in appeal and historical occurrence – the 'high' or intellectual magic that attracted many Renaissance and late-Renaissance European thinkers and their patrons by its promise of universal wisdom. In between, is sandwiched an account of what might be called the textual life of witchcraft – its representation in the literature known as 'demonology' between the fifteenth and eighteenth centuries. At first sight, these aspects of our subject may well seem as bizarre and irrational as the witch trials themselves, and such, indeed, has been their reputation in the past. The aim in what follows is to dispel this impression by showing that witchcraft and magic had a culturally and historically based rationality of their own. Even if they were always contentious matters, this too arose from circumstances internal and intrinsic to early modern culture.

CHAPTER 1

Popular Magic

MAGIC AT WORK

In 1517, a Castilian by the name of Alonso González de la Pintada presented himself to inquisitors in the diocese of Cuenca concerning a cure he had always used against haemorrhoids:

> Take the sick person to a certain fig tree and have him kneel facing the east with his hat off. Then you bless him, saying, 'In nomine patris et filii et spiritu sancti, what do I cut?' The sick one then says, 'The piles of so-and-so', and recites devoutly a Pater Noster and an Ave María, while you recite them as well. Together you recite the prayers three times, while you cut off nine figs from the fig tree. Then you take the figs to a place where neither sun nor smoke can get at them. While the figs dry out, the piles are cured.

González was punished as a Judaizer, but attempting to heal by sympathetic magic cannot have helped his cause (Nalle 1992: 14–15). In mid-sixteenth-century Rome, the prostitute Lucrezia the Greek was also using magic to gain customers and political allies in the city and to tap into the amatory powers of her rivals. In 1559, she was investigated by the governor's court on suspicion of making a young servant recite over and over again an incantatory 'prayer' addressed to an image of St Daniel. The prayer asked the saint, acting for God, the Virgin Mary and all the other saints 'of the sky, of the earth, of the air, fire, and water [to] work magic on one messer Giovanni Maria, a [domestic] servant of the pope, to make him love Lucrezia'. It had been bought for five scudi from a woman friend who had in turn inherited it from her mother. Another servant reported that Lucrezia also 'went to cut the cords of the bells and that she had them burnt in a lamp with oil and holy water so that messer Giovanni Maria might love her, and that she had earth taken from in front of the doors of the famous courtesans and brought to her house, saying that in such a way she would have good fortune come to her house' (Cohen and Cohen 1993: 190).

Thirty-five years later the people of an entire German district – Wiesbaden in the county of Nassau-Wiesbaden (Hesse) – were described by church visitation officials as habitual users of 'spells' and 'incantations' in every conceivable situation:

> To wit: when they are in pangs of childbirth, when an infant is picked up or laid down (to guard him against sorcery), when a child is taken to be baptized (at which time they bind amulets or bread crumbs into the baby's swaddling cloths to ward off enchantment), when cattle are driven out or brought home or are lost in the fields, when they shut their windows in the evening, and so on; also against all manner of sickness or misfortune. Whenever something has been mislaid, when a person feels sickly or a cow dries up, they make straightway for the soothsayer . . . to find out who has stolen the object or put a bad spell on the animal, and to procure from him some charm to use against the offender.

Names, words and rhymes were 'mumbled' or written on scraps of paper and then eaten or worn as amulets. 'Outlandish' signs and gestures accompanied strange deeds with 'roots, herbs, mandrakes, and Saint-John's-wort'. Every action, it was said, had its 'special day, hour, and secret place' (Strauss 1978: 304; cf. for Catholic Germany, Forster 1992: 236).

The early seventeenth-century inhabitants of Lower Brittany were apparently no different. The Catholic priest Michel Le Nobletz described a whole series of magical rituals practised during his 'missionary' work among them around 1610. Women swept dust from chapel floors and threw it into the air to secure the safe return of their fishermen husbands and sons. Objects with magical significance were strewn in fields to keep wolves away from straying livestock, and local fountains were given sacrificial offerings and used for divination. 'The people', he wrote, 'offered these fountains as many pieces of bread as there were persons in their families, and drew conclusions, from the way the bits they had thrown in in their name floated or not, as to who would die during the coming year' (Delumeau 1977: 162). Half a century later, in another part of Europe again, the peasants of the parish of Maarja-Magdaleena in Estonia were doing much the same kind of thing, but with fire rather than water. On Midsummer Eve 1667, they built a fire near a ceremonial stone and then set about healing their various afflictions:

> the sick come, who have internal ailments, and must take bandages with wax and tie one around their bodies and also pick up a dipper of ale, go around the fire three times and while doing this they must bow to certain places of the stone while saying 'O help us, St John.' Having done this, they remove their bandages and hand them to the same old woman who holds it before the patient's mouth to be kissed. Then the

bandage will be burned on the stone, the sick will drink from the dipper and pass it to the woman who will make the sign of the cross three times on the dipper and say, 'Help, dear St John, through these healing drugs this person', saying the sick person's name and ailment; afterwards she drank from the dipper and let the two widows drink also.

Other similar 'sacrifices' using wax and candles were prescribed for headaches and external injuries (Kahk 1990: 279–80).

These are not isolated or untypical instances – quite the contrary. During the early modern centuries, as in those before and after, individual men and women throughout Europe could draw on a very wide and versatile repertoire of communally shared practices of this sort (Wilson 2000). But, in addition, there were countless local experts in magic who provided extra help and resources when occasion demanded. In the Netherlands, for example, a region whose professional magicians have been much studied, one of them, Dirck Pieters, was banished from the province of Holland in 1550 for practising as a cunning man and conjuror. A century later, in Kampen, Jannigien Clinckhamers was likewise exiled for expelling ghosts, blessing cattle, and putting charms under thresholds and giving them to sick horses. And another century on, physicians in Amsterdam were complaining about a healer from Germany, Johann Christoph Ludeman, who, despite his university diploma, was still using many of the same 'cunning' techniques in the 1720s (Waardt 1993: 33–41; Waardt 1997: 142–5; Blécourt 1993: 52). In the 1570s and 1580s, the parishioners of the German margravate of Brandenburg-Ansbach-Kulmbach were travelling from a 35 mile radius to the village of Baiergrün to visit Margaretha Hohenberger, who treated sicknesses, provided abortions, recovered stolen goods and practised general soothsaying and divination. Meanwhile, in Ergersheim in Rothenburg ob der Tauber, the local cunning man Georg Kissling was being punished for using a crystal ball to find stolen goods and herbal protections for animals (Dixon 1996: 179–81; Rowlands 1996: 111–12).

In the Italian city of Modena in 1595, a 60-year-old healer called Antonio Coreggi confessed to local inquisitors that he had treated hernias for half a century without realizing that his special cure for the condition was sinful. It was performed at daybreak, either on the feast of St John the Baptist or on Good Friday. The sufferer had to be passed three times through an opening in a freshly split nut tree to readings from John's Gospel. A fellow healer, Diamente de Bisa, also from Modena, reported that her cure for worms involved the sign of the cross and the saying: 'On Holy Monday, Holy Tuesday, Holy Wednesday, Holy Thursday, Holy Friday, Holy Saturday, Easter Sunday, the worm dies and decays' (O'Neil

1987: 93, 97). And in 1632, in Kõlleste in Estonia, the authorities from Tartu indicted a popular sorcerer called Pudell for using spells and magical objects, including a stick, a coin, rings, and pieces of yarn and moss (Madar 1990: 268).

In England, and in the British Isles generally, cunning men and women were just as plentiful and just as popular. An Elizabethan cunning man from Dorset, John Walsh, was examined and tried in 1566 (as a suspected sorcerer) for a range of magical practices that included finding lost goods and consulting fairies (Thomas 1971: 215, 634; Gibson 2000: 25–32). In North Moreton in Oxfordshire in 1604, the 20-year-old Anne Gunter, seemingly bewitched, was seen by John Wendore of Newbury, 'being a person supposed to be cunning in matters concerning witchcraft', and by another cunning man called Blackwall, and her case was discussed with a third named Palliser. All of them were well known in the area. A doctor summoned to examine her, Roger Bracegirdle, even recommended that her family seek 'some cunning men to do [her] good'. Anne's neighbour, Alice Kirfoote, who was similarly afflicted, received 'a little bag' to hang around her neck and 'a little green vial glass' with liquid in it to drink, both supplied by Goodwife Higgs of Ashampstead, who had a reputation for helping bewitched cattle. 'Few settlements', says James Sharpe, 'could have lain more than five miles from the residence of one of these good witches' (Sharpe 1999: 72, 57–9, 46). On the borders of Sussex and Kent, in the town of Rye around the same time, the widow Anne Bennett and her daughter Anne Taylor were both well known as 'cunning folk' and the daughter attended their neighbour Susan Swapper who was afflicted by spirits in 1607, only to be accused herself (and acquitted) of practising witchcraft (Gregory 1991: 35–8). In 1634, the JPs in Lancashire investigated the activities of one Henry Baggilie, who used charms and spells to heal clients despite becoming ill with the same afflictions himself (Sharpe 1996: 67). Across the Pennines in Yorkshire, assize depositions mention the general services of charmers and healers such as Joan Jurdie (1605), Elizabeth Hodgson of Scarborough (1651) and a 'widow Gransley' (1655) (Sharpe 1992: 13–14). Such individuals even appeared in the imaginative literature of the period, another telling indication of their place in English culture. At the conclusion of George Gifford's fictional yet documentary book, *A Dialogue Concerning Witches and Witchcraftes* (1593), a character meant to capture the essence of local Essex expertise in magic, 'Good Wife R', enters the debate and attempts to confound its main arguments. The dramatist and poet Thomas Heywood even wrote a play called *The Wise-Woman of Hogsden* (1638), in which its central figure describes herself as a fortune-teller and a dealer in 'Physick and Fore-speaking, in Palmistry, and recovering of things lost', as well as a pimp and abortionist (Beier 1987: 29).

Individually identified magicians like these are scattered in great abundance through the ecclesiastical records of early modern Europe. But a whole typology is also evident in the collective terms that contemporaries used to describe them. Magic was a recognized ingredient in the rituals of Italian healers such as the *benandanti* of Friuli, the wandering *pauliani* (who specialized in snakebite cures) and the *ciarlatani*, as well as of those cunning folk known in the kingdom of Naples under the names *janare*, *magare* and *fattucchiare* (Burke 1987: 209, 213–17; Gentilcore 1998: 22–3). In Hungary, the equivalents of the western European magical practitioners were the *táltos*, men and women who were treasure seekers, fortune-tellers and enemies of witches, as well as healers. But Hungarians also knew the seer (*néző*), the wise man (*tudományos*) and the soothsayer (*javasasszony*) (Dömötör 1980; Klaniczay 1990: 254). French magicians were known as *devins*, *conjureurs* and *leveurs de sorts*, while in Portugal it was the *saludadores*, men with innate powers, who dominated rural magic (especially the healing of livestock) and the 'sorcerers', usually women, who dealt with the management of love and marriage by divination, often in urban environments. In some Portuguese cities there were even informal networks of sorcerers – 23 of them in Alcácer do Sal and 62 in Évora (Bethencourt 1990: 421–2). In early eighteenth-century Debrecen in Hungary – and no doubt in many other early modern communities – fierce rivalries broke out between the 'wise women' who made up a substantial proportion of those accused of witchcraft in the city (Kristóf, 1991/92: 107–9). In the Netherlands, and in Finland and Iceland, men have been found to predominate among the 'cunning folk'; in Modena, most of those investigated by the Inquisition for magical healing were women.

We can already see from many of the examples given so far what sort of actual techniques made up the magical practices of both private individuals and specialists. To attempt a comprehensive survey of them would be an endless task and not especially enlightening. To some extent – greater, perhaps, than one might imagine in the context of oral transmission – the techniques were uniform. All over Europe, men and women practised divination with scissors and sieves, or books and keys, or by peering into the flat surfaces made by water or mirrors or 'crystals'. They scrutinized the natural fluids of humans and animals, especially urine, they cast lots, they read 'signs' in the heavens and in nature, they consulted with the dead and with spirits, they spoke conjurations over crops or dwellings and they diagnosed illnesses and even cured them by measuring the bodies of the sick. The psychological skills of professional magicians in articulating the fears, suspicions and diagnoses of their clients also seem similar wherever they practised; so too do many of their practical ones. On the other hand, there was seemingly no limit to the words and things deemed to have special powers or to the ingenuity shown in manipulating them for magical gain. In Zwickau in the early sixteenth century a healer applied fried onions and incantations to a patient's head in order to cure him. A peasant from Saint-Dié in Lorraine offered to heal a neighbour's dislocated hip 'by begging manure from nine different stables, filling the peasant's breeches which he had been wearing at the time of the accident with it', and then hanging them up in the church of St Benedic in Brecklange. Jesuit visitors to Untergrombach in the bishopric of Speyer in the later seventeenth century were shocked to discover a traditional cure that involved the sick person saying a sacrilegious prayer and walking naked round the church altar (Karant-Nunn 1987: 201; Delumeau 1977: 163; Forster 1992: 236). Mary O'Neil reports of eight prostitutes tried in Modena in 1593–4 that they 'knew scores of devices to induce passion in another person'. One of them was a love charm calling on St Martha to go

> to that wood where Our Lord Jesus Christ baptised with his twelve Apostles. . . . Cut three branches of fire and flame and for love of me send them to the heart of N.N. Send them through the veins of the heart, of the head, of the lungs, through the marrow of the bones, the flesh of the legs, with such love that it beats and scourges, so that for my love he should suffer incessantly. . . . For love of me, take away from him drink, food, sleep, power that he might not go or stay, nor ride nor drive nor walk, nor have relations with any woman, until he should come to me to satisfy all my desire and do all that which I will ask of him. (O'Neil 1987: 102)

In Tallinn in 1526, less glamorously, three people were ordered to be whipped for 'stealing clothes off a hanged man, which they believed would improve their sale of beer' (Madar 1990: 259).

In addition, one can sense that particular professions and particular regions knew their own types of magic. Love magic, for example, was not unnaturally a speciality of prostitutes and courtesans in their attempts to attract and keep their clients and lovers (Ruggiero 1993: 24–56, 88–129). Although 'signing' (using *segnamenti*) was current in many places in Italy and elsewhere, the Modenese Inquisition archives studied by O'Neil reveal a fascinating local form of it in cases of healers' cures for *mal di pediga*. This was the potentially fatal sickness of the missing or 'lifted' footprint, thought to be caused by malefice (itself often in response to suspected theft). The sick person had to be measured, using thread freshly spun by a virgin. Should one leg turn out to be longer than the other, or if ashes stuck to the sole of the sick person's foot, a 'lifting' of the footprint by magic had occurred. The missing footprint was replaced in the following manner:

The healer would have the sick person place his foot on some ashes, creating a new footprint. These ashes were then gathered with a silver coin, placed in a piece of new cloth, and taken outside, where the bundle was thrown backwards into a well or running water. In some accounts, the person throwing the bundle was instructed to run away before it hit the water to avoid hearing the sound of the impact. One client who could not travel even managed to have her footprint lowered at a distance; she sent her shoe to the healer, and [?] ashes were sent back to be thrown in the water.

Once a person was cured, he or she then acquired the power and the legitimacy (and the technique, of course) to make the same cure for others (O'Neil 1991/92: 128–9; for similar details of magical practices from the late medieval archives in Lucca, see Meek 2000; for Terra d'Otranto, see Gentilcore 1992: 211–17).

THE MEANING OF MAGIC

The habit of describing all these social phenomena as 'magical' is now virtually universal – and I have obviously conformed to it. But what the label actually designates remains highly elusive, since neither social scientists nor social historians have succeeded in defining it. This is because what magic has signified has varied from age to age and context to context. It is a classic example of a concept whose meaning and application are always a function of local circumstances. The reason for this is that magic has most often been something disapproved of, and 'magical' a term of refusal. This is especially true in the sphere of religion, where magic has invariably been a concept employed either to stigmatize competitor faiths or to proscribe beliefs or behaviour deemed to be irreligious – both these uses being widespread among early modern churchmen. It is in this sense that magic has been the 'other' of Judaeo-Christian religious tradition from biblical times through to the present day. Western science has also had a major part in investing magic with oppositional meanings, in this case between the cogency and rationality of orthodox scientific or medical practice on the one side and the error and irrationality of the magician on the other. Here, magic has mostly been bad or pseudo-science, as defined by the scientific establishment of the day.

We shall see in the last section of this volume that this last point has to be qualified in the light of the enthusiastic endorsement of a certain kind of magic – *magia* and natural magic – by the scientists (the 'natural philosophers') of the early modern period *themselves*. But for the time being the point holds – and, certainly, the popular magic we have just been considering has usually been condemned in the name of 'higher' forms of knowledge as popular error (see, for example, in the field of medicine, Joubert 1989). Naturally, modern scholars too have indulged in the same labelling. The early academic history of anthropology, for example, was marked by the adoption of distinctions between magic and religion and between magic and science that were almost entirely stipulative and dismissive of the practices of other cultures. More recently, historians of religion have been charged with the same fault, in their case one of categorizing large swathes of pre-Reformation and early modern lay piety as 'magical', without thought to the condescension that this implies (Davis 1974; Frijhoff 1979: 71–88; Clark 1983; Bossy 1985: viii; Scribner 1993).

In general, then, magic has invariably been thought of in terms of what it is *not*, varying in direct relation to whatever its positive counterpart is taken to be. This is even true of the definition still most often adopted, which continues to distinguish magic from religion; the latter is characterized by 'human dependence on, and deference toward, the divine' and its supernatural power, the former by 'human attempts to appropriate divine power and apply it instrumentally' (Scribner 1993: 477, drawing on Flint 1991: 3). At present, it is probably best to assume that describing an aspect of any culture, past or present, as 'magical' runs the risk of begging serious questions. Indeed, we have come to see magic as a cultural construction, there being nothing in our attitudes to ourselves or to the world that is inherently 'magical'. In the case of Renaissance Europe there is even a suggestion that it fails to designate anything distinctive. Of the world of healing practitioners and their practices, for example, Katherine Park has written that the boundaries between 'medicine', 'magic' and 'religion' 'often did not correspond to modern ones, and in many cases are hardly to be discerned at all' (Park 1998: 132). In these circumstances, the task of the historian becomes that of understanding how such constructions have come about and been utilized and discussed in various sociocultural settings. In this particular essay, they continue to be adopted for the sake of conformity rather than from conviction, and in full awareness of all the pitfalls that have been indicated.

Perhaps the most obvious question begged by the terms 'magic' and 'magical' has to do with the issue of efficacy. All too often in the past it has been assumed that magic is a false belief in the sense that magical techniques are completely incapable of producing the effects they aim at. This, indeed, has been the principal reason for calling them 'magical' in the first place. In religion, they were 'superstitions', in science, falsehoods. In classic anthropology – as well as in the anthropologically influenced history of the 1970s – magic was the use of ineffective techniques to allay the anxiety caused by the absence of effective ones (Thomas 1971: 668).

Yet historians, at least, no longer feel that they have to take up a position of their own on this issue before writing about the history of magic. Instead, they prefer to leave the issue in the hands of those they study. In the case of the early modern centuries, there was in fact a lively debate among contemporaries about the efficacy of what they called magic. This, however, only reinforces the need for neutrality, since to decide now whether magic was efficacious or not is to take sides in the very thing being studied.

The sheer ubiquity of magic alone suggests that those who used it assumed, in principle, that it worked – in this important sense it was not a false belief at all. It was resorted to in all types of situation, by every kind of person and with a regularity that made it endemic. 'No man or woman', wrote the Hessian church visitors, 'begins, undertakes, does, or refrains from doing, desires or hopes for anything without using some special charm, spell, incantation–'. Every action, we recall, had its 'special day, hour, and secret place' (Strauss 1978: 304). Professional specialists in magic were known and could be found, if not in the next house, then in the next street, village or district. 'Their sheer numbers and ubiquitous presence', writes Robin Briggs, 'at once sustained the world view they represented and clogged any official attempt at repression' (Briggs 1996: 174). In recent years, indeed, the historiography of early modern magic has typically been concerned not just with individual specialists but with whole networks of them – not only among the urban sorcerers of Portugal but, for example, in Essex (Macfarlane 1970), in the regions of France (Briggs 1989: 21–31), in Lorraine (Briggs 1996), in the rural parishes of Germany (Dixon 1996: 181–3), and in the province of Holland (Waardt 1991).

The purposes for which magical techniques were adopted do certainly fall into a pattern. They were used typically to find lost or stolen goods, buried treasure, and missing persons, to heal a wide variety of ailments and illnesses in animals as well as humans, to procure or inhibit love and affection and to influence family affairs, to 'divine' or otherwise foretell the future, and to diagnose and counteract witchcraft. But this too hardly suggests a useless or futile resource. These were often matters of vital importance and urgency to those involved and they can hardly have given so much time and energy to magical solutions unless they expected – and, indeed, received – a positive outcome from them. Sheer need drove many 'cunning folk' to offer their services for a small fee or a gift of food but, even so, the sense that they were pressured by a large and demanding clientele is strong. It is not the absence of more effective (and to modern eyes more rational) services that led to magic's popularity but a combination – certainly in some contexts – of the absence of much else and its own effectiveness. Where different levels and types of healing practice *were* available, for instance, magic simply took its place alongside these other versions in an eclectically employed 'hierarchy of resort' (Park 1998: 133). The argument that magic is a substitute for real technology is no longer plausible in its anthropological form, and there seems to be little reason to go on accepting it in its historical form either.

Many magical techniques possessed their own kind of general rationality, quite apart from the intricate rules for performing them individually. In a famous review of Keith Thomas's *Religion and the Decline of Magic*, criticizing him for failing to see this, Hildred Geertz wrote: 'These practices are comprehensible within the framework of a historically particular view of the nature of reality, a culturally unique image of the way in which the universe works, that provides a hidden conceptual foundation for all of the specific diagnoses, prescriptions, and recipes that Thomas describes' (Geertz 1975: 83; cf. Thomas 1975). Neither anthropologists nor historians spend as much time as they used to working this rationality out, but Jean Delumeau, for example, has spoken of an underlying animism and a resort to the three laws of contact, similarity and contrast (contagion, sympathy and antipathy in other versions). It is not difficult to see the first of these in the use made of earth collected from a courtesan's doorstep or the dust swept from a chapel floor. The second is just as clearly at work in Alonso González de la Pintada's imitative rite for curing haemorrhoids or in Antonio Coreggi's for treating hernias. It is tempting, again, to think of the efficacy here as symbolic, but, as Robin Briggs has recently remarked, contemporaries must have believed the actions involved 'to have direct physical effects, through the principles of sympathy which permeated their vision of the natural world' (Briggs 1996: 181).

Magic also depended on other principles that evidently made as good sense, such as the idea that the cure for an illness consisted of the inverse of its cause (also found in the more traditionally learned medicine of the period) and the supposed equivalence of healing and harming (to which we shall return). Thus, the successful diagnosis of *mal di pediga* depended on the view that the foot's contact with the ground represented 'a strategically located, magical opening in the body . . . through which its vitality was drained', while the successful cure for the condition by 'lowering' of the footprint was simply the opposite of the original 'lifting' (O'Neil 1991/92: 129, 134). Other ingredients in magic's 'ontology' have been said to be a blurring of the natural and supernatural, a resistance to neutrality (in the sense that everything becomes potentially significant), the use of reversals of causality and the organization of time into auspicious or inauspicious moments rather than linear directions (Geertz 1975: 85, following Thomas). Above all, magic rested on the perceived power of words. Those who believed in this power did not necessarily have to think that there was a causal connection between words and their referents; they may simply have been exploiting the expressive capacities of language in a technological context heightened by ritual (Tambiah 1985). Nonetheless, the assumption that words, simply by virtue of being uttered, had a mechanical power at least to assist in the causation or prevention of events seems to have been an intrinsic element of many of the procedures we noted earlier. The most important instrument of supernatural power in early modern Iceland, according to Kirsten Hastrup, was words: 'Words were the main vehicles of magic influence, whether expressed in love-poetry, defamatory prose, or in secret codes' (Hastrup 1990: 387).

In most cases, as the earlier examples also show, the words spoken or written for magical purposes were religious in origin and character – blessings, prayers, Pater Nosters, Ave Marias and so on. Living at a time when religions gave sacred words a kind of agency, the users of them might be forgiven for taking this more literally than was intended. But this raises another vexed question in the history of magic – its relationship to the religious belief-systems that condemned it (Scribner 1984: 61–77). Many of the other things that made up magic – objects, rituals, occasions and places – were also derivations from (or, as Delumeau called them, 'folklorizations' of) religious practice. Lucrezia the Greek's love magic involved a prayer, a blessed candle, an image of a saint, holy bells and holy water, while the charm of the Modenese prostitutes was to be said 'kneeling and fasting for nine mornings with nine Pater Nosters, [and] nine Ave Marias . . .' (O'Neil 1987: 102). Among the borrowings of religious metaphors in the love magic of Venice was one which gave new meaning to the consecration 'For this is my body' and another that appealed to Christ on the cross: 'I bind and pierce the hands and feet of you N. with my love just as were bound the holy hands and feet of Our Lord Jesus Christ so that you cannot love another person in the world excepting M.' (Ruggiero 1993: 93, 105). The spell-casters of Wiesbaden mixed 'the names of God, the holy Trinity, some special angels, the Virgin Mary, the twelve apostles and the three kings, also with numerous saints, with the wounds of Christ and his seven last words . . . with gospel verses and certain prayers' (Strauss 1978: 304). In Lower Brittany, saints' statues were whipped, the Lord's Prayer was addressed to the moon and the devil was propitiated as a cereal-god. In Portugal, the *saludadores* mimed Catholic rites of blessing and aspersion and mixed this with popular motifs: 'Their procedure was usually based on the miraculous blessing of water in a bowl with a cross of salt, together with an invocation of the Holy Trinity or, sometimes, of demons; this water was then sprinkled over the "damned livestock" with a branch of spurge-laurel' (Bethencourt 1990: 410). Again, these instances could be multiplied endlessly from the literature. Across Europe, throughout the centuries we are discussing, magic often seems indistinguishable from religion.

The clergymen whose task it was to make the distinction knew exactly where it lay, as we shall see later. At least some of their colleagues, particularly in the lower ranks of the Church, did not, making the cleric who behaved like a wizard or magical healer by no means a rarity at the time (Waardt 1993: 36–8, for a comparison of techniques; cf. Briggs 1989: 23; Bethencourt 1990: 409; Gaskill 2000: 56). The very first user of magic we came across, Alonso González de la Pintada, turns out to have been a 'beato' and a lay Franciscan for 40 years (Nalle 1992: 14–15). None of this, however, allows *us* to say where religion ended and magic began, unless we are simply to adopt the definitions of theologians arguing 400 years ago. Hildred Geertz's other main charge against Thomas was that he had imposed a conceptual language of his own on magic that made it less comprehensive, less organized and less coherent than religion and more concerned with utilitarian ends – with 'practical solutions to immediate problems' (Geertz 1975: 72). But it remains the case today that virtually any criterion that we settle upon to separate these two cultural forms – major institutional and financial considerations apart – turns out to yield statements that are equally true of both of them (Scribner 1993).

With so many reservations about the very identity of something called 'magic', it might be thought better to dispense with the term altogether – to regard it, as Geertz did in her exchange with Thomas, as an entity only in the ideological weaponry of the past (Geertz 1975: 88). If, for its users, magic was efficacious, then it can presumably be dissolved without residue into its various practical purposes and be called simply 'healing', 'cultivation', 'household management', 'forecasting' and so on. What then would the addition of the predicate 'magical' – as in 'magical' healing, 'magical' cultivation, etc. – indicate, except our own ignorance of how these practices were thought to work?

> For a person to employ a certain procedure that is conventionally considered by all around him to be the acceptable thing to do in his situation, does not necessarily indicate that he is motivated by an attitude of self-deception and wishful distortion of reality, even though others, contemporaries or historians, may term that procedure 'magical'. (*ibid.* 1975: 82)

If, on the other hand, 'magical' relates not to efficacy in general but to the precise methods and techniques used by magicians – sympathy, antipathy, contagion, and so forth – then what is to separate these from the procedures warranted by any knowledge system?

What might prove a helpful guide in this context is the vocabulary used at the time to describe what we habitually refer to as 'magic'. One of the striking consequences of magic's role as a term of attribution is that it can be quite difficult to find anyone in the past who accepted it as a correct description of what they thought or did, let alone who called themselves a 'magician'. Significantly, perhaps, the labels most generally adopted in the sixteenth and seventeenth centuries to describe what we are discussing were simply 'cunning' or 'knowledge' – a usage first made generally known to modern scholars by Alan Macfarlane (Macfarlane 1970: esp. 115–34). In Iceland, according to Hastrup, the boundary between wisdom and magic was 'totally absent in the category of "knowledge"', while the literal meaning of the category used for witchcraft (*fjölkyngi*) was 'much knowledge' (Hastrup 1990: 387–8). In the 1640s, Jannigien Clinckhamers from Kampen in the Netherlands spoke of her power to charm and bless as 'the art' (Blécourt 1993: 52). Other contemporaries caught up in investigations of their 'magic' talked (or at least were reported to have talked) of simply having 'skill'. Of course, they may just have been evading the more dangerous word or simply dressing up their actions as a kind of mysterious speciality. Nevertheless, what seems to have been implied here was a more than usually difficult, or powerful or effective way of doing things, based on special wisdom and technique, but not one that was necessarily different in kind from the way they were usually done.

It is important not to exaggerate the case for the coherence of popular magic, to rationalize it excessively, or otherwise overcompensate for its poor reputation hitherto. One of the foremost current scholars of the subject, Robin Briggs, prefers to describe it as 'a flexible and polymorphous vision of the world, whose internal logic was often rickety or non-existent'. Everyday events were assumed to have many possible meanings and the world was full of significance and power for those who could understand and use it. But to the extent that this meant 'superenchantment', it was, he adds, 'quite impossible as a permanent context for ordinary life' (Briggs 2001: 176). Yet flexibility was also a marked feature of those contemporary beliefs and practices with which magic most closely competed – notably those of religion and medicine. The health strategies of the pre-modern world were particularly marked by improvisation and choice. And magical practices do seem to have enjoyed an integral place in the culture of fortune and misfortune that made up so much of popular life at this time. It was, it seems, pluralism and eclecticism that marked people's attitudes to the vagaries of existence and how to react to them, and magic was obviously well suited to this way of seeing things (on magic and medical pluralism in particular, see Park 1998; Gentilcore 1998).

MALEFICIUM AND MAGIC

One of the key reasons for the popularity of magical practices was that they were deployed to detect and counteract the harmful effects of witchcraft. Only the curing of illnesses occupied as important a place in the tasks for which magic was singled out – and, of course, many of these were attributed to *maleficium* anyway. Indeed, so intimate was the relationship between protective (or remedial) magic and malevolent witchcraft that historians have come to see them more and more as the two inseparable halves of the world of popular culture in this period. Gábor Klaniczay remarks that the 'two poles of the popular magical universe – the beneficial [in which Klaniczay includes religion] and the harmful, or the positive and the negative – have in fact always developed in relation to each other.' According to Mary O'Neil too, the merit of studying counter-witchcraft (and the counter witch) is that it puts witchcraft back into its original context, where it comprised 'only one half of a more elaborate system of beliefs'. And, more recently, Robin Briggs has spoken of the 'symbiosis' of witches and witch doctors, two categories that always accompanied each other and were always liable to be reversed (Klaniczay 1990: 240–1; O'Neil 1991/92: 123, cf. 137, 139; Briggs 1996: 171; cf. O'Neil, 1987: 104).

There was, moreover, a precise sense in which magical healing and maleficent harming were linked in the popular mind – they were equivalents. It was assumed as a matter of course that those with the special power to heal by magic must know how to harm by the same means. To reverse the effects of witchcraft was to understand how it worked in the first place. The idea crops up in many witchcraft trials, where defendants charged with *maleficium* often returned the plea allegedly made by Ursley Kempe to Grace Thurlowe in the Essex village of St Osyth sometime before 1582: that 'though shee coulde unwitche shee coulde not witche.' (Gibson 2000: 78). Nor was this association made only by the unlettered; we find it even among Lutheran church visitors and inquisitors of the Holy Office. The former reported indiscriminately of the people of Wiesbaden that their 'signs' and 'spells' were employed 'to inflict harm or do good to men, women, animals, and crops, to make things better or worse, to bring good or bad luck on themselves and their fellow creatures' (Strauss 1978: 304). In Modena in 1601, an inquisitor told a healer of *mal di pediga*, who had presumably protested her innocence of witchcraft in much the same terms as Kempe, that her statement lacked 'verisimilitude, for those who know how to lower one [i.e. a footprint], also know how to lift one'. In a later example from 1624, Maria Priora was similarly warned 'to beware of lies because it is the sad and common rule among witches "that who knows how to heal, knows also how to harm"' (O'Neil 1991/92: 131, cf. 126–8, 134).

If the arts of healing and harming were themselves equivalent, the principle of transference likewise encouraged the idea that no bewitchment was removed without the *maleficium* being shifted elsewhere. Furthermore, those healers whose magical remedies for illness failed to bring relief or made things worse were naturally likely to be suspected of witchcraft. In Modena, where accusations of *maleficium* were invariably against healers, the pressure to see things this way came mostly from client-witnesses who thereby hoped to turn cases almost into suits for malpractice (O'Neil 1987: 95, 97). The Italian inquisitors did not share this priority, but in the Lorraine archives Robin Briggs has discovered several examples of 'witch doctors' who ended up at the stake for this reason (Briggs 1996: 171; Briggs 2001). In general, historians have found it impossible to agree over the question of how many of the accused in witchcraft cases had previously practised as 'cunning folk' of one kind or another in their communities. But the correlation is sufficiently strong to suggest that those who practised 'cunning' ran a definite risk in this respect, even if they were never remotely in a majority. What can be agreed upon, given the cultural values current among the general population of the time, is that there was an ambiguity intrinsic to what they did (Blécourt 1994: 288–98, for the best discussion).

Such cultural values have recently become much more central to the historiography of witchcraft than they once were. As long as prosecutions were deemed to be inspired by government institutions or churches, the views of the general population were not thought to matter. But as William Monter emphasized at the outset of this volume, study after study has now shown that it was pressure from the communities to which alleged witches belonged that lay behind a great deal of 'witch-hunting', with the institutions of central government, the higher ranks and appellate courts of the judiciary and the church courts – especially the Inquisition – usually acting far more cautiously. Summarizing the work of historians such as Walter Rummel, Eva Labouvie and Rainer Walz, Wolfgang Behringer has written:

> The major shift in German witchcraft studies in recent years has been the recognition of a massive desire for persecution stemming from the general population. One apparent peculiarity of Central Europe is the role of communities, the self-appointed protagonists of witchcraft persecutions who placed their superiors under massive pressure to conduct them. (Behringer 1996: 88–9)

Remarkable instances of this have been discovered in the village committees, notably in the region around Trier, elected by communities to organize the detection and persecution of witches (Briggs 1996: 340–51; Monter, Part 1 of this volume). Further evidence of pressure 'from below' of this sort is offered by the findings of Al Soman concerning local justice in the regions of France (Soman 1992). Clearly, what seems to have mattered in the initial stages of a witchcraft case was, above all, the personal conviction on the part of victims that *maleficium* was something very real and that they were genuinely afflicted by it. This applied equally throughout the many thousands of episodes that never came to trial at all, as well as to those which carried on generating both accusations and protective counter-measures after the decriminalization of witchcraft altogether. In the Netherlands, for example, where the last execution took place in 1608, the resort to specialists in counter-witchcraft and the defamation suits brought by those still popularly accused of the crime bear witness to the long continuance of the belief in *maleficium* and its practitioners. The case notes of the English astrological physician Richard Napier likewise reveal sincerely expressed accusations of bewitchment on the part of hundreds of his patients (Sawyer 1988/89).

What witchcraft *meant* to most ordinary people, after all, was that it caused misfortune, not that it led to devil-worship. What was important was the harm it could do to themselves, their livelihoods and their families and communities. Witches disrupted the weather, wasted crops, ruined the production of beer and butter and, above all, brought sickness and death. This was not usually traced to demonic agency – except perhaps in the case of the English belief in witches' 'familiars' – nor was the witch automatically thought of as a servant of Satan. The detailed ethnography of these convictions, inspired originally by *Religion and the Decline of Magic*, is still being worked out. While malevolence itself and the often poisonous social rivalries that accompanied it were hardly rarities in early modern communities, to identify it as the inspiration for *witchcraft* required a particular set of cultural traits. While by no means unique to this period of European history, these traits were manifested in terms of witchcraft's association with particular individuals, occasions and misfortunes. However, establishing just *which* individuals, occasions and misfortunes were most likely to be selected is proving to be more and more difficult, as historians break down the stereotypical expectations about witchcraft (both among contemporaries and among modern scholars) and substitute a picture that is marked by the 'complexities, contingencies and ambiguities' of everyday experience (Gaskill 2000: 50). The process by which a person became a witch was itself long and complex, involving many intricate judgements about behaviour and reputation over a period of time. In the past, the sorts of interpersonal conflicts that occasioned accusations were found by anthropological historians to be concerned with indigence and the exercise of charity (Thomas 1971: 535–69; Macfarlane 1970:

147–207). More recently, feminist historians and historians of gender have linked them to the management of the household and the anxieties of motherhood (Roper 1994: 199–248; Purkiss 1995; Willis 1995: 27–81). The latest analysis of the English cases speaks more broadly of 'competition for power and resources' (Gaskill 2000: 55).

The means allegedly used by witches for harming their neighbours were likewise intelligible in terms of popular beliefs about such things as the maleficent powers of language and of bodily gestures, notably touching and looking (Thomas 1971: 435–49; Bethencourt 1990: 414–15). Certain kinds of misfortunes, and particularly certain kinds of illnesses, were more likely to be attributed to witchcraft than others. If a sickness was not immediately recognized or otherwise thought to be 'unnatural', if it was slow and lingering and failed to respond to treatment, if it occurred suddenly or violently in a previously healthy person, then *maleficium* was its likely cause (Briggs 1989: 29–31). Napier's patients, for example, complained typically of being 'strangely or sorely afflicted' by disturbances of the mind, fits, swoonings, tremblings and convulsions (especially in children), and lameness, pining and consuming (Sawyer 1988/89: 468–9). Provided such ailments coincided with an 'episode' involving a neighbour thought to be a witch and the resulting suspicions were confirmed by (as Briggs 1996: 171 has termed them) those 'key figures in the whole nexus of belief and practice' – the cunning folk – then an accusation of witchcraft was likely to make sense.

These features of the experience of witchcraft – in thought and practice alike – were subject to an infinite number of variations across the expanses of Europe. Yet a fundamental constant can still be asserted: whatever we may think about the social realities behind these episodes, discovered by historians looking 'through' them to features that contemporaries them-selves may not have grasped, their ingredients took the form they did as the consequence of the consciously shared assumptions and expectations that circulated in the cultures of the time. As far as illness is concerned, it has been said that accusations of witchcraft were 'ineluctably connected to the purposeful action and behaviour of patients who were actively seeking care for their afflictions' (Sawyer 1988/89: 466). We may talk here of a 'popular mentality' of witchcraft, or speak (as Marijke Gijswijt-Hofstra does in the next volume in this series) of 'cultures of misfortune'. What we cannot any longer say is that the accusations were made out of ignorance – ignorance of the real causes of disease, or of bad weather, or of poverty or of poor human relationships. On the contrary, the world of witchcraft accusations was a world of *knowledge* – indeed, a world rich in the particular forms of knowledge that allowed diagnosis, identification of those responsible and therapy all to take place, as they undoubtedly did, without any form of legal prosecution whatsoever.

RELIGIOUS REFORMATION AND POPULAR MAGIC

Unfortunately, the wardens of ordinary people's culture at the time – the clergy – did not agree. For them these were indeed forms of ignorance. They were lamentable displays of the lack of real religion and faith in God. Maria Priora, the Modenese healer, was told by her inquisitors that her skill had to involve a demonic pact, 'because ashes or flour do not of themselves have the power to heal the sick, especially those *in extremis*'. If, according to their own testimony, her clients were healed nevertheless, either God or the devil must have intervened, and 'since God holds superstitions in abomination, it is necessary to affirm that it was done by the power of the devil'. Antonio Coreggi was dealt with in the same terms as an apostate 'from God to the devil' for misappropriating holy words and holy days for 'superstitious' purposes – that is, purposes without efficacy (O'Neil 1991/92: 132; O'Neil 1987: 93–4). Such cases, and such opinions, multiplied in thousands of similar instances, represent, at grass-roots level, the impact on popular magic of the most fundamental and most sustained of all the changes experienced in the early modern centuries – those wrought by religious reformation. For while 'Reformation' has long been known as a far-reaching doctrinal, liturgical and ecclesiastical phenomenon, those involved also saw it as the refashioning of other equally fundamental aspects of human piety to do with day-to-day conduct and moral discipline. These embraced such things as sexual behaviour and the regulation of families, the proper use of language and speech codes, sabbath observance, and all the other matters that came under the heading of 'manners'. But they also included lay attitudes to fortune and misfortune, since securing the one and avoiding the other, and dealing with misfortunes when they came, raised issues that went to the heart of contemporary spirituality. Popular attitudes to magic and *maleficium* thus entered into Reformation debate from the outset as an urgent clerical priority. They became caught up in the process already described by William Monter (Part 1, above) whereby confessional rivalry turned the major European faiths into competing vehicles for the expression of religious zeal.

In essence, what reformers did with these matters was to spiritualize them – internalizing all their traditional ingredients until they became spiritual problems. For both Protestant and Catholic clerics, the real significance of witchcraft, as of all misfortunes, was not the immediate, this-worldly harm that it brought but the way the victim was give an opportunity for introspection and spiritual improvement. Misfortunes were a test or a punishment, sent by God, and the proper response to them was to reflect patiently on faith and sin, move on to repentance and then seek divine, clerical and eventually other approved forms of help. To think in terms of *maleficium* and to blame witches was therefore to miss the point. An affliction by witchcraft was not really a case of misfortune at all; it was a case of conscience – and, indeed, witchcraft turns out to be included in a great many early modern discussions and collections of 'cases of conscience'.

Popular *counter*-witchcraft, moreover, was itself superstitious and, so, idolatrous. People who resorted to magic were not merely ignoring the spiritual significance of fortune and misfortune, they were themselves appealing – like Maria Priora and Antonio Coreggi – to the devil. It is important to realize that this entire argument was built – as I indicated earlier – on a criterion of natural efficacy. Early modern clerics were being utterly naturalistic in this respect – given that their naturalisms were not ours. In the cultural milieu they inhabited, magic was specious in the sense that it attributed to persons, or places, or times or things causal properties that had no existence in nature (as well as no warrant in orthodox religious practice) and could therefore have no natural effects. If natural effects did nevertheless occur, then – as Maria and Antonio were told – it was the devil who had stepped in to bring them about. A demonic pact that was at least implicit was necessarily involved. As we shall see in a moment, magic was in this sense both 'superstitious', which was the term for inefficacy in this context, and also idolatrous, which meant an appeal to a false God. In love magic, in addition, the theological objection (in Italy, for example) was to the coercing of the victim to commit sin by subverting his or her free will. Many churchmen therefore came to think that what was done by magic – ostensibly a beneficial practice – to avoid or respond to misfortune, and especially to *maleficium*, had much more serious implications than maleficent witchcraft itself. The fact (as we saw earlier) that so many magical practices involved the use – or rather, misuse – of orthodox religious language and practice only served to make it more hateful. For all these reasons, nothing less than the general spiritual welfare of the laity seemed to be at stake in its widespread adoption.

These clerical arguments and opinions can be traced and illustrated in many forms and idioms of Reformation literature (Clark 1997: 445–525; Delumeau 1974). Churchmen of both the major faiths published sermons and treatises on the proper response to witchcraft that placed equal emphasis on its providential purpose, its key role in the economy of faith, sin and redemption and the duty of Christians to act like Job when faced by *maleficium*. Job's attitude to tribulation was so crucial to the argument that the Book of Job may be regarded as its spiritual cornerstone. The German Lutheran Johann Brenz preached in this manner in 1539 in a well-known sermon on hailstorms (Midelfort, 1974: 213–19) and so too did other pastors in later sermon-series on witchcraft – for example,

Joachim Zehner in Thuringia, Daniel Schaller in Brandenburg and Hermann Samson in Riga. The Geneva pastor Lambert Daneau said typically that it was the duty of the bewitched to 'patiently abyde and looke for ye helpe of God, and depende onely upon his providence' (Daneau, 1575: sig. Lii[r]). English Calvinists like William Perkins and George Gifford likewise devoted whole books to replacing popular views about the sources of misfortune with arguments that gave witches the least significant role, the devil a more important one and God the only one that really mattered (Macfarlane 1977: 140–55). Among the Catholic providentialists who shared this aim with their Protestant opponents – sharing also an enthusiasm for St Augustine in the process – were the nominalist Martin Plantsch, the Freiburg theologian Jodochus Lorichius and the suffragan bishop of Bamberg Friedrich Förner (Oberman 1981: 158–83; Midelfort 1972: 60–1; Clark 1997: 453–4). It seems that in this respect the two competing religions had exactly comparable evangelistic aims.

The same is true of their reactions to popular magic itself – to the sorts of things we began this chapter by considering. If Job was one biblical model to be commonly deployed against ordinary notions of misfortune, King Saul – for resorting to the 'witch' of Endor (a pythonness or Old Testament cunning woman) – was another. The perception of an unbridgeable gulf between *what they saw as* religion and magic came to dominate the sensibilities of churchmen and their evangelical efforts. Indeed, their hostility to the malevolent, devil-worshipping witch of the classical stereotype often seems to have been quite overshadowed by their hatred of her benevolent counterparts – the professional magicians and 'cunning folk' – towards whom greater severity was often shown (for examples of this from Germany, Denmark and Hungary, see Rowlands 1996; Johansen 1991/92; Kristóf 1991/92). This, of course, is because these too were regarded as witches, and of a more insidious and dangerous kind. Over and over again in the literature we find the term 'witch' being applied to *anyone* who practised the 'cunning' arts, whether as private individual or professional expert. Gifford, for example, explained that the conjuror, the enchanter, the sorcerer and the diviner were all 'compassed' by it. His *A Dialogue Concerning Witches and Witchcraftes* was largely taken up with the role in Essex villages of what he revealingly called the 'other sort of Witches, whome the people call cunning men and wise women' – that is, local experts in healing, divination, theft-detection and counter witchcraft. His fellow Englishman William Perkins was even more explicit; 'by Witches', he wrote, 'we understand not those onely which kill and torment: but all Diviners, Charmers, Juglers, all Wizzards, commonly called wise men and wise women . . . and in the same number we reckon all good Witches, which doe no hurt, but good, which doe not spoile and destroy, but save and deliver' (Gifford 1587: sig. Bii[r]; Gifford 1593: sig.

A3^r; Perkins 1610: 255). Such sentiments must have been shared in the Calvinist Low Countries, where cunning men and women continued to be targets of clerical disapproval long after the cessation of trials for malevolent witchcraft (Gijswijt-Hofstra 1989; Blécourt 1993: 49–55).

This means that 'witchcraft' turns out to have been an interest of many reformers not usually thought of as 'demonologists', Luther and Calvin among them (Haustein 1990; Jensen 1975), and in many countries, like Wales and Portugal, not normally associated with the diabolical witchcraft of the sabbat or where it was treated with scepticism. Quite simply, reformers saw witchcraft and demonism in many other contexts than those we normally associate with the terms, notably among the traditional resources favoured by ordinary people in need. Instead of Exodus 22:18 ('Thou shalt not suffer a witch to live'), or perhaps in addition to it, they turned to Deuteronomy 18:10–11 ('There shall not be found among you any one that maketh his son or his daughter to pass through the fire, or that useth divination, or an observer of times, or an enchanter, or a witch, Or a charmer, or a consulter with familiar spirits, or a wizard, or a necromancer'). This again can be illustrated from treatises denouncing magic by Lutheran clergymen and theologians such as Conrad Platz of Biberach in Württemberg, Bernhard Albrecht of Augsburg and Niels Hemmingsen of Copenhagen, or from the Calvinist demonology of English ministers such as Henry Holland and Richard Bernard. The Catholic Reformation's contribution to the anti-magical polemic was enormous. By 1679, when the Jansenist abbé Jean-Baptiste Thiers started to publish his *Traité des Superstitions (Treatise on Superstitions)*, he was able to list countless official denunciations of divining, astrology, soothsaying and magical healing by the central and regional institutions of the Church all over Europe. Catholic casuistry found ample space for these sins and there were many individual monographs on the subject, for example by the Spaniards Martín de Arles and Pedro Ciruelo and the Netherlanders Jacob van Hoogstraten and Johannes David. Pierre Massé's *De L'Imposture et tromperie des diables (On the Trickery and Deceit of Devils)* (1579) was an extended discussion of the *devins* and astrologers, the wearers of amulets and the interpreters of dreams who (in his view) seemed to be as popular in sixteenth-century France as in pagan times. Ciruelo spoke for all these, and many other authors, when he wrote that the folk healers of Spain were 'enchanters' (*ensalmos*) who destroyed the souls of those they cured even while they removed their bodily afflictions: 'Since this is true, any man or woman who seeks a cure through spells tacitly accepts a return to health with the aid of the devil and thus makes a pact of friendship with the enemy of God and man' (Ciruelo 1977: 208).

Two other features of this cross-party campaign indicate its extent and its seriousness. One is the way in which popular magic was classed as a 'superstition', a word that implies trivialization in our language but was far more ominous at the time. A 'superstition' could be many things in early modern theology, including an exaggerated, superfluous or otherwise incorrect devotion, but when applied to magic it meant natural inefficacy – the appeal to cause and effect relationships that were spurious in nature. As we have already seen, it was this inefficacy in magic that made it demonic; an appeal to magical causation was always necessarily an appeal to demonic causation as well, since it was only the devil who made magic actually work. Gregorius de Valentia, author of a set of *Commentariorum Theologicorum* (*Theological Commentaries*) published at Ingolstadt in 1591–7, wrote that an implicit demonic pact occurred 'whenever anyone employs, as capable of effecting something, such means as are in the truth of the matter empty and useless' (Valentia 1591/97: iii: col. 1985). This made magic a kind of witchcraft (hence 'white' witchcraft) but it also made it a form of idolatry, one of the major categories of superstition, and allowed the classifying of many of its practices as either *divinatio/divination* or *vana observantia/vain practice*, idolatry's two theological subdivisions. But superstition, we should always remember, was the reformers' main target where the laity was concerned – it was the most serious of religious transgressions, religion's 'opposite' – and endlessly debated and discussed throughout the dogmatics and casuistry of the Protestant and Catholic Reformations. Magic's assimilation to it thus meant the rejection of whole areas of popular life and thought as fundamentally illicit. By means of the notion of an implicit pact, an extraordinarily wide application of demonism to lay culture occurred. Given this, one is almost surprised by how little witch-hunting there was in Reformation Europe, not how much.

What there was may well be partly attributed – at least as far as its religious significance is concerned – to a second feature of the reformers' campaign against magic. This is their classification of magic as a sin against the First Commandment. Again, this recurs throughout the literature of the two great Reformations but it is particularly noticeable in the catechisms and guides to using them (and to confessing and hearing confessions) that multiplied in Europe in the period. Examples can be found in the Decalogue writings of Luther himself and the Marburg Lutheran Andreas Gerhard, in the Heidelberg catechism of 1563, in the highly popular confessors' manual by the French Franciscan Jean Benedicti, the *Somme des pechez* (*A Summation of Sins*) (1584) and in the individual catechisms written by English Calvinists like Alexander Nowell and John Mayer and continental Catholics like Peter Canisius and Robert Bellarmine. The growing dominance of the Decalogue in the 'moral system' of western Europe in this period has been argued by John Bossy (Bossy 1988), who stresses that, once the obligation to worship God correctly was put at the summit of Christian ethics, and idolatry was made a prime offence, witchcraft became a far more serious matter than it had been when still subsumed under one or other of the Deadly Sins. But Reformation catechisms and Decalogue treatises were not directed at witches who flew to sabbats and worshipped the devil in a ritualized anti-religion. From Luther's *A Short Exposition of the Decalogue* onwards, the witchcraft, magic and superstition that occur in them were the sorts that were supposed to lie covertly in the way ordinary people regulated their lives – in their use of charms and talismans, in their resort to healers, blessers, diviners and exorcists in sickness or loss, in their appeals to the treasure seekers and procurers of love.

In these ways and by these means, then, the patterns of thought and behaviour we started out with – calling them 'magic' out of habit, rather than conviction – became one of the major cultural battlegrounds of the early modern period. 'Magic', labelled and defined by clerics as spurious and irreligious, was at the heart of what many have seen as the most concerted attempt there has ever been to standardize the lives and ideas of ordinary Europeans – and by no means just the uneducated or unlettered among them. In texts disseminated on a gigantic scale, written by some of the leading reformers of the time, magic and religion were redefined in confrontation and opposition, as belonging to incompatible belief structures. Whether they did indeed belong to such different belief structures – or whether popular magic was rejected simply as a version of religion that clerics could not control – are different issues which this chapter has tried to leave open for debate.

It is not clear, in any case, that practice followed suit – that clerics successfully prosecuted their moral campaign in the church courts or in the consciences of individuals. Certainly, most of what we know about the magic we began with arises from the reports of hostile clerical witnesses or investigations; the Inquisition, in particular, became far more concerned with magic and superstition towards the last third of the sixteenth century. But even if it proved to be impractical and ineffective, the campaign succeeded in reaffirming one of the abiding distinctions on which European modernity and its sense of its origins have been built.

CHAPTER 2

Demonology

THE LITERATURE OF WITCHCRAFT

Alongside the legal prosecutions described earlier in this volume, Europe witnessed an equivalent upsurge of intellectual interest in witchcraft. As witches were being questioned in hundreds of courtrooms, so their crimes were being interrogated in as many texts. It is as if the trial took place of theories about witchcraft, as well as of those actually accused of it. The result was a literature of witchcraft – a demonology – spanning the fifteenth to eighteenth centuries, in which educated contemporaries explored and debated the complexities of the subject and its implications for their lives and culture. From the Council of Basel to the publication of the *Encyclopédie*, theologians and clerics, philosophers and moralists, lawyers and physicians argued about how to come to terms with it. Here, then, lies a further opportunity to consider the history of witchcraft and magic as a matter of beliefs.

The preceding two volumes in this series make clear the important role of demonology in early Christian and medieval theological and ecclesiastical thought. Indeed, one of the striking things about reading the texts from the early modern era is realizing how dependent they were on concepts of the devil elaborated by Church Fathers such as Augustine and philosopher-theologians such as Thomas Aquinas. Nevertheless, as Edward Peters also shows in Volume 3, it is possible to date the first textual accounts of witchcraft as a devil-worshipping cult with remarkable precision to the 1430s. In that decade a series of five texts, recently brought together in a new Latin–French edition by Martine Ostorero and her colleagues at the University of Lausanne, described the elemental features that came to dominate representations of the cult. Witches were now associated with ritual dedication to Satan, the practice of infanticide and anthropophagy, the aim of destroying Christian society and attendance at their notorious assemblies or 'sabbats' (Ostorero *et al.* 1999; Peters 2001: 231–3). Single works on demonology and witchcraft multiplied from this point onwards, with titles like *Lamiarum sive Striarum Opusculum* (*A Brief Work on Lamia or Witches*), *Flagellum Maleficorum* (*The Lash Against Those Who Commit Maleficia*), and *Quaestio de Strigis* (*An Investigation of Witches*) – titles which in themselves indicate the development of a genre. A good example of this emerging pattern and of the typical questions that were addressed is *Tractatus de Pythonicis Mulieribus* (*Treatise Concerning Women Who Prophesy*), published in 1489 by Ulrich Molitor, a legal professor at Constance. The work takes the form of an imaginary conversation between the man who commissioned it, Archduke Sigismund of Austria, Molitor himself and a magistrate of Constance, Conrad Schatz. The topics they discuss rapidly became standard in early modern demonology: Do witches have powers over the weather? Can they cause diseases and sexual impotence? Can they transform others or be transformed themselves into animals? Are they physically transported to their sabbats and are these real events? How do demons assume human shape and act as incubi? Can procreation take place between demons and witches? Can demons and witches predict the future? (Lea 1939/1957: 348–53; Maxwell-Stuart 2001: 32–41). Apart from the question of the sabbat, these were the sorts of issues that dominated what has come to be seen as the summary work of this period, *Malleus Maleficarum* (*Hammer of Witches*), a modern perspective produced in part by the tendency of modern commentators to read this text and little else. Certainly its authors had already encountered opposition to their views and jurisdiction when attempting to put both into practice, and the work itself was also much less immediately influential than has often been supposed.

The fact that Molitor cast his treatise in the form of a *debate* is particularly significant. So, too, is the asking of questions deemed to be answerable in contradictory ways (although this was, in fact, a habit of scholastic discourse). From the very outset, one gets the overwhelming impression that witchcraft was regarded as a controversial and difficult topic, on which many reservations and doubts might be expressed. Indeed, to say simply that early modern intellectuals *believed* in it is to miss the way in which they invariably struggled to come to terms with it. Those who did, on the whole, accept its reality always knew that there were serious objections that had to be overcome. Central to this first phase of the literature, for example, were many attempts to interpret the ninth-century capitulary known as the canon *Episcopi* which had stated,

> that some wicked women, perverted by the Devil, seduced by illusions and phantasms of demons, believe and profess themselves, in the hours of the night, to ride upon certain beasts with Diana, the goddess of pagans, and an innumerable multitude of women, and in the silence of the dead of night to traverse great spaces of earth, and to obey her commands as of their mistress, and to be summoned to her service on certain nights. (Peters 1978: 73; Peters 2001: 201–2)

The experience was in fact imposed on their minds, said the canon, by 'the malignant spirit' who transformed himself into the 'species and similitudes' of various people and exhibited other delusory things to them while they were asleep.

Discussions of the canon *Episcopi*, focusing on the nocturnal flight (or 'transvection') of witches to their sabbats, are common in this first phase of early modern demonology and seem almost to have dominated it. If the canon applied to the new fifteenth-century witches as much as to earlier ones, it made their crimes illusory; but if the latest sect was unlike the previous ones, then the text could be disregarded. Questions like these were frequently asked in the period between Johannes Nider's *Formicarius* (*The Antheap*), dating from around 1437 and Bernard of Como's *Tractatus de Strigibus* (*Treatise on Witches*), written around 1510. The Franciscan Samuel de Cassini and the Dominican Vincente Dodo clashed over the canon's implications in the first decade of the sixteenth century, and another cycle to the debate occurred in the 1520s between Paolo Grillando (*Tractatus de Sortilegiis* (*Treatise of Witchcrafts*), written *c.* 1525, published in 1536), who argued that sabbats and sabbat attendance were real and not the product of 'illusion in dreams', and Gianfrancesco Ponzinibio (*Tractatus de Lamiis* (*Treatise of Witches*)), who took the opposite view (Lea 1939/ 1957: 260–5, 366–7, 367, 370–3, 395–412, 377–82; for de Cassini and Dodo, see also Max 1993).

From the 1560s onwards, the literature of witchcraft may be said to have entered a fresh phase, marked by two developments. On the one hand, scepticism regarding the reality of the crime became even more systematic. To the reservations based on the canon *Episcopi*, which focused on the possibility of wholesale self or demonic delusion, the early and mid-sixteenth century added various forms of more general doubt regarding witchcraft. Considerable philosophical damage was inflicted (at least in theory) on the whole principle of demonic agency by a demon-free treatment of the power of incantations by the Padua-trained, purist Aristotelian thinker, Pietro Pomponazzi, in his *De Naturalium Effectuum Causis, sive de Incantationibus* (*On the Causes of Natural Effects, Or of Incantations*), which first appeared in 1520. This was a form of naturalism that later had a powerful appeal to the English witchcraft sceptic Reginald Scot. Another Italian, the lawyer Andrea Alciati, managed to achieve a Europe-wide reputation as a witchcraft sceptic as a result of just one memorable sentence reported in his *Parergon Juris* (*A Law Supplement*) (1538). Asked by an inquisitor for an opinion regarding the burning of witches in the Italian Alps, he had answered that they ought to be purged not with fire but with hellebore – the treatment for diseases of the mind (Lea 1939/1957: 374–5). Even inquisitors themselves could express the most serious doubts on the subject, as revealed by a letter issued in 1538 by the Inquisition in Madrid suggesting that not everything in the *Malleus Maleficarum* should be accepted as true (Henningsen 1980: 347). Above all, perhaps, there were the general cautions regarding occultism and 'superstition' and the punishment of heretics that one associates with the name of Erasmus and with Erasmians across Europe. Later in the century these were to be powerfully supplemented by a revival of interest in ancient philosophical scepticism among European intellectuals. Under its influence, Montaigne denounced the credulity of witchcraft believers in his 1588 essay *Des Boîteux* (*Of Cripples*), and the Spanish humanist Pedro de Valencia argued that witchcraft was a crime that it was impossible either to prove or disprove (for Montaigne, see Kors and Peters 2001: 402–6; for de Valencia, see Henningsen 1980: 6–9).

Nevertheless, it was with the publication of the first version of Johann Weyer's *De Praestigiis Daemonum* (*On the Tricks of Devils*) in 1563 (it was considerably expanded in later versions) that early modern scepticism about witchcraft found its first major voice. Weyer was the court physician to the Duke of Cleve-Mark, Jülich and Berg between about 1550 and 1578 and he worked in a political environment whose culture was thoroughly Erasmian. He also cited Erasmus extensively in attacking the prosecution of witches (Margolin 1974; Béné 1979). Essentially, Weyer explained witchcraft away in accordance with a medicine of gender. While admitting that men (*magi infames*) could deliberately and rationally co-operate with devils to perform feats of magic (not necessarily real ones), he insisted that every case in which *women* claimed or were accused of the same thing should be rejected as legally invalid. The women themselves were mad, senile or ill and thus a prey to wholesale demonic delusion, to which Weyer attributed both the witches' pact and their sabbats. As for the 'bewitched', they were afflicted by illnesses that were either purely natural or caused by demons using natural causes. To prosecute in these circumstances was a travesty of justice, since the defendants lacked 'the rational spirit required for "offending"' (Weyer 1991: 572). Instead, confessing 'witches' should be offered spiritual counselling and medical treatment. Weyer had, in effect, introduced the insanity defence into cases of witchcraft, in so doing 'fundamentally altering the terms of legal discourse' (Midelfort 1999: 196, see also 196–213; Clark 1997: 198–203; extracts from Weyer in Kors and Peters 2001: 280–9).

Weyer's audacious attempt to exempt all except poisoners from the charge of witchcraft was built on the physical powers of demons and (what he saw as) the physical weaknesses of women – to this extent he was a traditional demonologist (and misogynist). Much later in the debate, it was said that he had tried 'to load the Divell as much as he [could], his shoulders being more able to bear it, and so to ease the Haggs' (More 1653: 133). Twenty years after Weyer, a member of the Kentish farming gentry, Reginald Scot, took witchcraft scepticism that much further by picking up on Pomponazzi's arguments and giving demons no agency

whatsoever in the physical world. In a 'Discourse on Divels' added to his
The Discoverie of Witchcraft (1584) he assigned them a purely non-corporeal
status, making physical collusion with human beings – men or women –
an impossibility. With perhaps understandable lack of clarity, Scot spoke
of demonic spirits only as 'ordeined to a spirituall proportion', the exact
nature of which was unknown. This pseudo-Sadduceeism left him free to
explain away all the phenomena associated with witchcraft in non-
demonic terms. 'Witches' were either innocent victims of ignorance and
legal barbarity or they were deluded by their own illnesses and senility, by
their imaginations or by their Catholicism. A great deal of witchcraft was
no more than 'prestigious juggling', by which Scot meant the creation of
optical or other illusions by human trickery, and the rest was attributable
to strange but ultimately natural causes. The only people who took it
seriously were 'children, fools, melancholic persons [and] papists' (Scot
1584: 472; on Scot, see Anglo 1977b; West *c.* 1984; Estes 1983; and
extracts in Kors and Peters 2001: 394–401).

The arguments of Weyer and Scot systematized the grounds for *not*
believing in witchcraft that had been in existence from the beginning. But
the second development that marked the literature of witchcraft after the
1560s was the publication, and republication, of a far greater number of
texts asserting the general reality of the crime and the need to eradicate it
from European society. These claims were still not always made uncriti-
cally, devoid of all qualification or discrimination. On the contrary, most
authors opted for a middle way between credulity and scepticism –
between accepting too much and accepting too little. They were thus
usually as ready to question as to affirm and knew the dangers of
misattributing phenomena when trying to assign them to natural, preternatural or supernatural causes. Most authors continued to disavow aspects
of witchcraft that contravened either theological or natural philosophical
propriety, like the supposed metamorphosis of witches into animals or the
possibility of miscegenation involving witches and demons. Both of these
were invariably treated as popular misconceptions and explained away.
Most, while insisting on demonic agency, restrained it within the bounds
of nature, although all were agreed that demons could *seem* to go beyond
these limits by means of various delusions of the external or internal senses.
The actual arts of witchcraft – words and gestures, ceremonies and rituals
– were universally thought to be inefficacious in themselves, though not
if they were linked with genuinely natural effects by, for example, the use
of poisons. The culpability of the witch was therefore thought to consist
in the implicit or explicit collusion with devils that was needed to intrude
the additional causes that made these arts seem to work. The mere
pronunciation of words, for example, was never granted the power to
cause physical *maleficium* but, instead, seen as a sign (literally a sacrament)

for the devil to step in and bring about the intended effect by natural means. All this meant that most defenders of the reality of witchcraft knew that individual confessions could nevertheless contain things that were not real. Indeed, distributing the subject across a grid of possibilities and impossibilities seems often to have been the major purpose of their texts.

But if belief was always combined with scepticism in demonology, this still left plenty of scope for the vigorous denunciation of witches and the demand that they be punished. Probably the best-known group of writings in this respect comprised the books published by magistrates or judges in witchcraft trials who wished to pass on their experiences and reflections to their legal colleagues and the reading public (Houdard 1992). From the French-speaking lands – based on trials in the duchy of Lorraine, in Burgundy and in Labourd (the French Basque country) respectively – came Nicolas Rémy's *Daemonolatreiae Libri Tres* (*Three Books of Demonolatry*) (1595), Henri Boguet's *Discours des Sorciers* (*A Discourse on Witches*) (1602) and Pierre de Lancre's *Tableau de l'Inconstance des Mauvais Anges et Démons* (*A Display of the Inconstancy of Evil Angels and Devils*) (1612). These texts offered the by now standard arguments concerning the full range of witchcraft issues – the act of apostasy, the powers of demons and spirits, *maleficium*, travel to the sabbat and its ceremonies, banquets and dances, sexual dealings between witches and devils, the possibility of metamorphosis and so on – citing all the time individual cases purporting to come from the judicial archives. Even the legally trained Jean Bodin, who had little to do with any actual trials and whose demonology was vastly more abstract and philosophical, opened his *De la Démonomanie des Sorciers* (*On the Demon-Mania of Witches*) (1580) with the case of Jeanne Harvillier, executed at Ribemont in 1578. The largely unoriginal and rather unphilosophical work entitled *Daemonologie*, published by James VI of Scotland in 1597, falls into the same category. It originated in trials in Edinburgh in 1590–1 at which James himself had partly officiated, reportedly saying that God himself had made him 'a King and judge to judge righteouse judgmente' (*Calendar of State Papers Relating to Scotland etc., x, 1936*: 521–5; text in Normand and Roberts 2000: 353–426; extracts from Rémy and Bodin in Kors and Peters 2001: 322–9, 290–302; abridged trans. of Bodin in Bodin 1995)

Naturally, all these writings expressed religious convictions as well as judicial experience. But it is also helpful to think of other contributions to this later phase of the witchcraft debate in confessional and clerical terms. The Protestant and Catholic reformers, for example – whose work we have already seen impacting on popular magic – tended to see maleficent witchcraft through the same evangelical and spiritualizing lens. In attempting to turn *maleficium* into a case of conscience they played down the physical damage done by witches and saw their crime much more as an act of apostasy – a crime of which, as we have also seen, those who practised *counter*-witchcraft might be equally guilty. For Protestant writers in particular – men like William Perkins and George Gifford – secular laws that stressed the doing of harm by witchcraft were, therefore, somewhat wide of the mark. This meant that, while they often lamented the vengefulness of witchcraft victims and pointed to legal abuses and the convicting of innocent people, they would undoubtedly have strengthened the witchcraft legislation had they been able to. In this sense, religious reform contributed to the belief in the reality of witchcraft and the pressures to prosecute it that developed from the 1560s onwards (on Protestant demonology, see Clark 1990).

A further substantial contribution was made by Catholic intellectuals committed to the aims and programmes of the Counter-Reformation. In this category were prominent bishops, like the two suffragans Pierre Binsfeld of Trier, whose demonology appeared in 1589, and Friedrich Förner of Bamberg, who published 35 sermons on superstition, magic and witchcraft in 1625. So also were the Catholic theologians who wrote on witchcraft – men such as Martín de Azpilcueta, Gregory Sayer and Francisco de Toledo. The orders were well represented, particularly those with a keen sense of the Church in danger and the need for a militant response to lay indifference or error. The Dominicans had been prominent among witchcraft theorists from the beginning (including Johannes Nider, Johannes Vineti, Girolamo Visconti, the authors of *Malleus Maleficarum*, Bartolommeo Spina, Jacob van Hoogstraten and Silvestro Da Prierio), and in demonology's heyday they were represented by the eventual vicar-general of the French order, Sebastien Michaëlis. Other Frenchmen in this category included the Benedictine René Benoist, the Celestine Pierre Crespet and the Franciscan Jean Benedicti (whose views on witchcraft appeared in a popular confessors' manual). It was, however, the Jesuits who contributed most in this later period, men who, according to Marjorie Reeves, 'saw the world as the battlefield of two mighty "opposites", under whose banners of good and evil the whole of human-kind was encamped' (Reeves 1969: 274). They included Juan Maldonado, and Martin Del Río, whose huge study of magic and witchcraft, the *Disquisitionum Magicarum Libri Sex* (*Six Books of Disquisitions on Magic*) appeared first in Louvain in 1599. Such men were absolutely central to the intellectual strategy and direction of the Counter-Reformation. Maldonado had studied at Salamanca and taught at both the Jesuit College in Rome and at the Collège de Clermont in Paris, and was a highly respected Aristotle scholar (Lohr 1978: 562–3). The colleges and universities where Del Río spent a lifetime of study were among the most active and influential in the new Catholic Europe – the Collège de Clermont, Douai, Louvain, Salamanca and Graz. Significantly, such men saw the spread of witchcraft throughout Europe as an inevitable accompaniment of Protestant heresy (for Del Río on this theme, see Kors and Peters 2001: 331–4; on Catholic demonology, Caro Baroja 1990).

The combined impact of all these publications must have been to encourage witchcraft prosecutions, or at least to justify and explain them – even if the nature of the relationship between texts and events remains elusive. It is striking, for example, how the intensification of discussions of witchcraft in print from the 1560s onwards coincides with the opening of the period chosen by William Monter earlier in this volume as the key century of witchcraft trials. But if intellectual disbelief in witchcraft seems more muted in this period it was certainly still an important option (Lehmann and Ulbricht 1992). Many of Weyer's arguments were endorsed in Germany in the 1580s and 1590s, notably by the Lemgo preacher Jodocus Hocker, the Bremen physician Johann Ewich and the Heidelberg Greek and mathematics professor Hermann Witekind, whose book on witchcraft (published under the pseudonym 'Augustin Lercheimer') was scathing in its attack on popular credulity and clerical zeal. A particularly effective advocate of legal caution and the need for discrimination between real crimes and those which (as he said) 'never existed in nature' was Johann Georg Godelmann, a law professor at Rostock, whose lectures on witchcraft appeared in 1591 as *Tractatus de Magis, Veneficis et Lamiis deque his Recte Cognoscendis et Puniendis* (*A Treatise on Magicians, Poisoners, and Witches and How Properly to Identify and Punish Them*). In Trier in 1593, Cornelius Loos, a Catholic priest and theologian who sympathized with Weyer, was also forced to recant what seems to have been a more extreme denial of the physical existence of devils (Lea 1939/1957: 602–3).

Scepticism and opposition to witchcraft trials had come to take a variety of forms by this stage, each varying in its effectiveness (Clark 1992: 15–33). Firstly, as we have already seen, doubt could be strictly demonological in nature. Here the main issue was whether witchcraft was a crime for which any human agent could be held responsible. Did witches have the powers to commit the actions of which they were accused or were they caused directly by devils? Were they the victims of complex delusions brought about by illness and demonic deception? Could a natural explanation be given of the phenomena associated with them that precluded demonic agency? And most fundamental of all, did devils have a physical presence in the world to match their spiritual existence? These were questions about the very nature of witchcraft and what it was possible and impossible for witches and devils to do in the real world. Essentially, they fell within the realms of theology and natural philosophy.

Second, scepticism could also take what may be called a methodological form. Here criticism was directed at the evidence cited in support of the reality of witchcraft and the need to prosecute witches. Was it right to use episodes from the poetry of the ancient world as authority on matters of fact? Did the Bible really contain unambiguous references to demonic witchcraft or had translators misconstrued the Hebrew words for such things as 'poisoning' and 'divining'? Were any of the reports and narratives of witchcraft acceptable as testimony, or were they all corrupted by hearsay? These were questions about the reliability and interpretation of sources; in effect, they were questions about texts. As such they became the concern of exegetics and literary scholarship. A further considerable section of Weyer's *De Praestigiis Daemonum* was devoted to applying the findings of Hebrew scholars to various biblical labels for the black arts and showing that the usual conversions into Latin were mistranslations. In this he was followed extensively by Scot and, to a lesser extent, by Robert Filmer, whose sceptical tract *An Advertisement to the Jury-men of England, Touching Witches* appeared in 1653, in the wake of witchcraft executions at Maidstone in Kent the year before, with the subtitle: 'A Difference Betweene an English and Hebrew Witch'. It is noticeable, too, that a humanist attention to the construction and interpretation of historical texts is at the heart of Gabriel Naudé's attack, published in 1625, on the misattribution of the term 'magician' to many of the great figures of the European intellectual tradition – including Pythagoras, Socrates, Roger Bacon and Giovanni Pico della Mirandola (Naudé 1625).

Finally, there were legal forms of doubt, such as those voiced by Godelmann. Here scepticism was aimed at the whole conduct of witchcraft investigations and trials. Did not the fact that witchcraft was supposedly *crimen exceptum*, an exceptional, even unique, crime, imply stricter limits to the professional discretion of judges and greater control over the influence of clerics? Could the use of torture ever yield results that were not prejudicial to the accused? Was not the protection of the innocent more important as a judicial criterion than the punishment of the guilty? And should not many of those convicted of witchcraft suffer milder penalties than was customary? These were questions concerning rules of criminal procedure and points of law and their terms of reference were evidently those of jurisprudence. At a time when prosecutions were reaching a new peak in Germany, Godelmann himself complained of basic miscarriages of justice brought about by inexperienced judges who actually neglected or were ignorant of the correct laws relating to witchcraft and who therefore sent many innocent 'witches' to their deaths without proper evidence or proof. On matters of detail, he denounced the search for the witch's mark and the use of the water ordeal (as did many other legal theorists and theologians), demanded that the character and motives of hostile witnesses be scrutinized and that the accused be given copies of the charges and evidences against them and insisted that *corpus delicti* be conclusively established. Godelmann clearly believed that judges should always remember that defendants needed defending.

It was undoubtedly these legal scruples that made the greatest headway in the early to mid-seventeenth century – so much so that, in Volume 5 of this series, Brian Levack cites judicial scepticism and procedural caution as 'the starting point for any investigation of the decline of witch-hunting' (Levack 1999: 7). This is probably because it was perfectly possible to take a radically questioning position concerning the legal issues while remaining much more orthodox or indifferent with regard to the demonological ones. A string of published works critical of the handling of witchcraft cases (works that Levack also considers) emerged in this period, notably from the German opponents of witch trials (none of them lawyers), Adam Tanner, Paul Laymann, Friedrich Spee von Langenfeld and Johann Meyfart. Each paid at least lip-service to the possibility of witchcraft and, thus, of true convictions while virtually ruling out guilty verdicts as unjust in the present legal circumstances. Spee's *Cautio Criminalis seu de Processibus Contra Sagas* (*A Warning on Criminal Justice, or About the Trials of Witches*), published anonymously in Rinteln in 1631, and Meyfart's *Christliche Erinnerung* (*A Christian Reminder*), which appeared in Schleusingen in 1636 (the one by a Jesuit who experienced the prosecutions at Würzburg as a confessor to the condemned, and the other by a Lutheran who saw them at Coburg in Franconia), have come down to us as among the most passionate and eloquent denunciations of excessive religious zeal and barbaric legal procedures from this period – themselves built, said Spee, on 'popular superstition, envy, calumnies, back-bitings, insinuations, and the like' (Kors and Peters 2001: 425). These were men who thought that witchcraft *trials*, not witches, were demonic. Moreover, their reservations were gradually absorbed by the legal professionals themselves, such that we find them repeated or matched by jurists like Hermann Goehausen of Rinteln and Justus Oldekop of Hildesheim.

Demonological scepticism, by contrast, was much less clear-cut. It was much more difficult for critics to distance themselves intellectually from orthodox demonology than to attack trial procedures and investigative techniques such as torture. If restricted to the relative powers (and responsibilities) of witches and devils and the role played by trickery and delusion, the arguments could seldom be decisive, since no believer in witchcraft ever thought witches *themselves* had occult powers or denied that they could be deceived. In this way, negative arguments were already anticipated among the positive ones. The same was true of the naturalistic alternatives proffered for witchcraft phenomena; since devils were acknowledged by all to be inside nature and natural causation, to give a natural explanation for witchcraft effects was not as damaging as it might now seem. To get rid of devils altogether, or at least their physical powers in the physical world, would certainly have delivered a knockout blow to the acceptance of witchcraft but was far too radical a step for most to take, opening the door, as it was perceived to do, to atheism. Across the European intellectual community the aphorism voiced by the Englishman Henry More in 1653 held good throughout the seventeenth century: 'assuredly that Saying was nothing so true in Politicks, No Bishop, no King; as this is in Metaphysicks, No Spirit, no God' (More 1653: 164).

Yet even if legal criticisms were easiest to mount and most effective overall, notable individual attempts to sweep witchcraft beliefs away by restricting or reconceptualizing the powers of demons did multiply in this final period too. In England, where Scot's arguments were in abeyance for about three-quarters of a century, they were eventually taken up again by the physician Thomas Ady in the 1650s, by the one-time religious radical John Webster in the 1670s and by Francis Hutchinson in 1718. By 1690, when Balthasar Bekker began publishing his complete repudiation of witchcraft, *De Betoverde Weereld* (*The Enchanted World*), it was possible for this Dutch Calvinist pastor to combine all the misgivings previously felt about miscarriages of justice and misreadings of texts with a radical demonology that left no place for a devil who made a mockery of Providence. The same was true of the total scepticism of Christian Thomasius, the Prussian jurist, whose *De Crimine Magiae* (*On the Crime of Magic*) appeared in 1701. In a later work of 1712, his *Historische Untersuchung vom Ursprung und Fortgang des Inquisitions Prozesses* (*Historical Investigation into the Origins and Continuation of the Inquisitorial Trial*), Thomasius even went so far as to demolish the very genre that was demonology by treating every one of its canonical texts as critically unsound.

WITCHCRAFT AND INTELLECTUAL HISTORY

As Thomasius clearly understood, then, the history of early modern witchcraft beliefs is in one sense a story of individual texts and the specific ideas and arguments their authors wielded against each other. It is indeed the history we have just been tracing. But there is another way to approach it that seems ultimately more rewarding, in the sense that it reveals much more about the very possibility of witchcraft belief and its limitations and makes interpreting the texts less a matter of giving a blow-by-blow account of their contents and more a search for the congruities and incongruities that characterized early modern thought as a whole. Even identifying the texts themselves becomes less predictable and more open-ended. For this different approach we need to think more broadly about the intellectual and cultural history of Europe in the early modern period and, indeed, about intellectual and cultural history *itself* as a way of accessing early modern meanings.

What constituted the crime of witchcraft and the culpability of those charged with it were undoubtedly key issues in the long history of demonology. But witchcraft was able to raise issues across a much wider terrain, making demonology an unusually revealing guide to early modern intellectual and cultural values in general. For this reason, historians of witchcraft are now beginning to take a fresh look at it after a long period of relative neglect. In the 1970s and 1980s, at a time when witchcraft studies were being generally modernized, traditional intellectual history was in decline and the study of pure ideas discredited. Witchcraft historians also looked back with disapproval to a much earlier phase of study when conditions on both sides of the Atlantic led to a concentration on demonology and little else. The culture wars of mid- and later nineteenth-century Germany had turned the scholarship of pioneers like Wilhelm Gottlieb Soldan, Johann Diefenbach and Nikolaus Paulus not just into battles of books but into battles *about* books. In America, progressivists like Andrew Dickson White and George Lincoln Burr (and later rationalist historians like Henry Charles Lea and Rossell Hope Robbins) again saw the essence of what they deplored in witchcraft as the ideas expressed about it in writings. It seemed typical of these men that the 'materials toward a history of witchcraft' left behind by Lea in 1909 and first published by Arthur Howland in 1939 should have comprised notes taken almost entirely from demonological texts – the same texts collected by White while he was Cornell University's first President and by Burr his librarian, so that scholars might rid the world of intolerance and superstition by reading them (they are now in the magnificent rare books collection in Cornell's John M. Olin Library; Crowe 1977). As late as 1978 Robert Muchembled was complaining of what he called the 'intel-lectual' view of witchcraft, which he associated with Robert Mandrou (1968) and Hugh Trevor-Roper (1967), on the grounds that it privileged the opinions of a cultural élite remote from the social experiences of those most directly concerned with the crime (Muchembled 1978a). By this time, indeed, historians of witchcraft everywhere were refocusing on such things as the magical elements in popular culture, the social pressures and tensions behind witchcraft accusations in small communities and the fact that most of the accused were women. Their adoption of sociological and anthropological perspectives, some of them highly functionalist in charac-ter, also led to less and less attention being given to what demonology was best at revealing – the meaning of witchcraft.

Witchcraft studies today are an exciting blend of many innovative approaches and no one would wish to return to the days when what contemporaries wrote about witches was taken to be the key to everything

else about them. On the other hand, neglect has not been good for the
study of demonology either. For too long it remained unreformed, out of
date and subject to misreadings and misinterpretations. Trevor-Roper
himself expressed a crude form of rationalism in which the witchcraft
beliefs of intellectuals were seen as 'hysterical', 'lunatic' and so much
'rubbish'. In a survey published in 1972, the American scholar Wayne
Shumaker spoke similarly of 'delusions', 'stupidities', insanity and the lack
of 'hard intellectual argument' in early modern demonology (Trevor-
Roper 1967: 97; Shumaker 1972: 61, 101–2). Until very recently,
educated concepts of witchcraft, especially those expressed by magistrates
and clergymen, were still regarded as little more than rationalizations for
'witch-hunting'. Relatively few texts were well studied – a complaint
made by Sydney Anglo in one of the first modern attempts to remedy the
situation (Anglo 1977a: vii, 1–3) – and disproportionate attention was
given to the sceptics and opponents of witch trials, presumably on the,
again rationalist, grounds that they merited more attention than those
writers who supported prosecution. Shumaker spoke typically of their
'healthy tough-mindedness' (Shumaker 1972: 61). Finally, it was usually
assumed (and often still is) that 'demonologists' discussed only witchcraft –
and only the classic, highly stereotyped diabolism of the sabbat – and
studied it to the exclusion of anything else.

For, above all, Renaissance demonology has been read out of context –
its *Renaissance* context. Modern readers have had difficulty in appreciating
that educated beliefs about witchcraft were not held in isolation but were
dependent on other intellectual commitments, as well as on a whole series
of social and institutional practices. This is not just a matter of intellectual
processes and styles of argument and scholarship – the kinds of mental
habits that made the Bible, the Ancients and the Fathers authoritative (and
cumulative) sources of belief and the 'argument from authority' itself a
form of proof and persuasion in every Renaissance field (Shumaker 1972:
70–85, 100–2; Anglo 1977a: 6–14). Rather, it is a matter of substance.
Most 'demonologists' were not interested exclusively in demonology and
if the label implies that they were it ought to be used only with caution
or not at all. Take, for example, the Spaniard Maldonado, whom we have
already noted as one of the leading Jesuit intellectuals of the Catholic
Reformation – a philosopher, theologian and an authority on Aristotle; or
the Englishman William Perkins, the most prolific and influential of the
'Puritan' authors of the Elizabethan age, who wrote on every aspect of
Calvinist theology and morality; or the Swiss intellectual Thomas Erastus,
holder of the chair of philosophy, theology and medicine at Heidelberg
University, author of a classic refutation of Paracelsus and immortalized as
a proponent of 'Erastianism' in Church–state relations. It would be wrong
to think of these men as 'demonologists' simply because Maldonado's

lectures in Paris gave rise to a *Traicté des anges et demons* (*Treatise on Angels and Demons*), published posthumously in 1616, because some of Perkins's hundreds of sermons were turned into one of England's best-known witchcraft tracts, *A Discourse of the Damned Art of Witchcraft*, which also appeared posthumously in 1608, and because, in addition to denouncing Paracelsus, Erastus also denounced Johann Weyer and defended witch-hunting in his *Repetitio Disputationis de Lamiis seu Strigibus* (*A Renewed Examination of Lamiae or Witches*) (Basel 1578). To do so would run the risk of isolating their interest in demonology from their other pursuits – in fact, from precisely the things that help to explain why they were interested in demonology at all.

There were others, of course, who do seem to have written (or at least published) little besides demonology and who may well have been preoccupied by it. Examples might be the *procureur général* of the duchy of Lorraine, Nicolas Rémy, or his magistrate colleague at Saint-Claude in Franche-Comté, Henri Boguet, or, again, Bishop Peter Binsfeld from the city of Trier, all of whom were mentioned earlier as authors of specific works. But we still cannot read their books on magic and witchcraft without being struck by the way their demonology was linked conceptually to other aspects of their thinking – for example, their views about the natural world, about the course of human history, about the nature of legal and political authority and so on. Here, too, we need to treat educated witchcraft beliefs in a rounded way, resituating them among the other beliefs with which they were associated and which made them seem rational to those who held them. Most illuminating of all, in fact, are those occasions when we find extensive discussions of witchcraft in texts that are concerned with precisely these other ingredients of Renaissance belief – and which for this very reason have invariably been missed by witchcraft historians. The material on witchcraft in Book 5 of Johannes Nider's fifteenth-century treatise, *Formicarius*, has often been analysed, but there is just as much embedded in the Decalogue theology contained in his *Praeceptorium Legis sive Expositio Decalogi* (*Instruction in the Law, or an Exposition of the Decalogue*), written a few years later in about 1440. There is a substantial demonology in the French political theorist Pierre Grégoire's tract on government, *De Republica* (*On Government*) (1578), and another in the section on 'occult' diseases in a textbook for physicians by the leading medical authority in early seventeenth-century Wittenberg, Daniel Sennert. Casuists on both sides of the religious divide, like the Benedictine Gregory Sayer or the irenicist François Baudouin, included extensive sections on witchcraft and magic in their guides to the perfect conscience. In the same way, the Würzburg Jesuit Gaspar Schott inserted a great deal of witchcraft material into the natural philosophical discussions he published in 1662 entitled *Physica Curiosa, sive Mirabilia Naturae et Artis*

(*A Curious Physics, or The Wonders of Nature and Art*). The question 'what is witchcraft doing in these books?' may be prompted initially by the false expectation that it ought not to be present in any of them. But it is still a question well worth considering, if by answering it we are able to place witchcraft in its true intellectual surroundings.

Another reason why this wider context has often been missed is the tendency to relate witchcraft beliefs *solely* to witchcraft trials, as if these were their only point of reference. Naturally, many witchcraft texts did originate either in specific episodes or in waves of prosecutions, provoked into being by reflection on or the desire to justify what had occurred in the courtroom. The magistrates who acted in trials and later wrote books based on their experiences are obvious cases in point, with Boguet's *Discours des Sorciers* actually concluding with 70 'articles' of advice about how other judges should proceed in trying witches. In his contribution to this volume, William Monter makes clear how the writings of Binsfeld and Förner were intimately related to the 'superhunts' in Trier and Franconia which they helped to co-ordinate. Many adverse reactions to witch prosecutions, like those of Scot, Godelmann, Spee and Filmer already mentioned, arose likewise in response to individual cases or longer episodes of witch-hunting that struck these critics as grossly unjust. Conversely, there are numerous examples of individual witchcraft texts being brought into play during the course of prosecutions. This happened most often when lawyers sought help with legal technicalities directly from professional manuals or indirectly from the legal faculties of neighbouring universities in the form of what in Germany was called a *gutachten* (e.g. Lorenz 1995). Many other general forms of guidance and advice could be found in demonologies should judges and magistrates choose to consult them – as, for example, they were invited to do by the English preacher Thomas Cooper and by Pierre Nodé in France. Indeed, for this reason, there has even been an assumption among modern historians that demonology was one of the principal causes of witchcraft prosecutions and that its profile as a scholarly genre rose and fell exactly as they did in seriousness and frequency.

Yet discussions of witchcraft in print also had a life that was independent of the trials (Closson 2000). They flourished in some contexts – in the Dutch Republic in the 1690s or in England on the eve of the repeal of the witchcraft legislation in 1736, for example – where prosecutions had actually ceased. They appeared in texts – texts such as catechisms or published university dissertations or biblical commentaries – whose primary purpose had little to do with either encouraging or reflecting upon the legal process. And they were written by authors – authors like Joseph Glanvill and Henry More in English philosophical circles – who showed little interest in apprehending and punishing witches. Throughout the

European scientific community, indeed, witchcraft excited a theoretical interest that bore little relation to the practice of witch-hunting. At the same time, works that we habitually identify as witchcraft texts turn out to contain many other things, to which witchcraft was neverthless thought at the time to be integrally linked. A work like Del Río's ranges over a truly vast intellectual terrain that quite outreaches anything as focused as a witchcraft trial. On many occasions, then, one has the impression that the subject of witchcraft was being used as a kind of intellectual resource – as a means for thinking through problems that originated elsewhere and had little or nothing to do with the legal prosecution of witches. What witchcraft scholars are currently looking for in demonology has much to do with these various features. At the same time, intellectual and cultural history itself has also changed, insisting on far less – if any – segregation between the sorts of things that used to be pigeon-holed as 'religion', or 'science' or 'politics' and, at the same time, ready to acknowledge the strangeness that marked many aspects of the early modern world, not just its witchcraft beliefs.

THE POLITICS OF WITCHCRAFT BELIEF

If Renaissance witchcraft belief is to be made intelligible in its original intellectual surroundings, a good place to begin is with the political (and linked religious) ideologies of the age. A number of recent studies have shown how demonology could never be merely a set of abstract theories about witchcraft or 'demonologists' a group of ideologically disinterested or unattached observers of the crime – or simply members of some undifferentiated 'élite'. Attitudes to witchcraft were always mediated by the complicated and fluctuating allegiances of dominion and faith, party and faction, and in turn help to reveal these to us historically. In later sixteenth-century and early seventeenth-century France, for example, those who were most zealous about witch-hunting were deeply commit-ted – through conviction and connection alike – not just to Tridentine Catholicism but to the Holy League of the 1580s and 1590s and to the *dévot* party thereafter. 'Their point of view', says Jonathan Pearl, 'was not just a worldview or religious inclination, but a party allegiance in a time of bitter sectarian violence.' At their heart was a group of Jesuits, heavily influenced by Maldonado's lectures on witchcraft in Paris in the 1570s, who in their demonologies went on to write propaganda for a cause, rather than anything that had a direct influence on the pace or severity of French witchcraft trials. Indeed, the latter better reflected the moderation of the Gallican lawyers and magistrates who staffed France's parlements, both in Paris and in the provinces. In the end, Pearl has argued, the zealots, their impact already blunted by their very factionalism, were gradually marginalized as a minority of extremists in a political culture increasingly given over to *politique* values (Pearl 1999: 6 and *passim*; cf. Soman 1992).

A similar analysis of attitudes to witchcraft in England in the same period has yet to be completed, although an approach based on mapping the ideological significance of believing in or denying witchcraft for particular groups caught up in the ever-changing flow of national and local affairs has been sketched (Elmer 2001). What has been clear for some time is that, in France and England alike, both the theoretical debates about possession and exorcism and also the unfolding of individual episodes were heavily factionalized in terms of the complex religious and political controversies of the time. This was an aspect of the demonic that was linked to witchcraft through accusations that witches or sorcerers had caused possessions in the first place and could therefore be denounced by their victims during exorcism. It was not just that possession and exorcism were contentious subjects dividing Protestants from Catholics; they divided the faiths *internally* as well, together with the political configurations of faction and party. In Elizabethan England, the credibility of specific cases involving Jesuit and Puritan exorcists and the ideological capital that could be gained (and lost) when they were proved genuine or fraudulent became central to the fortunes of the settlement and survival of religious consensus (Walker 1981: 43–73, 77–84; cf. MacDonald 1991). In France, the case of the demoniac Marthe Brossier in 1598–9 was caught up in exactly the same way in the public fortunes of the Edict of Nantes, after she disclosed that Satan himself approved of tolerating Huguenots. To the Catholic opposers of the Edict, especially the Capuchins, she was genuinely possessed and, thus, of great propaganda value; to Henri IV and the *Parlement* of Paris she was emphatically not (Mandrou 1968: 163–79; Ferber 1991; Walker and Dickerman 1991). Perhaps the best illustration of this point – and undoubtedly the most brilliant exposition of it by a modern historian – lies in Michel de Certeau's account of how the conduct of the exorcisms of the possessed Ursulines of Loudun in the 1630s and the resulting trial of Urbain Grandier were affected by the intervention of the French government, with its royalist and centralist aims, in the form of a commission from Richelieu to the *intendent* Jean Martin, baron de Laubardemont. De Certeau best makes the point that emerges from all such cases, and from the world of witchcraft beliefs in general – that it was the very reality of the phenomena (what it was possible to believe or disbelieve, accept or reject), and not merely what action to take, that was determined by ideological positioning. The diabolical, he says, became 'the metaphor of politics'; political conflicts organized the 'vocabulary' of the Loudun episode, revealed themselves in it, used it and then moved on (Certeau 2000: 65 and *passim*).

To talk this way about 'use' seems too reductive, perhaps. Even so, evidence of how the political use of the idioms and vocabulary of witchcraft – indeed, their *overuse* – eventually damaged the credibility of witchcraft and led to its ideological appeal becoming exhausted comes in the form of the most sophisticated and original of all recent histories of early modern demonology, Ian Bostridge's *Witchcraft and Its Transformations c.1650–c.1750* (1997). One aim of this study is to account for witchcraft's resonance in England long after it is usually supposed to have been in inevitable decline – indeed, Bostridge seeks to avoid the assumption of inevitability altogether. The other is to achieve this by tracing witchcraft's place in public life as a function (even the creation) of political debate, its fortunes being much more dependent on this political context than on abstract intellectual arguments (in the case of scepticism, broadly unchanged since Reginald Scot) or the onset of the rationalism and the science of the Enlightenment – or, once again, the actual occurrence or intensity of prosecutions. The book is a series of case studies, reaching from the Civil Wars and Interregnum, through the Restoration and the 'rage' of party, to the repeal of English witchcraft legislation in 1736. Bostridge pits the covenantal witchcraft of Perkins against the politics of the Arminian and absolutist Filmer, the political theology of demonology against the Church–state relations envisaged by Hobbes, the royalist traditionalism of Meric Casaubon against the radicalism of John Webster and the freethinking Hobbism of John Wagstaffe, and the *Spectator* of Joseph Addison against the *Review* of Daniel Defoe. Party narrowly defined is not necessarily seen as the key to these differences of view, though the trial of Jane Wenham in 1712, when she was found guilt by the jury and reprieved by the judge, did lead to a spate of pamphleteering in which the High Church Tory Francis Bragge asked for conviction and his Whig respondents the opposite. After her pardon, writes Bostridge, she became 'part of the Whig mythology of Tory superstition' (Bostridge 1997: 135).

What these various studies reveal, then, are examples of the specific contexts in which writers and others positioned themselves with regard to witchcraft in relation to the major public issues of their times. But even if we recede somewhat from the intricacies and practicalities of public affairs to the more abstract patterns of argument discernible in demonology itself – that is to say, even if we recede from contingency to theory – we can still detect correlations between attitudes to witchcraft and particular styles or languages of political commitment. In fact, these may very well be the more general correlations that lay behind the ideological choices made by individuals in the particular situations they confronted. It was always impossible, after all, to arrive at a theory about witchcraft and its treatment by public officials without some kind of attention to political values of one sort or another. Conversely, any formulation of a theory of government necessarily implied a view about what kind of social and moral order it was designed to secure and what kind of social and moral disorder it was expected to prevent. Demonology and ideology, we might say, were always mutually entailed, whatever the level of generality we approach them at.

Speaking in very broad terms, we can identify three major traditions of political theorizing in the sixteenth and seventeenth centuries. The first, the most familiar and predictable, consisted of defences of theocratic absolutism and the 'divine right' of rulers. Here, authority was said to originate in – and 'descend' from – a divine gift of grace that made it literally charismatic. Political forms stemmed directly from God and were bestowed on men as divine favours via the temporal authority of rulers acting in his image and as his lieutenants or viceregents. Rulership in fact lay wholly outside the intentions of human agents, its force and ability to command depending solely on supernatural qualities and powers. Far removed from this way of theorizing, and in many ways diametrically opposed to it, were attempts to demystify politics by offering naturalistic accounts of its supposed supernaturalisms, and justifying all political actions in terms of pragmatism and rational calculation. One important strand of this was derived from Machiavelli's account of the social and political functions of religious belief in ancient Rome, which openly or surreptitiously was then extended to cover the political utility of Christianity itself. Another was the political vocabulary of what Richard Tuck has described as the 'new humanism', combining scepticism with Stoicism and stressing the importance of prudence, necessity and *raison d'état*. What emerged was an unscrupulous, instrumentalist ethic – almost an anti-ethic, says Tuck – which permitted citizens and their princes to concentrate on their own interests, effectively self-preservation, at the expense of traditional norms. Notoriously, religion, along with laws and constitutions, might be subordinated to the demands of political necessity (Tuck 1993: 31–119). Midway between these two traditions – rejecting the Augustinianism of the first and the individualism and relativism of the second – lay the kind of politics that has come to be called 'constitutionalist'. Here the main stylistic trait was to place political responsibility in the community, whether as the originator of power or as one of its participants. Actual rulers were said to be hedged about with legal and institutional, and not merely moral, other-worldly restrictions – their power was 'limited'. Constitutionalism often spoke the language of social contract and of popular sovereignty. It was committed to the normative value of human institutions and traditions, and owed much to the rehabilitation of human

reason. Political society and its forms of domination came about, hypo-
thetically, when men, living in a state of natural liberty, and acting for
reasons of utility, freely agreed to delegate their sovereignty to rulers while
yet reserving the collective right to remove them if they were not
conducive to the public good.

It is difficult to see how a crime like witchcraft could have meant the
same thing in these three very different theoretical contexts (Clark 1997:
596–612, 668–82, from which much of this present discussion is taken).
And, indeed, the varying significance attached to witchcraft by those who
wrote directly about it – the authors of the demonological texts we have
been discussing – seems to bear this out. Those who took it most seriously
did so in terms of the first political tradition, adopting its concepts of
government and magistracy. Here, witchcraft assumed the terrible proportions of a threat to cosmological order. Service to the devil and the
disorder that it produced were heinous criminal offences to those who
assumed that God was the direct author of political forms. Witchcraft
appealed to a source of authority which parodied the type that God had
actually created in his own image, and it reverberated with all manner of
damaging implications for the sense of order and hierarchy on which
divine politics ultimately rested. A special enmity – even a kind of
symmetry – could be said to exist between magistrates conceived of as
agents of divine authority and justice and the witches they tried; they
were similar vehicles of antithetical powers. This is the reason why so
many witchcraft theorists could plausibly claim that magistrates were
actually immune from *maleficium* – inviolable to direct assaults on their
authority by the devil or his agents (Clark 1997: 572–81).

Mainstream demonology is full of these ideas and sentiments. But we
can now also see why standard witchcraft theory found a natural place in
a work like Grégoire's *De Republica*, which argued that 'since the king was
no less than the actively inspired agent of the Deity, the people had no
choice but to give reverence to their ruler as to the divine majesty itself'
(Church 1941: 247–8). The best illustration of all lies in the absolute
congruity between Jean Bodin's two major publications of the late 1570s,
his *Six Livres de la République (Six Books of the Commonwealth)* (1576) and
his *De La Démonomanie des Sorciers* (1580), making them virtually one
book and explaining, in particular, Bodin's harsh and punitive attitude to
witches.

In stark contrast, witchcraft played almost no role at all in the arguments
of those who were so cynical – or at least instrumentalist – about politics
that they turned supernaturalism into a useful form of statecraft and
relativized religious orthodoxy to the needs of policy. Mystical and quasi-
sacerdotal views of magistracy were absent from the writings of Machiavelli and those of 'new humanists' like Montaigne, Lipsius and Charron,

relying heavily as they did on models of power drawn from Tacitus and Seneca. For them the charisma of princes was a product of artifice and superstition, leading, in the words of Gabriel Naudé (who, significantly, was deeply sceptical about such things as the witches' sabbat; Mandrou 1968: 124, 298–301, 310–11, 336) to 'feigned Dieties [sic], pretended Conferences, imaginary Apparaitions ... to lay a surer foundation of future Empire' (cited by Clark 1997: 597). As a crime defined in antithesis to mystical rulership, witchcraft made no sense in this non-mystical context. The awfulness of witches ceased to be inherent in their deeds and became a political construction. Mostly, then, they were either ignored in this way of talking about politics, or laughed at as crude attempts to frighten people into compliance. This is why we can see witches being dismissed as serious deviants by the most important 'new' political humanist of the sixteenth century, Montaigne (in the essay *Des Boîteux*, mentioned earlier), and in a book by the later seventeenth-century English 'libertine' thinker John Wagstaffe, entitled *The Question of Witchcraft Debated* (1669, 1671).

On the one hand, a summation of everything that was evil in the world; on the other, the product of dreams and trickery. But was there a midway position on witchcraft and did it correspond to the third form of political theorizing – constitutionalism? This is a more difficult question to answer, given the current state of research. In the context of man-made politics, witchcraft could never assume the importance given it by the political theology of divine right, but there was no reason for it to disappear altogether. It became a different crime – less portentous, certainly, and less Mosaic – but still a real one. In a commonwealth erected to ensure the citizens' security and well-being, its seriousness depended on the threat it posed to these goals. Witchcraft lost the overtones of rebelliousness and antimonarchism and became primarily a menace to life and property. What mattered were not the symbolic overtones of apostasy and the devil worship of the sabbat but the actual harms caused by *maleficium*. That these could still occur through demonically inspired actions – without being reduced entirely to non-demonic causes – meant a continued belief in witchcraft's reality as a phenomenon, if not in its more sensational aspects.

We can see the political weighting at work here in the way English Royalists of the 1640s turned to the subject of witchcraft – and in particular to the biblical verse in 1 Samuel 15:23; 'For rebellion is as the sin of witchcraft' – in order to bring out the awfulness of armed opposition to the king. This, indeed, exemplifies again witchcraft's relationship to the first of the three political traditions we have been examining here – as does the use made of this text by other Crown supporters in the seventeenth century, from Isaac Bargrave in 1627 defending the 'forced loan' of Charles I, to the tracts and sermons concerned with the Exclusion

Crisis and Monmouth's rebellion in the 1680s. But what is especially striking is the contrast drawn by the royalists of the 1640s between their own linking of demonology with politics and the way their constitution-alist opponents made the connection. The suggestion was that those who defended the parliamentarian cause in terms of the notion of popular sovereignty were comparable to those who were sceptical about the reality and seriousness of witchcraft. Diminishing the significance of witchcraft was like diminishing the significance of resistance to Charles I.

Searching for overt constitutionalism in demonologies that did indeed play down the seriousness of witchcraft while still regarding it as a crime is a task that has hardly begun. But a good indication of what to look for comes in another text that was mentioned earlier, Godelmann's *Tractatus de Magis, Veneficis et Lamiis*. Clearly, this work contains the main elements of the midway position on witchcraft – in particular, a concentration on the inflicting of actual harm, a concern to distinguish real *maleficium* from crimes that were illusory and fictitious (the term 'witchcraft' itself being reserved, in this case, for the latter), and a distaste for the public disorder and judicial abuses of trials and ordeals conducted by poorly qualified and 'superstitious' magistrates. Many other German jurists came to share some or all of Godelmann's misgivings; so too did the magistrates of the Parlement of Paris, and so too did many Protestant clergymen through Europe (Godelmann himself was a Lutheran), inviting the question as to what role constitutionalist leanings may have played in this. But in Godelmann's own case, endorsement was given to his arguments by a fellow jurist who went on to enunciate a political theory that became synonymous with constitutionalism. At the conclusion of Part 1 of the *Tractatus* there is a 'Warning to the Judge', contributed by Johannes Althusius, at the time a teacher in the law faculty of the Calvinist academy of Herborn, and later the author of *Politica Methodice Digesta* (*Politics Methodically Set Forth*), published in 1603. This juxtaposition of identical views expressed by an intellectual normally thought of as a demonologist and one normally thought of as a political theorist itself invites the kinds of questions we have been considering about the, at least cognitive, relationships that existed between the two fields. But more precisely it allows us to match the mainly legal reasons for questioning witchcraft trials with the kind of politics that was congruent with them (Clark 2000).

LANGUAGES OF WITCHCRAFT

Congruence and incongruence are in fact the key to the kind of intellec-tual history of demonology that is being proposed here. If we move beyond politics to religious ideology and to views about the Church and about salvation; if we move beyond these to conceptions of history, of historical time, agency and process; and if we move beyond these to questions about natural causation and physical reality; if, indeed, we reconstruct the issues raised by demonology in each of these other overlapping areas of early modern thought, the same general pattern keeps recurring – the belief in witchcraft was congruent with particular styles of religious, historical and scientific thinking and incongruent with others. Those who, on the whole, believed in witchcraft and wanted it eradicated derived their view of religious deviance from a providential interpretation of misfortune, a pastoral and evangelical conception of piety and conformity and a preoccupation with sins against the First Commandment. This is why there is so much demonology stored up in texts such as catechisms and casuistical treatises. They were not supporters of what Ernst Troeltsch called the 'sect-type' churches of Anabaptists and other independents or of their spiritualist and antinomian theologies – churches which paid much less or little attention to the physical presence of devils and to the association of witchcraft with heresy. Hence, by contrast, the significance of the links which the two most radical witchcraft sceptics in England *do* seem to have had with this kind of religious radicalism, Scot with the Familists and Webster with the Anabaptists and antinomians (Wootton 2001: 119–38; Elmer 1986, 2–12).

Again, with regard to their views about history, believers in witchcraft (and demonic possession) espoused a linear, apocalyptic and prophetic understanding of the past and the demonic events of their own times, derived from Revelation, which gave a prominent place to the Antichrist. To cleanse societies of their witches (and to exorcise demoniacs) was to prepare the way for the end of the world, an incentive to witchcraft prosecution whose powerful appeal has only recently begun to be recognized (Behringer 1997: 113, 115–21; Crouzet 1990: ii. 340–1; Boyer and Nissenbaum 1974: 174–5). However, this view of history was rivalled in the sixteenth and seventeenth centuries by the quite different style of Renaissance Ciceronianism, with its more cyclical, more secular concentration on human motivation and the provision of lessons for the conduct of public life. This was the sort of humanistic history-writing we associate with the Florentines Leonardo Bruni, Machiavelli and Francesco Guicciardini, with de Thou in France, and with Francis Bacon and the Earl of Clarendon in England. The contrast here is equally instructive; eschatological history found a natural, intelligible place for witchcraft but could we imagine any of the humanist historians paying serious attention to devils, the Antichrist and witches as agents of historical change?

Finally, those who believed in witchcraft operated with a natural philosophy that blended in a flexible way the up-to-date Aristotelianism of the European universities and the theory and practice of natural magic, of which demonic magic – the physical means by which the devil produced witchcraft effects – was considered the exact analogue (on natural magic, see Chapter 3 below). But their acceptance of demonic intervention in natural events rested on notions of causation that purists of both the Aristotelian and corpuscularian philosophies would have liked to rule out. Once again, then, we are presented with a situation in which demonology matched up with one version of things but not with others – in this case, one account of nature and natural knowledge rather than the alternatives on offer at the time. Of the purist Aristotelians, the most threatening to witchcraft belief – as we saw earlier – was Pomponazzi; among the corpuscularians were philosophers like Marin Mersenne and Pierre Gassendi. For René Descartes and Thomas Hobbes, nature consisted entirely of matter in motion, and incorporeal causes and preternatural effects were physically impossible. Although many English admirers of this 'mechanic' philosophy found it hard to do without spirits (or witches), no pure Cartesian would have been expected to defend the physical reality of demonism and witchcraft.

Relating witchcraft belief much more broadly to the intellectual and cultural history of Europe in this manner helps us to grasp two important features of it. On the one hand, we can better see the reasons for its strength and resilience between the fifteenth and eighteenth centuries. Its essential congruence with so many other ways of thinking explains its appeal and the nature of its coherence and rationality for contemporaries. On the other hand, congruence also helps to account for the rise and decline of witchcraft belief. It became possible to 'think' witchcraft as and when the intellectual positions that were allied to demonology themselves became available as options for intellectuals to adopt. It ceased to be possible when they lost their appeal, to be replaced by others with which witchcraft belief was *in*congruent. Bostridge, for example, speaks of the eventual loss of witchcraft's ideological roots in religion and politics, notably with the waning of commitment to the ideal of divine order in Church, state and society. More importantly, he indicates a kind of ideological exhaustion at work in early eighteenth-century Britain, whereby the habitual association of witchcraft with transparently 'party' passions acted to discredit its very authenticity, especially at the time of the trial of Jane Wenham in 1712 (Bostridge 1997: 108–38).

This, of course, is a modern historian's insight. But among the most interesting features of early modern writings on witchcraft are the, first occasional and then ever-growing, indications that contemporaries grasped this idea too – first, identifying in the acceptance of witchcraft a specific ideological position and then using this very partiality as a reason for scepticism. Probably, this could not happen before the Protestant Reformation introduced radical religious partisanship into European intellectual life. Indeed, the earliest example of this sort of scepticism seems to be the Protestant Johann Weyer's accusation that many of the things witches were supposed to do were merely anti-*Catholic* transgressions – that is, things that no one but Catholics could take seriously (Weyer 1991: 177–9). Further impetus was given by the emergence of so-called 'libertinism' in early seventeenth-century France and by the adoption of *cui bono* arguments among intellectual radicals and freethinkers in mid- to later seventeenth-century England. Following Hobbes, 'policy' came to be urged as a reason for creating and maintaining the fear of witches, with John Wagstaffe, in particular, explaining demonology away as a politically useful tool (Hunter 1995). Eventually, Francis Hutchinson was to repeat Weyer's point but in a now all-embracing manner, remarking that 'the Numbers of Witches, and the suppos'd Dealings of Spirits with them', increased or decreased according to 'the Laws, and Notions, and Principles of the several Times, Places, and Princes'. For him (writing in 1718), 'a Hebrew Witch, a Pagan Witch, a Lapland Witch, an Indian Witch, a Protestant Witch, and a Popish Witch [were] different from one another' (cited by Clark 1997: 144). Today we would say that Hutchinson was seeking to destroy the belief in witchcraft by turning it into a cultural construction. But this form of relativism had begun at least 150 years before.

CHAPTER 3

Intellectual Magic

'THE GREATEST PROFOUNDNESSE OF NATURAL PHILOSOPHIE'

The two preceding chapters have been very much concerned with the twin questions of reputation and interpretation, and this last one continues the theme. We saw firstly how, in recent years, popular magic has had to be rescued from various kinds of rejection at the hands of both contemporaries and modern scholars; and then, in the last chapter, how demonology, likewise, has suffered in the past from the depredations of rationalism and historical isolation and only now is being read in a context that begins to make sense of it. In the case of popular magic, those who accepted it and used it left little record of their reasons for doing so, let alone their way of conceptualizing it; the sense it undoubtedly had for them has largely to be inferred. Indeed, as was noted earlier, it can be difficult in this context to find anyone in the early modern period who would have agreed that 'magic' was the best (or, certainly, the safest) description of what he or she did or who would have called him/herself a 'magician'. With learned witchcraft beliefs (though not, of course, the beliefs of those actually accused of witchcraft) the case is quite different. We have an abundance of published statements about why it was important to take witchcraft and its legal prosecution seriously, and in this sense there is no silence in the historical record or lack of self-confessed 'demonologists'.

The subject of this last chapter – the intellectual magic of the Renaissance centuries – has also experienced wild fluctuations in fortune and so its history too must, in part, be the history of a reputation and the problems of interpretation this has caused. But unlike its popular counterpart it was certainly not lacking a voice of its own. As the name usually given to it suggests, it was a theory and practice of magic enunciated by intellectuals. Like demonology, indeed, it was described and debated in a multitude of texts – sometimes, the same texts. Initially, at least, there is no need for inference in discovering what it was. Before considering its reputation, therefore, it will be best to let the intellectual magicians of Renaissance Europe speak for themselves.

A good place to start is with a work known throughout the period as a kind of encyclopaedia of intellectual (or 'high') magic, *De Occulta*

Philosophia Libri Tres (*Three Books Of Occult Philosophy*) by Heinrich Cornelius Agrippa (1486–1535) (the work is described and discussed by Yates 1964: 130–43, and by Shumaker 1972: 134–56). Agrippa was a student and teacher of philosophy, theology and medicine (which he also practised, for a time at the French court), who moved between France, Italy, Switzerland, Germany and the Low Countries in the course of a lifetime of study. For a while, the witchcraft author Johann Weyer served as his assistant. In *De Occulta Philosophia*, which appeared between 1531 and 1533 and in manuscript long before that, Agrippa gave a definition of magic that was widely shared by his contemporaries:

> Magic is a faculty of wonderful power, full of most high mysteries. It contains the most profound contemplation of things which are most secret, together with their nature, power, quality, substance and virtues, and the knowledge of the whole of nature. It instructs us in the way things differ and agree with each other and thus it produces wonderful effects by applying the virtues of one thing to another and thus uniting them. It also joins and knits firmly together compatible inferior objects by means of the powers and virtues of superior bodies. This is the most perfect and principal branch of knowledge, a sacred and more lofty kind of philosophy, and the most absolute perfection of every most excellent philosophy. (Maxwell-Stuart 1999: 116)

This definition repays close attention since it refers to many of the key features of intellectual magic and captures its characteristic mentality. Self-congratulatory as it may sound, this kind of magic was always described as the summation of knowledge and wisdom, as something 'high' and 'more lofty'. It was not just another kind of science, but its apogee ('the most perfect and principal branch of knowledge'). In another work, Agrippa described it as 'the greatest profoundnesse of natural Philosophie, and absolutest perfection therof'. Francis Bacon, tracing it like everybody else to the ancient Persians and their word *magia*, explained that they regarded it as 'a sublime wisdom, and the knowledge of the universal consents of things' (cited by Clark 1997: 216).

Generally, many contemporaries shared this notion of the seriousness, the importance and the stature of intellectual magic. However we may think of it, it was certainly not regarded as routine, everyday knowledge. One reason for this, as we shall see in a moment, was that it was all-embracing; it was 'the knowledge of the whole of nature' – indeed, of the whole of creation. Another was that it dealt with the most profound and mysterious aspects of the created world, those 'which are most secret'. In many ways, intellectual magic was synonymous with the attempt to grasp what was hidden – literally 'occult' (Latin = *occulta*) – about nature's workings. It specialized, in particular, in uncovering what were known as 'occult virtues', whose remarkable effects were manifest to experience in the form of natural marvels but whose causes remained beyond the reach of human intellect, and so could not be rationally explained. In the third part of his *De Vita Libri Tres* (*Three Books on Life*), the Italian Neoplatonist (and high magic's greatest Renaissance theoretician), Marsilio Ficino, spoke about the example of talismanic stones whose power depended not just on 'the qualities recognized by the senses, but also and much more on certain properties . . . hidden to our senses and scarcely at all recognized by reason' (cited by Copenhaver 1984: 525). Another Italian humanist, Giovanni Pico della Mirandola, described the magician's craft as to bring forth 'into the open the miracles concealed in the recesses of the world, in the depths of nature, and in the storehouses and mysteries of God, just as if she herself were their maker' (cited by Grafton 1990: 111). Agrippa himself explained that, in addition to the qualities of the four elements, there were natural 'virtues' that could be admired but not seen or known. Of all these occult agents, perhaps the most discussed were the sympathies and antipathies that drew natural things together in 'friendship' and drove them apart in 'enmity' ('the way things differ and agree with each other'). Magicians hoped, above all, to master these universal inclinations in things, hoping thereby to manipulate artificially the interactions that resulted.

Also considered crucial among them were the relationships between the 'inferior' and the 'superior'. Intellectual magic had a hierarchical notion of causation and influence, captured elsewhere in *De Occulta Philosophia* by the statement: 'It is clear that all inferior things are subject to higher and (as Proclus says) in a certain fashion each is present inside the other, i.e. the highest is in the lowest and the lowest in the highest' (Maxwell-Stuart 1999: 96). Later in the sixteenth century, another Italian philosopher, Giambattista della Porta, renowned as an exponent and promoter of this kind of magic, quoted Plotinus to the effect that the study had only originated at all 'that the superiors might be seen in these inferiors, and these inferiors in their superiors; earthly things in heavenly . . . likewise heavenly things in earthly' (cited by Clark 1997: 218). Obviously, this was the ultimate rationale that guaranteed the workings of astrology in all its various manifestations.

Finally, Agrippa's definition speaks of producing 'wonderful effects', another aspiration central to intellectual magic and which also explains its elevated self-image and its considerable appeal. This kind of magic was intensely utilitarian as well as intensely cerebral. The magician – the *magus* – was one who could imitate and manipulate nature's most fundamental and challenging operations in order to create powerful and dazzling works of his own. Something of this is captured in the subtitle which della Porta gave to his highly influential book on magic, which first appeared at

Naples in 1558 – *Magiae Naturalis, sive de Miraculis Rerum Naturalium* (*Natural Magic, or the Miracles of Natural Things*).

With an illustrious pedigree stretching back to ancient Persia, therefore – and, in addition, to a mythical Egyptian philosopher, Hermes Trismegistus, and a series of very real Neoplatonists that included Proclus, Porphyry and Plotinus – magic signified the pursuit by adepts of a highly elevated and esoteric form of wisdom based on the perceived presence in the world of secret patterns and mysterious intelligences possessing real efficacy in nature and human affairs. In the *De Occulta Philosophia*, as well as in the writings of Ficino, this causation was seen in terms of an organically related hierarchy of powers divided into three levels. Influences descended from the highest level of the angelic or intellectual world of spirits, to the stellar and planetary world of the heavens, which in turn governed the behaviour of earthly things and their physical changes. The magician was, in consequence, someone who sought to ascend to knowledge of these superior powers and then accentuate their normal workings by drawing them down artificially to produce amazing effects. 'The Agrippan Magus', writes Frances Yates, 'aims at mounting up through all three worlds . . . and beyond even that to the Creator himself whose divine creative power he will obtain' (Yates 1964: 136). In effect he needed three sets of abilities and achieved three kinds of insight. Agrippa's definition continues in this way:

> So whoever wishes to study this faculty must be skilled in natural philosophy in which is to be found the qualities of things and the hidden properties of everything which exists. He must also be expert in mathematics, and in the aspects and figures of the stars, upon which depends the sublime virtue and property of everything; and in theology in which are manifested those immaterial substances which regulate and administer all things. Without these, he cannot possibly be able to understand the rationality of magic. (Maxwell-Stuart 1999: 116)

Natural philosophy; mathematics and astrology; theology and religion. Magic's claim to be the highest form of wisdom depended on its ability to embrace all three aspects of the world order, elementary, celestial and supercelestial, and all forms of access to its truths. At the highest level, it became as much an act of mystical illumination as a piece of science. Here, the magician aimed at a priest-like role and his wonders competed with the miracles of religion. Indeed, another of the characteristic features of intellectual magic is its invariably intense religiosity and sense of piety, even if this was often construed as misplaced or superstitious. It liked to trace its doctrines to ancient sages (or *prisci theologi*) and contemporaries of Moses, of whom Hermes, who himself was both natural philosopher and priest, was only one (a tendency shared by Isaac Newton: McGuire and

Rattansi 1966). Its conception of the world that it struggled to comprehend and master was always as a religious entity – something created by a divine intelligence that was the ultimate model for the magician's own creative intelligence. Agrippa himself thought that the mysteries of the angelic intelligences above the stars could only be grasped by rites – by what he called in Book 3 of the *De Occulta Philosophia* 'Ceremonial Magic'. Herein lie some of the most notorious and esoteric aspects of intellectual magic, captured particularly in the cabbalistic principle of the power lying encoded in the names of God and in holy language in general. 'The Kabbalah', wrote the German humanist Johannes Reuchlin in 1517, 'is the reception, through symbols, of a divine revelation handed down so that we may contemplate, to our salvation, both God and the individual Forms' (Maxwell-Stuart 1999: 139).

However, 'ceremonial magic' and cabbala were always less prominent in intellectual magic than the study of the two lower levels of Agrippa's tripartite world – that is to say, 'Celestial Magic' and 'Natural Magic'. Communing with angels and tapping their knowledge and powers were very different and vastly more dangerous than dealing with the properties of terrestrial things or the effluvia of the planets and stars, and it was with these joint inquiries that magic was mostly occupied and in which it made its biggest impact. They were joint because of the relationship between 'superior' and 'inferior' things on which magic, as we have seen, was fundamentally based. Magic, said many commentators, was the 'marrying' of heaven and earth. Besides astrology, the key ingredient of 'Celestial Magic' was mathematics, linked to artificial and mechanical marvels and to numerology. Book 2 of *De Occulta Philosophia* dealt accordingly with the creation of 'living' statues and other marvellous mechanical feats (classed as mathematical), the virtues of single numbers and of arrangements of them (more like numerology), universal harmony and the effects of music, images for 'talismans' corresponding to the planets and zodiacal signs and the nature and powers of incantations and 'Orphic' hymns. In Book 1, reserved for 'Natural Magic', Agrippa turned correspondingly to 'those things which are in the world', identifying in particular the studies of medicine and physics. These terrestrial matters were to be taken up above all with the four elements and their mixtures, the nature of the occult virtues of things, the idea of signatures stamped upon objects corresponding to their stars and the manipulation of sympathies and antipathies and other 'stellar virtues in natural objects' (Yates, 1964: 132).

None of these three 'levels' of magic was, or was intended to be, separate from the others; quite the contrary. The universe of virtues, powers and influences, whether these were deemed to be earthly, heavenly or spiritual, was organically and hierarchically integrated. One of the reasons why we tend to miss this point is that we have a much more exclusive understanding of the category of nature and feel that some of these topics do not belong in natural science at all. But in this respect we are largely inheritors of trends that post-dated the kind of knowledge that Agrippa sought. For him and many other Neoplatonists, the relationship between objects in the lower or material world and the celestial powers that ruled their behaviour was a genuinely natural relationship. When Ficino adoped the *spiritus mundi* as the link between the two, he was thinking of something substantial. The occult virtues that governed so many of nature's secret processes and produced so many of its wonderful effects stemmed from the natural powers of the heavens; Agrippa, like Ficino, derived occult events from the *spiritus mundi* and the rays of the heavenly bodies. The idea of signatures also contained the argument that the heavens stamped particular characteristics and uses onto natural things from above. Talismans could only be thought to work if pneumatic links were assumed between *spiritus* and *materia* and if the characters and figures placed on them were capable of natural activity. Even incantations and songs could draw down stellar influences through the channel of the *spiritus* – and there are wonderful accounts in Ficino of how this astrological music was to be achieved (Walker 1958: 12–24). Thus, despite Agrippa's restriction of the label 'natural magic' to the first or elementary level of the world, his depiction of its relationship to the second, celestial level – and of that level's relationship to the first – is entirely in what he conceived of as naturalistic terms. The angelic powers of the highest level of magic might be truly spiritual things, and only something like a religious discipline could engage with them. But everything else about magic was natural – it was *all* 'natural magic'. Besides its grandly astrological and mathematical foundations and its broad commitment to physics and medicine, the sorts of individual scientific fields that Agrippa associated with the marrying of heaven and earth were arithmetic, music, geometry, optics, astronomy and mechanics.

It has to be said, too, that down-to-earth naturalism is present in many of magic's individual pronouncements, no matter what we may think of the concepts and causalities that underpinned them. In 1608 we find Oswald Croll plotting out the various correspondences that existed between the microcosm and the macrocosm and suggesting, for example, that 'the generation of epilepsy in the lesser world is the same as that of storm and thunder in the greater'. In 1650 we find Athanasius Kircher explaining reports that fishermen captured swordfish in the Straits of Messina by talking to them by saying that 'whenever a sound meets an object with which it is in correspondence and harmony, it disturbs only this object and leaves other things, no matter how many there may be, undisturbed because there is no correspondence between it and them'

(Maxwell-Stuart 1999: 150–1, 129–31). Agrippa himself accounted for occult properties, their medical uses and 'magical rites' in similar terms:

> Anything which has within it an excess of any quality or property, such as heat, cold, audacity, fear, sadness, anger, love, hate or any other passion or virtue ... these things especially prompt and provoke a similar quality, passion or virtue. So fire occasions fire, water occasions water, and a bold quality occasions boldness. Physicians know that a brain helps the brain and a lung helps the lungs. Thus they say that the right eye of a frog cures inflammation of the right eye, when hung round one's neck in a piece of undyed cloth, while its left cures the left eye ... Therefore if we want to perform magical rites with a view to provoking some property or virtue, let us seek out living things, or other things in which such properties conspicuously exist, and from them let us take for ourselves the part in which such a property or virtue is most pre-eminently strong. (Maxwell-Stuart, 1999: 125–6)

Love was thus provoked by taking from particularly affectionate animals (pigeons, doves, swallows) the parts of them (hearts, genitals) where desire was most strongly concentrated at a time when their sexual appetites were at their height. Like its popular counterpart, intellectual magic clearly had a logic that guaranteed its practical efficacy in the eyes of its users and defenders.

There were those who sought out the highest forms of gnostic, theurgical enlightenment in magic, at Agrippa's third level. A recent study by Deborah Harkness of the Elizabethan *magus*, John Dee, for example, accounts for his attempts to talk to angels in terms of this kind of magic, set nevertheless in the context of an improved – indeed, a kind of ultimate – natural philosophy. Dee emerges from this book as very much a man of his age, sharing in its intellectual traditions. Despairing of conventional natural philosophy, convinced that the world was coming to an end and imbued with large doses of prophetism, perfectionism and universalism (and supported intermittently by powerful patrons), he sought to bridge the terrestrial and the supercelestial and ascend to true wisdom by means of divine revelations from angelic intermediaries and messengers. His was a science conducted as revealed theology and via spirit experiments. For him the world was an opaque holy text to be read in the light of the language that had originally created it and given it power – the true cabbala of nature. Dee tried literally to learn this language from the angel Raphael; he tried, that is, to speak God's language, hoping thereby to transform human knowledge and the declining world simultaneously. As another of his angels put it to him, this was 'to talk in mortal sounds with such as are immortal'. Predictably enough, God's language turned out to conform to no known rules of grammar, syntax or pronunciation, and to be utterable only as the world did actually end (Harkness 1999; cf. Clulee 1988).

Nevertheless, Neoplatonic magic was, on the whole, of more modest and more practical ambitions. Magicians mostly claimed to practise only natural magic – or *magia naturalis* – and concentrated on the understanding of material forms and the production of this-worldly effects. This cautious and restrained approach, often profoundly empirical and observational in character, gave their work a powerful appeal in early modern scientific circles (survey in Copenhaver 1988; Shumaker 1989, is a study of four typical discussions of natural magic between 1590 and 1657). It was a dominant influence on Paracelsus and on his seventeenth-century follow-ers and adaptors, including Daniel Sennert and Joan Baptista van Helmont, and it served to give coherence to the polymathic thinking of Girolamo Cardano which embraced the fields of medicine, natural philosophy, mathematics and astrology. In England it informed many of the projects associated with the circle of Samuel Hartlib during the 1640s and was one of the many tributaries feeding into the thought and activities of the Royal Society (Webster 1975; 1982). Both its range and its essentially operative and mimetic – that is to say, naturalistic – qualities are seen, above all, in the recognition given it by Francis Bacon. Bacon certainly criticized elements of the magical approach to knowledge, attacking Paracelsus, Cardano and, indeed, Agrippa as he did so. But his dislike was more of the way things had hitherto been done, not of the concept of magic itself, which he called 'ancient and honourable', placing it in the 'most excellent tier' of natural philosophy. Indeed, his understanding of it was, in Agrippan terms, as 'the science which applies the knowledge of hidden forms to the production of wonderful operations; and by uniting (as they say) actives with passives, displays the wonderful works of nature' (cited by Clark 1997: 222). Bacon built many of the ideals of magical intellectual enterprise into his depiction of the ideal scientific community in his *New Atlantis* (1624); he incorporated many individual natural magical enquiries and speculations into his *Sylva Sylvarum* (1624); and he even projected (but did not complete) a 'natural history' of sympathies and antipathies (on the magical elements in Bacon, see especially Rossi 1968: 11–35).

INTELLECTUAL MAGIC AND THE SCIENTIFIC REVOLUTION

The case of Bacon – and, indeed, of other 'mainstream' natural philoso-phers who adopted high magical concepts and procedures – raises ques-tions about the relationship between the history of intellectual magic and those transformations in scientific knowledge and practice conventionally known as the 'Scientific Revolution'. Such questions need not be seen as inevitable, however. We might choose instead to discuss the world of science in the sixteenth and seventeenth centuries, with all its many fluctuations and changes, without invoking the concept of 'revolution' and simply talking about the various loose conceptual schemes – Aristotelian, mechanistic and, yes, magical – that, competing or mingling, allowed individual thinkers to ground their explanations of phenomena in a preferred cosmology. Alternatively, should we wish to preserve the notion of a 'Scientific Revolution' in some form or other, we might still write an entirely convincing account of what was truly new and radical in early modern science without finding much space in it for intellectual magic (see, for example, Shapin 1996). Nevertheless, it has been the case historiographically that magic has most often been related to the yardsticks supposedly provided by the 'Scientific Revolution' – just as that revolution has been identified, in part, in terms of its capacity to disenchant the world. On the one hand, magic's reputation has varied according to whether it is seen to have advanced or retarded 'modern science'; on the other, 'modern science' itself has been variously judged in terms of its rejection or retention of magical elements. Inevitable or not, therefore, there seems to be a need to relate the magic we have been describing to the science we have come to recognize as definitional of early modern intellectual change (Henry 1997).

The process started immediately with the revolutionizers themselves, many of whom dismissed, or at least criticized, elements of the magical tradition. An essay by Roy Porter in the next volume of this series describes how this process continued throughout the period of the European 'Enlightenment' and, indeed, helped 'enlightened' thinkers and writers to establish their own intellectual and social identity (Porter 1999). During the following centuries of the ascendancy of modern science, magic was neglected altogether, even by historians, except as a misguided obstacle in the way of true knowledge. Between the two World Wars, especially in the work of Lynn Thorndike (Thorndike 1923–58), this approach began to be challenged, and then in the 1960s it was completely rejected by the historian Frances Yates – so much so that, for a time, the attempt to rehabilitate intellectual magic became known as the 'Yates thesis'. Yates conducted pioneering fresh research on central figures of the magical tradition, notably Giordano Bruno (Yates 1964), but it was in an essay edited by Charles Singleton (Yates 1967) that she made her central claims on behalf of the 'Hermetic tradition' as, if not scientific modernity itself, then an essential preparing of the ground. What distinguished the 'new science' of the seventeenth century, in her view, was the ideal of human intervention in, and dominion over, nature, an attitude prefigured by the aims of the *magus* set forth in the *Corpus Hermeticum* (*Hermetical Works*) translated by Ficino and in Agrippa's *De Occulta Philosophia* and also anticipated in the magical enthusiasm for mathematics and mechanics. As a manifesto for the 'advancement of learning' Yates preferred not Bacon's work of that name but the astrologer and 'conjuror' John Dee's preface to his edition of Euclid, although she did recognize in the *New Atlantis* an immensely influential rationalization and remoralization of the Hermetic ideals. She concluded:

> If one includes in the [Hermetic] tradition the revived Platonism with the accompanying Pythagoro-Platonic interest in number, the expansion of theories of harmony under the combined pressures of Pythagoro-Platonism, Hermetism, and Cabalism, the intensification of interest in astrology with which genuine astronomical research was bound up, and if one adds to all this complex stream of influences the expansion of alchemy in new forms, it is, I think, impossible to deny that these were the Renaissance forces which turned men's minds in the direction out of which the scientific revolution was to come. (Yates 1967: 273)

Thus, the 'Scientific Revolution', in her view, had two phases; first, the magical and animistic phase, and then the mathematical and mechanical one, each interlinked with the other.

Frances Yates herself – together with others who were prepared to suggest a more central role for the 'occult' sciences, like Allen G. Debus (on Paracelsianism: Debus 1966; on magic generally: Debus 1978), P. M. Rattansi, Charles Webster (especially Webster 1982) and Betty Jo Teeter Dobbs (on Newton and alchemy: Dobbs 1975; 1991) – succeeded in reassessing the significance of magic in the history of science in a manner that will never be altogether reversed. Nevertheless, the 'Yates thesis' itself is no longer thought to be convincing and has now been superseded by an approach to the history of early modern natural philosophy that stresses its eclecticism and heterogeneity and, thus, the lack of any 'single coherent story' to be told about it (Shapin 1996: 10). Partly, the problem was with Yates's own sometimes exaggerated arguments – particularly so in the case of her attribution to Rosicrucianism of a number of key seventeenth-century intellectual and cultural developments (Yates 1972; Vickers 1979). Another difficulty lay with the differences in kind that seemed to persist whenever intellectual magic and the new science were strictly compared, overruling the affinities that Yates had successfully identified. There is, after all, something conceptually irreconcilable between a nature seen as alive and purposive and a nature seen as inert and machine-like – yet the machine metaphor was at the very heart of what many new scientists thought they were trying to achieve. To this fundamental incompatibility may be added others; between the magical (and cabbalistic) idea that 'sounds and words have efficacy in magical operation because that by which Nature works magic first and foremost is the voice of God' (Giovanni Pico della Mirandola, cited by Maxwell-Stuart 1999: 147) and the opposite principle that language is related to the world only arbitrarily by human convention and agreement – adopted by Marin Mersenne, Robert Boyle, Thomas Hobbes, John Wilkins and John Locke; between treating analogy as a way of grasping actual relationships in the universe and seeing it as an heuristic tool, 'subordinate to argument and proof'; between saying that metaphor 'is not just a trope, but reality' and saying it 'is not reality, but only a trope' (Vickers 1984: 95–163, esp. 95, 135). To view the world as a work of art, full of mysteries and capable of surprise, was just not the same as viewing it as driven by regularity and predictability.

Above all, perhaps, it is now realized that appeal does not have to be made solely to the 'Hermetic tradition', or to Neoplatonism more generally, in order to account for the presence in early modern natural philosophy of a widespread enthusiasm for natural magic. It was discussed and evaluated by many whose cosmology and epistemology was still Christian Aristotelian and Thomist. The study of preternatural and artificial marvels had always complemented the study of nature's normal processes in scholasticism, since the latter allowed for the presence of occult qualities in nature of exactly the sort described by Ficino and Agrippa. For Aristotelians the sorts of things that governed normal natural processes were the four qualities of hot and cold, and wet and dry. Preternatural phenomena (events and behaviour that were 'beyond' or 'above' ordinary nature) were often caused by other qualities, not accessible to the senses, that operated in a secret manner. Because they were insensible they were unintelligible in Aristotelian terms – their effects could not be deduced from the perceptible (or manifest) qualities of the objects or creatures in question. But the effects *themselves* embraced some important natural phenomena that could clearly not be ignored. They included gravitation, magnetism, the generation of lower animal forms, the ebbing and flowing of the tides, the effects of electricity, the workings of poisons and their antidotes, and the strange behaviour of many individual plants, minerals and animals. In addition, Aristotelianism also allowed for (indeed, was built upon) purpose and appetite in nature and could therefore readily embrace 'sympathies' and 'antipathies' (as, for example, in the work of Girolamo Fracastoro, an astronomer and physician trained in Padua).

There was, therefore, what Bert Hansen has called a 'scholastic magic', more sober, perhaps, than its Hermetic counterpart, but still dedicated to investigating nature's innermost secrets, to manipulating actives and passives and to producing rare and wonderful effects (Hansen 1978; 1986). In this guise it crops up regularly in the pronouncements – and, indeed, the textbooks – of the early modern Aristotelians who still dominated university education in physics well into the seventeenth century. The occult causes of diseases were also widely discussed by the orthodox medical theorists and practitioners of the age, together with the commentators on Galen. Here, writers like Jean Fernel, who was physician to the French king Henri II, Levinus Lemnius, a physician in the province of Zeeland in the Low Countries, and Daniel Sennert, the leading professor of medicine in Lutheran Germany in the early seventeenth century, published important works with titles like *De Abditis Rerum Causis* (*Of the Secret Causes of Things*) and *De Miraculis Occultis Naturae* (*Of the Hidden Wonders of Nature*).

In a sense, natural magic was an attempt – shared, as we have just seen, by early modern 'Hermeticists' and Aristotelians alike – to deal more satisfactorily with the epistemological difficulties created by occult qualities. It tried to account for occult causes and effects and render them less mysterious, less unintelligible. In this respect it contributed to an intellectual enterprise, identified by Ron Millen as the 'manifestation' of occult qualities, that formed one strand of contemporary scientific innovation and which he describes as 'a serious effort . . . to bring occult qualities within the scope of natural philosophy' (Millen 1985: 190). Among the most prominent figures involved were Pomponazzi, Fracastoro, Cardano, Fernel, Bacon and Sennert. The overall aim was to break the connection between insensibility and unintelligibility – in effect, to retain the occult as a category of investigation, but to make manifest its features. In this way, science and natural magic would no longer be merely complementary but identical. We can see this happening in the many sixteenth- and seventeenth-century scientific textbooks that presented natural magic simply as a branch of physics and also in the popularity of natural magic as a subject for the dissertations defended by examinands in Europe's universities.

Occult causes could still be attacked and derided by the spokesmen of the newest, 'mechanical' approaches to natural philosophy, for whom they represented intellectual evasion as well as philosophical nonsense. 'Sympathy' and 'antipathy', in particular, were ridiculed as things that could not possibly cause motion between inert, insentient corpuscles of matter. But another striking argument by a historian of science – in this case John Henry – is that the onset of the mechanical philosophy did not necessarily mean the end of occult qualities anyway. Purely mechanical explanations for things like 'spring' (the supposed elasticity of air), the cohesion of matter and magnetism were extremely clumsy and implausible, and for the cause of weight a mechanical explanation could not be provided at all. Even transference of motion itself remained inexplicable to many, without the existence of active principles. In the end, Isaac Newton himself could only come to terms with gravitational forces by arguing that there must be 'occult active principles in the world to initiate and preserve motions'

(Henry 1986: 339). For this he was attacked by Leibnitz, who said in a famous accusation that Newton's gravity was a 'chimerical thing, a scholastic occult quality'. Henry suggests not only that Newton was able to distance himself from the kind of unintelligibility attached to the scholastic version of occult qualities, but that his stance on the whole issue had been anticipated by a series of natural philosophers among his older contemporaries. English new scientists, in particular, were able more and more to accept the fact that such qualities were not accessible to the senses as it became apparent that *many* natural qualities were insensible and that it was only their effects that needed to be accessible to empirical investigation. Insensibility was, after all, at the heart of the corpuscularian conception of matter. Many exponents of the new science were thus able to reconcile the idea of occult properties with mechanical explanations of phenomena – including Robert Boyle, Henry More, Robert Hooke, Walter Charleton and William Petty. They were helped in this by a desire, felt throughout the scientific circles of Restoration England, to develop a natural philosophy that would protect traditional Anglican theology and the orthodoxies that went with it. In this respect, the principles of activity and immateriality that were allied with occult aetiology represented important protections against atheism and subversive sectarian enthusiasm. What seems to have happened, then, was a continuation of a very old intellectual preoccupation by other means, rather than an abandonment of it. 'The mechanists of the seventeenth century', George MacDonald Ross has written, 'had a considerable problem if they wanted to maintain that they were different in kind from the magicians of old, and were not simply the first generation of *successful* magicians' (MacDonald Ross 1985: 102, author's emphasis; cf. Henry 1986; Hutchison 1982; Millen 1985: 186).

These are admittedly complicated matters to do with the intricacies of early modern natural philosophy – and they are still being researched by historians. But they do give a good idea of how scholars currently view the issues that Frances Yates was the first to raise openly. Essentially, there is now an unwillingness simply to confront the 'Hermetic tradition' with the 'Scientific Revolution' – let alone 'magic' with 'science' – or to think in terms of a single narrative of change. Instead, historians tend to talk much more about the multiple and diverse ways in which the natural world might be confronted and explained and to concentrate not on conceptual monoliths but on overlapping thematic strands that illuminate the conflicting, changing and essentially eclectic interests of the age. Two recent studies have made a considerable impact in this respect and will provide final examples of how some of the preoccupations of intellectual magic are now being related to their cultural and social contexts. William Eamon's book *Science and the Secrets of Nature*, published in 1994, traces the many collections of 'secrets' published in the sixteenth and seventeenth centuries, which embraced not only nature's spontaneous productions but also the recipes of the arts and crafts, medical remedies and mechanical devices. These works, he argues, impinged greatly on the general development of natural philosophy by presenting the secret as a tested and classified experiment with practical and theoretical applications, by suggesting that scientific knowledge was characterized by the pursuit and disclosure of things hidden in the world, and by contributing to the emergence of rigorous analysis and attention to detail. A more recent book of 1998 by Lorraine Daston and Katharine Park, entitled *Wonders and the Order of Nature, 1150–1750*, looks at both wonder itself as a collective scientific sensibility – as something felt – and at the things that medieval and early modern scientists found wonderful – monsters, gems that shone in the dark, petrifying springs, celestial apparitions and so on. The two authors suggest that natural magic was crucial to the way naturalists of all sorts envisioned their own activity and divided up the natural world into various orders of being and causation (Eamon 1994; Daston and Park 1998).

NATURAL MAGIC AND DEMONIC MAGIC

In stressing the successful reception of magical ideas and practices and their appeal to many early modern intellectuals engaged in natural philosophy, we should not forget the very strong lobby directed *against* them on religious and moral (rather than philosophical) grounds. Quite simply, intellectual magic was denounced as demonic as frequently as was its popular counterpart. The attack came from many quarters – indeed, from anyone sufficiently sceptical of the intrinsic powers of words and signs, or of amulets and talismans, to think that demons must be involved in their workings. It came especially from those whom D. P. Walker memorably called the 'evangelical hard-heads' of the age (Walker 1958: 145–85, discussing Gianfrancesco Pico della Mirandola, Johann Weyer and Thomas Erastus). In general, we can say that the religious reformers who belonged to the main churches of the period, together with a vast number of conservative moral and social commentators, were always likely to express opposition to 'high' magic. Sometimes it was denounced in its entirety; more usually it was said to have declined from its original integrity and purity in the ancient world, becoming corrupt and evil in its present form. In 1580, the French witchcraft writer (though not a church reformer) Jean Bodin defined the magician simply as 'someone who knowingly and deliberately tries to achieve something by diabolical means' (Maxwell-Stuart 1999: 122). Magicians were often said to be constantly teetering on the very edge of respectability, always liable to topple over it into outright devil-worship. Although perhaps an extreme case, it is hardly surprising that John Dee's 'angel diaries' should have been published by Meric Casaubon in 1659 with the aim of exposing them as records not of conversations with heavenly spirits but of consultations with 'false lying' ones – with demons. But even the more routine and naturalistic aspects of magic could attract the charge of demonism, since any attempt to trace and manipulate nature's most hidden processes in order to produce amazing effects smacked intrinsically of aid by extra-human powers. In this respect, the boundary between miracles and wonders (*false* miracles) was seen to be in need of constant redrawing. Additionally, occult disciplines like alchemy and astrology were subject to sustained criticism, as both irreligious and subject to charlatanry.

Mostly, these were aspects of the religious quarrels and divisions of the times, revealing only the (admittedly very important) extent to which the acquisition and distribution of knowledge about the natural world was subject to ideological interventions. However, probably the most common position was to distinguish natural magic and demonic magic as the two parallel expressions of a single *magia*, and this does have a number of important implications for the way we look back on the history of witchcraft and magic now (Zambelli 1988). The Portuguese Jesuit and inquisitor Benito Pereira is a typical example. In a treatise 'against the false and superstitious arts' he said that all forms of magic were of two sorts: 'The first is Natural Magic in which wonders are created by the individual artifice of certain people who make use of things which are natural. The second is Unnatural Magic which invokes evil spirits and uses their power for its operation' (Maxwell-Stuart 1999: 117). This statement, and hundreds of others like it, contained two implied comparisons. Most obviously, it expressed the cautions we have just noted; it allowed for a genuine form of magic but set it in proximity to a false version. In this way, it acted as a warning against 'the false and superstitious arts'. Less obviously, but just as significantly, it also placed the powers of evil spirits in proximity to those of magicians. In doing this it revealed an attitude to demonism, very common in the sixteenth and seventeenth centuries, in which the devil became the analogue of the natural magician.

In every Christian society the devil has meant different things to different people. In the Renaissance period he was the serpent of the Garden of Eden in the Old Testament, the roaring lion of the New Testament, the force behind the Antichrist, the model for tyrants, the figure who tempted Faustus, the ruler of the demons who ran through the streets at carnival time and many more besides. But if we restrict ourselves solely to natural philosophical questions, the devil *had* to be a natural magician. According to orthodox Christian theology, the devil had to be both a supremely powerful figure and at the same time inferior to God. He had to be able to achieve marvellous things in the created world but without ever rivalling God's own interventions; in other words, he too had to be able to perform wonders not miracles. In natural philosophical terms this made him the exact equivalent of the natural magician, who also specialized in preternature. A physician from Ferrara wrote in 1605 that magic was 'a single thing' and that the devil only worked through natural secrets just as the natural magicians did. In 1658 a colleague in Seville wrote similarly that diabolic magic was 'the ape of natural magic' (cited by Clark 1997: 234). Another way to put this is to say that the difference between Pereira's 'Natural Magic' and his 'Unnatural Magic' was one of intention, not one of substance. The same kinds of natural processes were manipulated in each case, but for completely opposite purposes; 'unnatural' magic was still natural, even if it was evil.

In the demonology we surveyed in the last chapter, portrayals of the devil as a natural magician, albeit a supremely gifted one, were actually quite precise. The theologian Hieronymus Zanchy said that there was 'in herbs and stones, and other natural things a marvellous force, although hidden, by which many strange things can be performed. And this force is especially well marked and perceived by the devil.' According to King James VI of Scotland, the devil was 'far cunninger than man in the knowledge of all the occult properties of nature'. Nicolas Rémy wrote that devils had 'a perfect knowledge of the secret and hidden properties of natural things' (all cited by Clark 1997: 245). Perhaps the best statement of all comes from the Elizabethan Puritan writer and preacher, William Perkins:

> Whereas in nature there be some properties, causes, and effects, which man never imagined to be; others, that men did once know, but are now forgot; some which men knewe not, but might know; and thousands which can hardly, or not at all be known: all these are most familiar unto [the devil], because in themselves they be no wonders, but only misteries and secrets, the vertue and effect whereof he hath sometime observed since his creation. (cited by Clark 1997: 246–7)

What then are the implications for historians of this early modern way of relating and comparing natural and demonic magic? One of them takes us back to witchcraft beliefs and to questions about opposition to them and their decline – questions that were raised in the previous chapter. For if natural magic and demonism were exact analogues, notably in terms of their causation, could not natural magic have posed a powerful threat to witchcraft beliefs? Could it not have accounted successfully for the puzzling effects blamed on witches by giving a non-demonic explanation of them that was just as causally complete? It was Hugh Trevor-Roper in his famous 'European witch-craze' essay who first suggested that natural magicians like Agrippa and Cardano and alchemists like Paracelsus and Van Helmont were among the enemies of witchcraft trials, while those who attacked Neoplatonism, Hermetic ideas and Paracelsian medicine were often keen defenders of them (Trevor-Roper 1967: 132). And it does make sense to assume that a demonic cause for witchcraft could have been made redundant – and the witchcraft itself explained away – if all the mysterious phenomena at issue were given purely natural explanations. What better source for this than the science that specialized in accounting for mysterious phenomena in terms of the secrets of nature?

There is undoubtedly evidence that supports this possibility but it is not decisive (see Clark 1997: 235–50 for a full account). Agrippa did indeed defend a peasant woman accused of witchcraft in 1519 and was said to mock the very idea of witchcraft as a delusion and a dream (Zambelli 1988: 137–8; cf. Zambelli 1974). Paracelsus, Cardano and Van Helmont all tried to give non-demonic accounts of witches' powers and Cardano (whose views were later borrowed by Johann Weyer) said that witchcraft could only be believed by those who were ignorant 'of natural causes and effects' (for Cardano on witchcraft see Maxwell-Stuart 1999: 174–6). The classic natural magician of the sixteenth century, della Porta, reported in the first edition of his *Magiae Naturalis* an experiment with the ointment that witches were supposed to smear on themselves to enable them to fly. He had tested it by physically beating an old woman after she had used it and fallen into a trance, so that he could show her the bruises when she regained consciousness. She still insisted that she had flown to the witches' sabbat but he was able to prove that she had dreamed the whole experience under the influence of the narcotics in the ointment. The outstanding English witchcraft sceptic of the seventeenth century, John Webster, drew heavily on the natural magical tradition and, once again, insisted that there was 'no other ground or reason of dividing Magick into natural and Diabolical, but only that they differ in the end and use'. If both were worked by natural agency, then men might do 'without the aid of devils whatsoever they can do' (cited by Clark 1997: 239).

When looked at more closely, however, the witchcraft beliefs of the magicians turn out to be ambiguous. Johannes Trithemius, to whom Agrippa presented a first draft of *De Occulta Philosophia*, discussed witchcraft in terms reminiscent of *Malleus Maleficarum*, and both Paracelsus and Cardano made remarks that suggest uncertainty rather than outright rejection. In any case, as we saw in Chapter 2, scepticism about witchcraft could derive from things that had little to do with 'high' magic' – the widespread attribution of witchcraft phenomena to the condition known as 'melancholy' and to dreaming, or doubts about the legal procedures employed in witch trials, for example. In the cases of Reginald Scot and

John Webster, it seems to have been unorthodox, even radical, theology that mattered more than the attempt to explain witchcraft away in terms of natural magical findings. Johann Weyer, who disbelieved in witchcraft altogether, also denounced the entire magical and Neoplatonic traditions, despite his time as Agrippa's servant and assistant; he is thus a major exception to Trevor-Roper's generalization. There is, too, the wider question of whether, in comparing the powers of devils to the powers of magicians, early modern writers were not *strengthening* the credibility of witchcraft, rather than weakening it. Witchcraft authors may, if anything, have been helped in their portrayals of the demonic efficacy that lay behind witchcraft by their increasing familiarity with its natural magical counterpart.

We cannot be sure, then, whether natural magical explanations sustained witchcraft beliefs or undermined them. But what is clear is the sheer level of interest shown in witchcraft matters by exponents of 'high' magic – and, indeed, by many natural philosophers who made a special study of the occult aspects of the natural world. Here we have another example of an aspect of demonology and witchcraft that was also discussed in the last chapter – the capacity of these subjects to arouse interest in a wide range of intellectual contexts *other than* the legal prosecution of witches. They obviously appealed to some of the brightest scientific talents of the day who showed a theoretical interest in them that bore little relation to witch-hunting. Whether these men ended up believing more or less in witchcraft than they would otherwise have done therefore seems less important than their use of the subject as a kind of intellectual resource.

What a statement like William Perkins's suggests is that the devil posed a particular epistemological challenge to the theorists – the challenge of accounting for both his knowledge of natural things and his capacity to operate in the natural world in terms of the concepts and categories of natural magic. As Girolamo Cardano said: 'No discussion is as difficult or as excellent as that which concerns demons.' But this meant that witchcraft too, which, after all, was one of the things the devil actually brought about with his occult powers, became a suitable subject for natural philosophers to analyse. Indeed, it was an especially revealing subject to analyse since it was full of precisely the sorts of phenomena that gave natural magic its reputation as the most demanding and yet most revealing branch of scientific inquiry. It was defined, as we have already seen, as the practical application of abstruse natural knowledge to produce wonderful effects. In the case of witchcraft, there were several demonically caused effects that conformed exactly to this definition – known both generally in terms of traditional expectations and, more precisely, from the confessions that were emerging from witchcraft trials. These effects were all quite clearly bizarre and abnormal in relation to nature's usual workings.

But they were nevertheless still natural rather than supernatural or miraculous; they were, again, preternatural phenomena. How then were they brought about? And what light did this shed on the natural world?

Let us look at some examples. First, there was the question of how witches were able to travel vast distances to their meetings (or 'sabbats') by flying. When they were also reported to be at home in their beds at the time, did this mean that they attended the sabbat in spirit only or did it mean that they merely dreamed that they were there? The natural philosophers and the demonologists gave an unhesitatingly naturalistic answer; they either travelled really to the sabbat, 'transvected' through the air at an enormous speed by the devil's prodigious (that is to say, natural magical) powers, or they were deluded about going altogether. Sometimes the devil put counterfeit bodies in their beds to confuse the issue, but, in general, transvection was either a true preternatural phenomenon or a product of dreams – for which, of course, preternatural explanations were likewise possible. Then there was the further question, also linked to the sabbat, of whether or not witches who had sex with devils could then bear demonic children. Again the answer was naturalistic; the devil had no procreative power but could borrow human semen and use it to inseminate witches so that they gave birth to human children. Monstrous demons might be instantly substituted for the babies delivered to pregnant witches but this was still a secondary complication, with no effect on the main claim. A third topic was metamorphosis; could witches turn themselves or their victims into animals, particularly wolves? With few exceptions no one accepted this as a real phenomenon. For the most part it was attributed to the strange effects of the human imagination, especially when inflamed by melancholy. Alternatively, the devil might replace lycanthropic humans with real wolves so quickly that transmutation appeared to occur, or represent illusory wolves to the senses either by 'wrapping' real humans in the required shape or condensing the air between eye and object in such a way as to produce a suitable effigy. But these illusions were allowed for as part of the devil's natural powers and so a consistently naturalistic explanation for lycanthropy was maintained. A yet further debate concerned the possibility of demons causing strange diseases, an idea accepted by most physicians of the period. The diseases included melancholy, epilepsy, paralysis and contortions, the vomiting of bizarre objects, impotence and the inflammation of all the human passions to the point of pathological disturbance. Finally, there was the issue of the apparently malevolent efficacy of words – whether witches could achieve their *maleficium* merely by the pronunciation of curses or charms. Once more, an apparently very bizarre form of causation was denied on the grounds that language was merely a human convention for conveying meanings and its apparent efficacy was explained as a demonic intervention. When witches cursed, the words themselves caused nothing; they were, instead, signs to the devil to step in and bring the desired misfortune about by natural means.

It is quite extraordinary how often these five topics were analysed, not merely in the pages of those who wrote directly on witchcraft but more generally in the field of early modern natural magic. We therefore have to ask ourselves what scientific purposes these analyses served. At one level, obviously, they were simply ways of accounting for witchcraft – of explaining it in accordance with the scientific criteria of the age. They were ways of answering doubts about the very possibility of witchcraft as a real activity with real effects. But there is, in addition, a deeper purpose in these discussions, a purpose indicated by a remark of Francis Bacon in his *The Advancement of Learning*, in the course of his defence of natural magic as a scientific field of interest. Arguing for a new study of natural marvels, he asked that the arts of witchcraft be included in it:

> from the speculation and consideration of them (if they be diligently unravelled) a useful light may be gained, not only for the true judgement of the offences of persons charged with such practices, but likewise for the further disclosing of the secrets of nature. (cited by Clark 1997: 254)

What Bacon was saying was that stories of witchcraft were not merely evidence in a legal sense – they were evidence in an empirical sense as well, what he called elsewhere 'experiments of witchcraft'. They contained the moral deviations of men and women but also the physical deviations of a nature under demonic control. Like the other marvels and prodigies, the secrets and wonders that preoccupied the natural magicians of Bacon's Europe, they afforded privileged access into nature's innermost workings. This is the reason why Giambattista della Porta included his witchcraft experiment in (at least the first edition of) his book on natural magic. The way we might put this today would be to say that the subject of witchcraft had become particularly rich in thought-experiments. Experimenting with it in any practical way was obviously not advisable – beyond the beating up of old ladies – but all manner of insights might be gained by imagining what would have to follow for such strange phenomena as transvection or metamorphosis or the instrumental power of words to be true and what needed to be the case for them to be false. What was at stake, it seems, was the issue of scientific intelligibility *itself*, and the various criteria by which it was achieved in a particular scientific community at a particular time in European history.

MAGIC AND POLITICS

In every such scientific community, there are those who want to work at the very limits of the discipline, even if the paradigmatic constraints classically described by Thomas Kuhn act as a brake in this respect. This, after all, is the most demanding, the most innovative and frequently the most rewarding kind of science to do. This is especially true in periods of rapid change in scientific thought and practice, when Kuhn's 'paradigms' are at their least effective. By its very nature, early modern natural magic provided such an opportunity, and this chapter has sought to explain why. Magic's very concentration on occult causes made it particularly challenging from an intellectual point of view, while its promise of marvellous effects made it exciting as an observational and empirical practice and offered material rewards as well as renown. It was also thought to be especially enlightening from a religious point of view, giving access to the most fundamental aspects of God's creation and improving closeness to the Creator himself. All these attractions were summed up in what the word 'magic' meant to those intellectuals who saw in it the sum of wisdom and insight.

What has also become apparent in the most recent research on intellectual magic and the occult sciences in general is that they also had considerable political appeal, especially in the circles in which many magicians moved and received patronage. For although one thinks of figures like Agrippa and Paracelsus as almost physical and intellectual nomads, many of the intellectuals who defended or practised high magic were linked to specific monarchical or princely courts and aristocratic households. This is a pattern recognizable in Ficino's relationship with the Medici, John Dee's with Elizabeth I and her courtiers and della Porta's with Luigi d'Este and Federico Cesi (on della Porta, see Eamon 1991: 39–40). We thus arrive finally at a politics of high magic to match – and in part explain – the politics of witchcraft belief that we looked at earlier. In one way, this discovery is not at all surprising. Magic could offer a vocabulary for rulership and the exercise of authority (even for Elizabethan imperialism, in the case of Dee), just as it provided a pattern for science. The powers and attributes of rulers were often seen in divine and mystical terms in Renaissance Europe and their ability to provide solutions to political problems was regarded as thaumaturgical and charismatic, as much as administrative and logistical (aspects of governing that could rest on very shaky foundations). Monarchs and princes who liked to think of themselves as removed from the scrutiny of their subjects and in possession of absolute or semi-absolute 'prerogatives' were, in many ways, *magus*-like figures. Just as the latter worked in secret ways and on secret matters, so did princes in the realm of *arcana imperii* (secrets of state). Just as the latter sought to achieve wonderful effects in the field of natural philosophy, so the magician–ruler – like Mercury with his caduceus, it has been suggested (Brooks-Davies 1983) – aimed at *mira* in the sphere of government. Religiosity, ritualism and even hints of hoped-for infallibility were common to both. This, after all, is the age in which French and English monarchs cured those suffering from 'scrofula' by means of the 'royal touch', a politically inspired miracle that repeatedly had to be distinguished from magical forms of healing that were otherwise identical to it in form (Bloch 1973).

Many modern commentators have remarked on the way in which court festivals and pageants – notably masques – embodied such ideals. In a ritual setting, they celebrated the magical power and aura of the ruler and his or her court by means of stage effects and other spectacles that were themselves marvels of hidden invention and technology (Parry 1981; Kogan 1986; Greene 1987). Often they pitted royal figures against evil forms of magic and witchcraft – *theurgia* versus *goetia* – in a manner that suggests ritual disenchantment (Clark 1997: 634–54). In another illustration of the links between magic and politics, it has also been noted how the processes of alchemy, in particular, were often applied allegorically to the problems of maintaining order and harmony in societies divided by religious and other conflicts (classically Yates 1972; Moran 1991b; recent reappraisal by Mendelsohn 1992). In the world of early modern literature there is, perhaps, no more effective portrayal of these various aspects of the political occult, including its ambiguity, than the figure of Prospero in Shakespeare's last play *The Tempest*. In some respects, Prospero is a Baconian figure, a natural magician seeking knowledge and control of nature's secret powers; he nevertheless renounces magic before returning to power as the Duke of Milan.

The fictional Prospero, according to Stephen Orgel, is a royal scientist and masque-maker who exemplifies Walter Raleigh's definition of magic as 'the connection of natural agents ... wrought by a wise man to the bringing forth of such effects as are wonderful to those that know not their causes' (Orgel 1987: 20). But even a real king could be fêted as a magician. Bacon addressed James I as a Hermetic figure, at once a ruler, priest and *magus*; the royal dedication of Robert Fludd's *Utriusque Cosmi ... Historia* (*The History of Both Worlds*) (1617) comes almost as close. Bacon thought highly of the ancient Persian practice of always training would-be governors in natural magical philosophy, and designed his own Utopian *New Atlantis* (which appeared in eight editions between 1626 and 1658) as a society ruled by *magi* who combined the functions of politicians, priests and natural philosophers. Yet another illustration of these associations and the patronage they created is the sustained interest shown in the magical and occult sciences at the court of the Emperor Rudolf II in Prague between 1583 and 1612 (Evans, 1973; cf. Evans 1979: 346–80). At the Danish court, the best-known Danish Paracelsian, Petrus Severinus, was supported by Frederik II (Shackelford 1991: 86). According to Bruce Moran, the court of the German landgrave, Wilhelm IV of Hessen-Kassel, 'stands out as a sort of scientific research institute at the end of the sixteenth century' (Moran 1991b: 170).

In this broad context, the more specific links between natural magic and court society – noted, for example, by Eamon – take on considerable significance. In his view, the idea of scientific discovery as a *venatio*, a hunt, mirrored the courtly self-image much more than the idea of knowledge acquired via the university and scholastic disputation. Curiosity and virtuosity likewise became common aims, and reputation a way of measuring importance. Marvels and secrets became the currency of courtly science. Natural magic helped to promote the keen interest in the setting up of *Wunderkammern* (cabinets of curiosities) that typified courtly and aristocratic notions of power and knowledge in this period. The political purpose of all this was to represent the prince 'as a repository of praeternatural, superhuman secrets, and as the rightful heir to a tradition of esoteric and hidden wisdom' that provided authority and control. The kinds of scientists who flourished in such an environment were those 'whose contributions were formerly considered to be only ancillary to natural philosophy, including engineers, craftsmen, and mathematicians, as well as those whose activities formerly carried the stigma of the forbidden arts, alchemists, magicians, and investigators of the occult sciences'. The key figure in Italy, for example, was della Porta and his ideal of natural magic 'the courtly science *par excellence*'. Like Bacon at the court of James I, della Porta thought that the understanding brought by natural magic had a direct bearing on the government of kingdoms and societies. The commonwealth of the whole world and the commonwealth of men and women operated according to the same principles, and the prince and *magus* were thus exactly alike in their powers and roles (Eamon 1991: 37, 28, 40; cf. Henry 1997: 46; Moran 1991a). We seem to have come a long way from the pronouncements of Agrippa in the 1530s but, in fact, we have not travelled any distance at all. The principles that ruled all affairs, natural and political alike, were, not unintelligibly, those of 'sympathy' and 'antipathy'. Friendship and enmity were indeed the universal inclinations of all things.

Bibliography

Anglo, S. (1977a) 'Preface' and 'Evident authority and authoritative evidence: the *Malleus Maleficarum*', in Anglo, ed. *The Damned Art: Essays in the Literature of Witchcraft* (London): vii–viii, 1–31.

Anglo, S. (1977b) 'Reginald Scot's *Discoverie of Witchcraft*: scepticism and sadduceeism', in Anglo, ed. *The Damned Art: Essays in the Literature of Witchcraft* (London): 106–39.

Ankarloo, B. (1971) *Trolldomsprocesserna i Sverige* (Stockholm), English summary, 2nd edn. 1984.

Ankarloo, B. (1988) *Att stilla herrevrede* (Stockholm).

Ankarloo, B. (1990) 'Sweden: the mass burnings (1668–1676)', in Ankarloo and Henningsen, eds. (1990): 285–317.

Ankarloo, B. (1991) 'Trolldomsprocesser, 1549–1722', in *Lima och Transtrand: Ur två socknars historia*, 3 (Malung).

Ankarloo, B. and Henningsen, G., eds. (1990) *Early Modern European Witchcraft: Centres and Peripheries* (Oxford).

Bader, G. (1945) *Die Hexenprozesse in der Schweiz* (Affolteren).

Behringer, W. (1987) *Hexenverfolgungen in Bayern: Volksmagie, Glaubenseifer und Staatsräson in der Frühen Neuzeit* (Munich).

Behringer, W. (1988) *Mit dem Feuer vom Leben zum Tod: Hexengesetzgebung in Bayern* (Munich).

Behringer, W. (1989) 'Erträge und Perspektiven der Hexenforschung', *Historische Zeitschrift*, 249: 619–40.

Behringer, W., ed. (1993) *Hexen und Hexenprozesse in Deutschland*, 2nd edn. (Munich).

Behringer, W. (1994) 'Allemagne, 'mère de tant de sorcières': au cœur des persécutions', in Muchembled, ed. (1994): 59–98.

Behringer, W. (1996) 'Witchcraft studies: Austria, Germany and Switzerland', in J. Barry, M. Hester, and G. Roberts, eds. *Witchcraft in Early Modern Europe: Studies in Culture and Belief* (Cambridge): 64–95.

Behringer, W. (1997) *Witchcraft Persecutions in Bavaria: Popular Magic, Religious Zealotry and Reason of State in Early Modern Europe*, trans. J. C. Grayson and D. Lederer (Cambridge); trans. of Behringer, 1987.

Behringer, W. (1998a) *Shaman of Oberstdorf*, trans. H. C. Erik Midelfort (Charlottesville).

Behringer, W. (1998b) *Hexen: Glauben, Verfolgung, Vermarktung* (Munich).

Beier, L. M. (1987) *Sufferers and Healers: The Experience of Illness in Seventeenth-Century England* (London).

Béné, C. (1979) 'Jean Wier et les procès de sorcellerie, ou l'érasmisme au service de la tolérance', in P. Tuynman, G. C. Kuiper, and E. Kessler, eds. *Acta Conventus Neolatini Amstelodamensis* (Munich): 58–73.

Bethencourt, F. (1987) *O imaginário da magia: feiticeiras, saludadores e nigromantes no século XVI* (Lisbon).

Bethencourt, F. (1990) 'Portugal: a scrupulous Inquisition', in Ankarloo and Henningsen, eds. (1990): 403–22.

Bethencourt, F. (1994) 'Un univers saturé de magie: l'Europe méridionale', in Muchembled, ed. (1994): 159–94.

Biesel, E. (1993) 'Les descriptions du sabbat dans les confessions des inculpés lorrains et trévirois', in Jacques-Chaquin and Préaud, eds. (1993): 183–97.

Biesel, E. (1997) *Hexenjustiz, Volksmagie und soziale Konflikte im Lothringischen Raum* (Trier).

Biondi, A. (1984) 'Gianfrancesco Pico e la repressione della stregoneria: qualche novità sui processi mirandolesi del 1522–23', in *Mirandola e le terre del basso corso del Secchia della Deputazione di storia patria per le antiche provincie modenesi, Biblioteca*, n.s. 76 (1984): 331–49.

Blécourt, W. de (1986) 'Van heksenprocessen naar toverij', in Blécourt and Gijswijt-Hofstra, eds. (1986): 2–30.

Blécourt, W. de (1993) 'Cunning women, from healers to fortune tellers', in H. Binneveld and R. Dekker, eds. *Curing and Insuring: Essays on Illness in Past Times: The Netherlands, Belgium, England and Italy, 16th–20th Centuries* (Hilversum): 43–55.

Blécourt, W. de (1994) 'Witch doctors, soothsayers and priests: on cunning folk in European historiography and tradition', *Social History*, 19: 285–303.

Blécourt, W. de and Gijswijt-Hofstra, M., eds. (1986) *Kwade Mensen: Toverij in Nederland*, Special issue of *Volkskundig Bulletin*, 12, 1 (Amsterdam).

Bloch, M. (1973) *The Royal Touch: Sacred Monarchy and Scrofula in England and France*, trans. J. E. Anderson (London).

Bodin, J. (1995) *On the Demon-Mania of Witches*, trans. R. A. Scott, intro. J. L. Pearl (Toronto).

Bossy, J. (1985) *Christianity in the West, 1400–1700* (Oxford).

Bossy, J. (1988) 'Moral arithmetic: seven sins into ten commandments', in E. Leites, ed. *Conscience and Casuistry in Early Modern Europe* (Cambridge): 214–34.

Bostridge, I. (1997) *Witchcraft and Its Transformations c. 1650–c. 1750* (Oxford).

Boyer, P. (1994) *The Naturalness of Religious Ideas: A Cognitive Theory of Religion* (Berkeley).

Boyer, P. and Nissenbaum, S. (1974) *Salem Possessed: The Social Origins of Witchcraft* (London).

Briggs, R. (1989) *Communities of Belief: Cultural and Social Tensions in Early Modern France* (Oxford).

Briggs, R. (1996) *Witches and Neighbours: The Social and Cultural Context of European Witchcraft* (London).

Briggs, R. (2001) 'Circling the Devil: witch-doctors and magical healers in early modern Lorraine', in Clark, ed. (2001): 161–78.

Brooks-Davies, D. (1983) *The Mercurian Monarch: Magical Politics from Spenser to Pope* (Manchester).

Burke, P. (1977) 'Witchcraft and magic in Renaissance Italy: Gianfrancesco Pico and his *Strix*', in S. Anglo, ed. *The Damned Art: Essays in the Literature of Witchcraft* (London): 32–52.

Burke, P. (1987) *The Historical Anthropology of Early Modern Italy: Essays on Perception and Communication* (Cambridge).

Burr, G. L. (1943) 'The literature of witchcraft', in L. O. Gibbons, ed. *George Lincoln Burr: His Life by R. H. Bainton. Selections from His Writings* (Ithaca, NY): 166–89.

Calendar of State Papers Relating to Scotland and Mary, Queen of Scots, 1547–1603, x. 1589–93, eds. W. K. Boyd and H. W. Meikle (Edinburgh).

Caro Baroja, J. (1990) 'Witchcraft and Catholic theology', in Ankarloo and Henningsen, eds. (1990): 19–43.

Certeau, M. de (2000) *The Possession at Loudun*, trans. M. B. Smith (Chicago and London); originally published 1970.

Chambers, D. S., and Pullan, B., eds. (1992) *Venice: A Documentary History, 1450–1630* (Oxford).

Church, W. F. (1941) *Constitutional Thought in Sixteenth-Century France* (Cambridge, MA).

Ciruelo, P. (1977) *A Treatise Reproving All Superstitions and Forms of Witchcraft Very Necessary and Useful for All Good Christians Zealous for Their Salvation*, trans. E. A. Maio and D'O. W. Pearson, ed. D'O. W. Pearson (London).

Clark, S. (1983) 'French historians and early modern popular culture', *Past and Present*, 100: 62–99.

Clark, S. (1990) 'Protestant demonology: sin, superstition, and society (c. 1520–c. 1630)', in Ankarloo and Henningsen, eds. (1990): 45–81.

Clark, S. (1992) 'Glaube und Skepsis in der deutschen Hexenliteratur von Johan Weyer bis Friedrich Von Spee', in Lehmann and Ulbricht, eds. (1992): 15–33.

Clark, S. (1997) *Thinking with Demons: The Idea of Witchcraft in Early Modern Europe* (Oxford).

Clark, S. (2000) 'Johannes Althusius and the politics of witchcraft', in L. M. Andersson *et al.*, eds. *Rätten: En Festskrift till Bengt Ankarloo* (Lund): 272–90.

Clark, S., ed. (2001) *Languages of Witchcraft: Narrative, Ideology and Meaning in Early Modern Culture* (London).

Clasen, C.-P. (1972) *Anabaptism: A Social History, 1525–1618* (Ithaca, NY).

Closson, M. (2000) *L'Imaginaire démoniaque en France (1550–1650): Genèse de la littérature fantastique* (Geneva).

Clulee, N. H. (1988) *John Dee's Natural Philosophy: Between Science and Religion* (London).

Cohen, T. V., and Cohen, E. S., eds. (1993) *Words and Deeds in Renaissance Rome: Trials before the Papal Magistrates* (Toronto, Buffalo, and London).

Copenhaver, B. P. (1984) 'Scholastic philosophy and Renaissance magic in the *De Vita* of Marsilio Ficino', *Renaissance Quarterly*, 37: 523–54.

Copenhaver, B. P. (1988) 'Astrology and magic', in C. B. Schmitt, ed. *The Cambridge History of Renaissance Philosophy* (Cambridge): 264–300.

Crouzet, D. (1990) *Les Guerriers de Dieu: la violence au temps des troubles de religion*, 2 vols (Paris).

Crowe, M. J., ed. (1977) *Witchcraft: Catalogue of the Witchcraft Collection in Cornell University Library*, intro. R. H. Robbins (Millwood, NY).

Daneau, L. (1575) *A Dialogue of Witches*, trans. attrib. to T. Twyne (London).

Daston, L., and Park, K. (1998) *Wonders and the Order of Nature 1150–1750* (New York).

Davis, N. Z. (1974) 'Some tasks and themes in the study of popular religion', in C. Trinkaus and H. A. Oberman, eds. *The Pursuit of Holiness in Late Medieval and Renaissance Religion* (Leiden): 307–36.

Debus, A. G. (1966) *The English Paracelsians* (New York).

Debus, A. G. (1978) *Man and Nature in the Renaissance* (Cambridge).

Delumeau, J. (1974) 'Les réformateurs et la superstition', in *Actes du Colloque l'Amiral Coligny et son temps* (Paris): 451–87.

Delumeau, J. (1977) *Catholicism between Luther and Voltaire: A New View of the Counter-Reformation*, intro. J. Bossy, trans. J. Moiser (London).

Delumeau, J. (1978) *La Peur en Occident (XIVe–XVIIIe siècles): une cité assiégée* (Paris).

Di Simplicio, O. (2000) *Inquisizione Stregoneria Medicina: Siena e il suo stato (1580–1721)* (Siena).

Dixon, C. S. (1996) *The Reformation and Rural Society: The Parishes of Brandenburg-Ansbach-Kulmbach, 1528–1603* (Cambridge).

Dobbs, B. J. T. (1975) *The Foundations of Newton's Alchemy: Or, 'The Hunting of the Greene Lyon'* (Cambridge).

Dobbs, B. J. T. (1991) *The Janus Faces of Genius: The Role of Alchemy in Newton's Thought* (Cambridge).

Dömötör, T. (1980) 'The cunning folk in English and Hungarian witch trials', in V. Newell, ed. *Folklore Studies in the Twentieth Century* (Woodbridge): 183–7.

Dupont-Bouchat, M.-S. (1978) 'La répression de la sorcellerie dans le duché de Luxembourg aux XVIe et XVIIe siècles', in M. S. Dupont-Bouchat, W. Frijhoff and R. Muchembled, *Prophètes et sorciers dans les Pays-Bas, XVIe–XVIIIe siècle* (Paris): 41–154.

Eamon, W. (1991) 'Court, academy, and printing house: patronage and scientific careers in late-Renaissance Italy', in Moran, ed. (1991a): 25–50.

Eamon, W. (1994) *Science and the Secrets of Nature: Books of Secrets in Medieval and Early Modern Culture* (Princeton).

Elmer, P., ed. (1986) *The Library of Dr. John Webster: The Making of a Seventeenth-Century Radical*, Medical History, suppl. 6 (London).

Elmer, P. (2001) 'Towards a politics of witchcraft in early modern England', in Clark, ed. (2001): 101–18.

Estes, L. L. (1983) 'Reginald Scot and his *Discoverie of Witchcraft*: religion and science in the opposition to the European witch craze', *Church History*, 52: 444–56.

Evans, R. J. W. (1973) *Rudolf II and His World: A Study in Intellectual History 1576–1612* (Oxford).

Evans, R. J. W. (1979) *The Making of the Habsburg Monarchy, 1550–1700: An Interpretation* (Oxford).

Fajardo Spinola, F. (1992) *Hechicería y brujería en Canarias en la Edad Moderna* (Las Palmas).

Ferber, S. (1991) 'The demonic possession of Marthe Brossier, France 1598–1600', in C. Zika, ed. *No Gods Except Me: Orthodoxy and Religious Practice in Europe, 1200–1600* (Melbourne): 59–83.

Flint, V. I. J. (1991) *The Rise of Magic in Early Medieval Europe* Oxford).

Forster, M. R. (1992) *The Counter-Reformation in the Villages: Religion and Reform in the Bishopric of Speyer, 1560–1720* (Ithaca, NY, and London).

Frijhoff, W. Th. M. (1979) 'Official and popular religion in Christianity: the late middle ages and early modern times (13th–18th centuries)', in P. H. Vrijhof and J. Waardenburg, eds. *Official and Popular Religion: Analysis of a Theme for Religious Studies* (The Hague): 71–116.

Gaskill, M. (2000) *Crime and Mentalities in Early Modern England* (Cambridge).

Gebhard, H. (1989) *Hexenprozesse im Kurfürstentum Mainz des 17. Jahrhunderts* (Aschaffenburg).

Geertz, H. (1975) 'An anthropology of religion and magic', *Journal of Interdisciplinary History*, 6: 71–89.

Gentilcore, D. (1992) *From Bishop to Witch: The System of the Sacred in Early Modern Terra d'Otranto* (Manchester).

Gentilcore, D. (1998) *Healers and Healing in Early Modern Italy* (Manchester and New York).

Gibson, M. (2000) *Early Modern Witches: Witchcraft Cases in Contemporary Writing* (London and New York).

Gifford, G. (1587) *A Discourse of the Subtill Practises of Devilles by Witches and Sorcerers* (London).

Gifford, G. (1593) *A Dialogue Concerning Witches and Witchcraftes* (London).

Gijswijt-Hofstra, M., (1989) 'Witchcraft in the northern Netherlands', in A. Angerman *et al.*, eds. *Current Issues in Women's History* (London): 75–92.

Gijswijt-Hofstra, M., and Frijhoff, W., eds. (1991) *Witchcraft in the Netherlands from the Fourteenth to the Twentieth Century*, trans. R. M. J. van der Wilden-Fall (Rotterdam).

Ginzburg, C. (1966/1983) *I Benandanti* (Turin), trans. J. and A. Tedeschi, *The Night Battles: Witchcraft and Agrarian Cults in the Sixteenth and Seventeenth Centuries* (London, 1983).

Grafton, A. (1990) 'Humanism, magic and science', in A. Goodman and A. MacKay, eds. *The Impact of Humanism on Western Europe* (London and New York): 99–117.

Greene, T. M. (1987) 'Magic and festivity at the Renaissance court', *Renaissance Quarterly*, 40: 636–59.

Gregory, A. (1991) 'Witchcraft, politics and "good neighbourhood"', *Past and Present*, 133: 31–66.

Hajnal, J. (1965) 'European marriage patterns in perspective', in D. V. Glass and D. E. C. Eversley, eds. *Population in History: Essays in Historical Demography* (London): 101–43.

Hansen, B. (1978) 'Science and magic', in D. C. Lindberg, ed. *Science in the Middle Ages* (Chicago): 483–506.

Hansen, B. (1986) 'The complementarity of science and magic before the Scientific Revolution', *American Scientist*, 74: 128–36.

Harkness, D. E. (1999) *John Dee's Conversations with Angels: Cabala, Alchemy, and the End of Nature* (Cambridge).

Hastrup, K. (1990) 'Iceland: sorcerers and paganism', in Ankarloo and Henningsen, eds. (1990): 383–401.

Haustein, J. (1990) *Martin Luthers Stellung zum Zauber- und Hexenwesen* (Stuttgart).

Heikkinen, A., and Kervinen, T. (1990) 'Finland: the male domination', in Ankarloo and Henningsen, eds. (1990): 319–38.

Henningsen, G. (1980) *The Witches' Advocate: Basque Witchcraft and the Spanish Inquisition (1609–1614)* (Reno, NV).

Henry, J. (1986) 'Occult qualities and the experimental philosophy: active principles in pre-Newtonian matter theory', *History of Science*, 24: 335–81.

Henry, J. (1990) 'Magic and science in the sixteenth and seventeenth centuries', in R. C. Olby *et al.*, eds. *Companion to the History of Modern Science* (London and New York): 583–96.

Henry, J. (1997) *The Scientific Revolution and the Origins of Modern Science* (London).

Hiegel, H. (1961) *Le Bailliage d'Allemagne de 1600 à 1632* (Sarreguemines).

Horsley, R. (1979) 'Who were the witches? The social roles of the accused in the European witch trials', *Journal of Interdisciplinary History*, 9: 689–715.

Houdard, S. (1992) *Les Sciences du diable: quatre discours sur la sorcellerie* (Paris).

Hunter, M. (1995) 'The witchcraft controversy and the nature of free-thought in Restoration England: John Wagstaffe's *The Question of Witchcraft Debated* (1669)', in M. Hunter, *Science and the Shape of Orthodoxy: Intellectual Change in Late 17th-Century Britain* (Woodbridge): 286–307.

Hutchison, K. (1982) 'What happened to occult qualities in the scientific revolution?', *Isis*, 73: 233–54.

Idoate, F. (1978) *La Brujería en Navarra y sus documentos* (Pamplona).

Jacques-Chaquin, N., and Préaud, M., eds. (1993) *Le Sabbat des sorciers en Europe (XVe–XVIIIe siècles)* (Grenoble).

Jensen, P. F. (1975) 'Calvin and witchcraft', *Reformed Theological Review*, 34: 76–86.

Johansen, J. Chr.V. (1990) 'Denmark: the sociology of accusations', in Ankarloo and Henningsen, eds. (1990): 339–65.

Johansen, J. Chr.V. (1991) *Da Djaevelen var ude . . . Trolddom i det 17. Århundredes Danmark* (Odense), French summary.

Johansen, J. Chr.V. (1991/92) 'Witchcraft, sin and repentance: the decline of Danish witchcraft trials', *Acta Ethnographica Hungarica*, 37: 413–23.

Joubert, L. (1989) *Popular Errors*, trans. and ed. G. D. de Rocher (Tuscaloosa and London).

Kahk, J. (1990) 'Estonia II: the crusade against idolatry', in Ankarloo and Henningsen, eds. (1990): 273–84.

Kamber, P. (1982) 'La chasse aux sorciers at aux sorcières dans le Pays de Vaud', *Revue historique vaudoise*, 90: 21–33.

Karant-Nunn, S. C. (1987) *Zwickau in Transition, 1500–1547: The Reformation as an Agent of Change* (Columbus, OH).

Kieckhefer, R. (1976) *European Witch Trials: Their Foundations in Popular and Learned Culture, 1300–1500* (London).

Kittredge, G. L. (1929) *Witchcraft in Old and New England* (Cambridge, MA; reissued New York, 1958).

Klaniczay, G. (1990) 'Hungary: the accusations and the universe of popular magic', in Ankarloo and Henningsen, eds. (1990): 219–55.

Klaniczay, G. (1994) 'Bûchers tardifs en Europe centrale et orientale', in Muchembled, ed. (1994): 215–31.

Kogan, S. (1986) *The Hieroglyphic King: Wisdom and Idolatry in the Seventeenth-Century Masque* (London).

Kors, A. C., and Peters, E. (2001) *Witchcraft in Europe 400–1700: A Documentary History*, 2nd edn. (Philadelphia).

Kristóf, I. (1991/92) '"Wise women", sinners and the poor: the social background of witch-hunting in a 16th–18th century Calvinist city of eastern Hungary', *Acta Ethnographica Hungarica*, 37: 93–119.

Kunze, M. (1987) *Highroad to the Stake: A Tale of Witchcraft*, trans. W. E. Yuill (London).

Labouvie, E. (1991) *Zauberei und Hexenwerk: Ländlicher Hexenglaube in der frühen Neuzeit* (Frankfurt/Main).

Larner, C. (1984) *Witchcraft and Religion: The Politics of Popular Belief* (London).

Lea, H. C. (1939/1957) *Materials toward a History of Witchcraft*, ed. A. C. Howland, intro. G. L. Burr, 3 vols (New York and London).

Lebigre, A. (1989) *L'Affaire des poisons* (Paris).

Lehmann, H., and Ulbricht, O., eds. (1992) *Vom Unfug des Hexen-Processes: Gegner der Hexenverfolgung von Johann Weyer bis Friedrich Spee* (Wiesbaden).

Lenman, B., and Parker, G. (1980) 'The state, the community and the criminal law in early modern Europe', in V. A. C. Gatrell, B. Lenman and G. Parker, eds. *Crime and the Law: The Social History of Crime in Western Europe since 1500* (London): 11–48.

Levack, B. P. (1995) *The Witch-Hunt in Early Modern Europe*, 2nd edn. (London).

Levack, B. P. (1999) 'The decline and end of witchcraft prosecutions', in B. Ankarloo and S. Clark, eds. *Witchcraft and Magic in Europe: The Eighteenth and Nineteenth Centuries* (London): 1–93.

Liljequist, J. (1992) *Brott, synd och straff: Tidelagsbrottet i Sverige under 1600-och 1700-talet* (Umeå), English summary.

Lohr, C. H. (1978) 'Renaissance Latin Aristotle commentaries: authors L–M', *Renaissance Quarterly*, 31: 532–603.

Lorenz, S. (1995) 'Zur Spruchpraxis der Juristenfakultät Mainz in Hexenprozessen: Ein Beitrag zur Geschichte von Jurisprudenz und Hexenverfolgung', in G. Franz and F. Irsigler, eds. *Hexenglaube und Hexenprozesse im Raum Rhein-Mosel-Saar (Trierer Hexenprozesse, 2)* (Trier): 73–87.

MacDonald, M., ed. (1991) *Witchcraft and Hysteria in Elizabethan London: Edward Jorden and the Mary Glover Case* (London).

MacDonald Ross, G. (1985) 'Occultism and philosophy in the seventeenth century', in A. J. Holland, ed. *Philosophy: Its History and Historiography* (Dordrecht): 95–115.

Macfarlane, A. (1970) *Witchcraft in Tudor and Stuart England: A Regional and Comparative Study* (London), 2nd edn. 1999, ed. J. A. Sharpe.

Macfarlane, A. (1977) 'A Tudor anthropologist: George Gifford's *Discourse* and *Dialogue*', in S. Anglo, ed. *The Damned Art: Essays in the Literature of Witchcraft* (London): 140–55.

McGuire, J. E., and Rattansi, P. M. (1966) 'Newton and the "Pipes of Pan"', *Notes and Records of the Royal Society of London*, 21: 108–43.

Madar, M. (1990) 'Estonia I: werewolves and poisoners', in Ankarloo and Henningsen, eds. (1990): 257–72.

Malinowski, B. (1954) *Magic, Science and Religion and Other Essays*, intro. R. Redfield (New York).

Mandrou, R. (1968) *Magistrats et sorciers en France au XVIIe siècle: un analyse de psychologie historique* (Paris).

Margolin, J.-C. (1974) 'La politique culturelle de Guillaume, duc de Clèves', in F. Simone, ed. *Culture et politique en France à l'époque de l'humanisme et de la Renaissance* (Turin): 293–324.

Martin, R. (1989) *Witchcraft and the Inquisition in Venice, 1550–1650* (Oxford).

Marwick, M., ed. (1990) *Witchcraft and Sorcery* (Harmondsworth).

Max, F. (1993) 'Les premières controverses sur la réalité du sabbat dans l'Italie du XVIe siècle', in Jacques-Chaquin and Préaud, eds. (1993): 55–62.

Maxwell-Stuart, P. G. (1999) *The Occult in Early Modern Europe: A Documentary History* (London).

Maxwell-Stuart, P. G. (2001) *Witchcraft in Europe and the New World, 1400–1800* (Basingstoke).

Meek, C. (2000) 'Men, women and magic: some cases from late medieval

Lucca', in C. Meek, ed. *Women in Renaissance and Early Modern Europe* (Dublin): 43–66.

Mendelsohn, J. A. (1992) 'Alchemy and politics in England 1649–1665', *Past and Present*, 135: 30–78.

Midelfort, H. C. E. (1972) *Witch Hunting in Southwestern Germany, 1562–1684: The Social and Intellectual Foundations* (Stanford).

Midelfort, H. C. E. (1974) 'Were there really witches?', in R. M. Kingdon, ed. *Transition and Revolution* (Minneapolis): 189–226.

Midelfort, H. C. E. (1999) *A History of Madness in Sixteenth-Century Germany* (Stanford).

Millen, R. (1985) 'The manifestation of occult qualities in the Scientific Revolution', in M. J. Osler and P. L. Farber, eds. *Religion, Science, and Worldview: Essays in Honour of Richard S. Westfall* (Cambridge): 185–216.

Monter, E. W. (1976) *Witchcraft in France and Switzerland: The Borderlands during the Reformation* (Ithaca, NY, and London).

Monter, E. W. (1990) *Frontiers of Heresy: The Spanish Inquisition from the Basque Lands to Sicily* (Cambridge).

Monter, E. W. (1997) 'Toads and eucharists: the male witches of Normandy, 1564–1660', *French Historical Studies*, 20: 563–95.

Monter, E. W. (1999) *Judging the French Reformation: Heresy Trials by Sixteenth-Century Parlements* (Cambridge, MA).

Moran, B. T., ed. (1991a) *Patronage and Institutions: Science, Technology, and Medicine at the European Court, 1500–1750* (Woodbridge).

Moran, B. T. (1991b) 'Patronage and institutions: courts, universities, and academies in Germany; an overview', in B. T. Moran, ed. (1991a): 169–83.

More, H. (1653) *An Antidote Against Atheisme* (London).

Muchembled, R. (1978a) *Culture populaire et culture des élites dans la France moderne (XVe–XVIIIe siècles)* (Paris); trans. by L. Cochrane, *Popular Culture and Elite Culture in France, 1400–1750* (Baton Rouge and London, 1985).

Muchembled, R. (1978b) 'Satan ou les hommes? La chasse aux sorcières et ses causes', in M.-S. Dupont-Bouchat, W. Frijhoff and R. Muchembled, eds. *Prophètes et sorciers dans les Pays-Bas, XVIe–XVIIIe siècle* (Paris): 13–39.

Muchembled, R. (1993) *Le Roi et la sorcière: l'Europe des bûchers XVe–XVIIIe siècle* (Paris).

Muchembled, R., ed. (1994) *Magie et sorcellerie en Europe du Moyen Age à nos jours* (Paris).

Naess, H. E. (1982) *Trolldomsprosessene i Norge på 1500–1600-tallet: En retts- og sosialhistorisk undersøkelse* (Oslo), English summary.

Naess, H. E. (1990) 'Norway: the criminological context', in Ankarloo and Henningsen, eds. (1990): 367–82.

Nalle, S. T. (1992) *God in La Mancha: Religious Reform and the People of Cuenca, 1500–1650* (Baltimore and London).

Naudé, G. (1625) *Apologie pour tous les grands personnages qui ont esté faussement soupçonnez de magie* (Paris).

Normand, L., and Roberts, G. (2000) *Witchcraft in Early Modern Scotland: James VI's* Demonology *and the North Berwick Witches* (Exeter).

Oberman, H. A. (1981) *Masters of the Reformation: The Emergence of a New Intellectual Climate in Europe*, trans. D. Martin (Cambridge).

Oestmann, P. (1997) *Hexenprozesse am Reichskammergericht* (Vienna–Munich–Cologne).

Ogden, D. (1999) 'Binding spells: curse tablets and voodoo dolls in the Greek and Roman worlds', in B. Ankarloo and S. Clark, eds. *Witchcraft and Magic in Europe: Ancient Greece and Rome* (London): 1–90.

O'Neil, M. (1987) 'Magical healing, love magic and the Inquisition in late sixteenth-century Modena', in S. Haliczer, ed. *Inquisition and Society in Early Modern Europe* (London): 88–114.

O'Neil, M. (1991/92) 'Missing footprints: maleficium in Modena', *Acta Ethnographica Hungarica*, 37: 123–42.

Orgel, S., ed. (1987) *The Tempest* (*The Oxford Shakespeare*) (Oxford).

Ostorero, M., Bagliani, A. P., and Tremp, K. U., eds. (1999) *L'Imaginaire du sabbat: édition critique des textes les plus anciens (1430c.–1440c.)* (Lausanne).

Park, K. (1998) 'Medicine and magic: the healing arts', in J. C. Brown and R. C. Davis, eds. *Gender and Society in Renaissance Italy* (London): 129–49.

Parry, G. (1981) *The Golden Age Restor'd: The Culture of the Stuart Court, 1603–42* (Manchester).

Pearl, J. L. (1999) *The Crime of Crimes: Demonology and Politics in France 1560–1620* (Waterloo, Ontario).

Perkins, W. (1610) *A Discourse of the Damned Art of Witchcraft* (Cambridge).

Peters, E. (1978) *The Magician, the Witch, and the Law* (Brighton).

Peters, E. (2001) 'The medieval church and state on superstition, magic and witchcraft: from Augustine to the sixteenth century', in B. Ankarloo and S. Clark, eds. *Witchcraft and Magic in Europe: The Middle Ages* (London): 171–243.

Pohl, H. (1988) *Hexenglaube und Hexenverfolgung im Kurfürstentum Mainz: Ein Beitrag zur Hexenfrage im 16. und beginnenden 17. Jahrhundert* (Stuttgart).

Porter, R. (1999) 'Witchcraft and magic in Enlightenment, Romantic and

Liberal thought', in B. Ankarloo and S. Clark, eds. *Witchcraft and Magic in Europe: The Eighteenth and Nineteenth Centuries* (London): 191–282.

Priester, P., and Barske, A. (1986) 'Vervolging van tovenaars(en) in Groningen, 1547–1597', in Blécourt and Gijswijt-Hofstra, eds. (1986): 50–76.

Purkiss, D. (1995) 'Women's stories of witchcraft in early modern England: the house, the body, the child', *Gender and History*, 7: 408–32.

Quaife, G. R. (1987) *Godly Zeal and Furious Rage: The Witch in Early Modern Europe* (London).

Reeves, M. (1969) *The Influence of Prophecy in the Later Middle Ages* (Oxford).

Robbins, R. H. (1959) *The Encyclopedia of Witchcraft and Demonology* (London).

Rochelandet, B. (1997) *Sorcières, diables et bûchers en Franche-Comté aux XVIe et XVIIe siècles* (Besançon).

Romeo, G. (1990) *Inquisitori, esorcisti e streghe nell'Italia della Controriforma* (Florence).

Roper, L. (1994) *Oedipus and the Devil: Witchcraft, Sexuality, and Religion in Early Modern Europe* (London).

Rosen, B., ed. (1969) *Witchcraft* (London).

Rossi, P. (1968) *Francis Bacon: From Magic to Science*, trans. S. Rabinovitch (London).

Rowlands, A. (1996) 'Witchcraft and popular religion in early modern Rothenburg ob der Tauber', in R. Scribner and T. Johnson, eds. *Popular Religion in Germany and Central Europe, 1400–1800* (London): 101–18.

Ruggiero, G. (1993) *Binding Passions: Tales of Magic, Marriage, and Power at the End of the Renaissance* (New York).

Rummel, W. (1991) *Bauern, Herren und Hexen: Studien zur Sozialgeschichte sponheimischer und kurtrierischer Hexenprozesse 1574–1664* (Göttingen).

Sawyer, R. C. (1988/89) '"Strangely handled in all her lyms": witchcraft and healing in Jacobean England', *Journal of Social History*, 22: 461–85.

Scheltema, J. (1828) *Geschiedenis der Heksenprocessen: eene bijdrage tot den roem des Vaderlands* (Haarlem).

Schöffer, I. (1973) 'Heksengeloof en heksenvervolging: een historiografisch overzicht', *Tijdschrift voor Geschiedenis*, 86: 215–34.

Schormann, G. (1981) *Hexenprozesse in Deutschland* (Göttingen).

Schormann, G. (1991) *Der Krieg gegen die Hexen: Das Ausrottungsprogramm des Kurfürsten von Köln* (Göttingen).

Schormann, G. (1992) 'Die Haltung des Reichskammergerichts in

Hexenprozessen', in H. Lehmann and O. Ulbricht, eds. *Vom Unfug des Hexen-Processes: Gegner der Hexenverfolgungen von Johan Weyer bis Friedrich Spee* (Wiesbaden): 269–80.

Scot, R. (1584) *The Discoverie of Witchcraft* (London).

Scribner, R. (1984) 'Ritual and popular religion in Catholic Germany at the time of the Reformation', *Journal of Ecclesiastical History*, 35: 47–77.

Scribner, R. (1993) 'The Reformation, popular magic and the 'disenchantment of the world'', *Journal of Interdisciplinary History*, 23: 475–94.

Sejr Jensen, K. (1982) *Trolddom i Danmark, 1500–1588* (Copenhagen).

Shackelford, J. (1991) 'Paracelsianism and patronage in early modern Denmark', in Moran, ed. (1991a): 85–109.

Shapin, S. (1996) *The Scientific Revolution* (Chicago and London).

Sharpe, J. A. (1992) *Witchcraft in Seventeenth-Century Yorkshire: Accusations and Counter Measures*, University of York Borthwick Institute of Historical Research, Paper 81 (York).

Sharpe, J. A. (1996) *Instruments of Darkness: Witchcraft in England 1550–1750* (London).

Sharpe, J. A. (1999) *The Bewitching of Anne Gunter: A Horrible and True Story of Football, Witchcraft, Murder, and the King of England* (London).

Shumaker, W. (1972) *The Occult Sciences in the Renaissance* (London).

Shumaker, W. (1989) *Natural Magic and Modern Science: Four Treatises 1590–1657* (Binghamton, NY).

Soman, A. (1978) 'The Parlement of Paris and the great witch hunt (1565–1640)', *Sixteenth Century Journal*, 9: 31–44.

Soman, A. (1981) 'La sorcellerie vue du Parlement de Paris au début du XVIIe siècle', *Actes du 104e Congrès national des Sociétés savantes*, 2 vols (Paris): i, 393–405.

Soman, A. (1992) *Sorcellerie et justice criminelle: le Parlement de Paris (16e–18e siècles)* (Bath).

Soman, A. (1993) 'Le sabbat des sorciers: preuve juridique', in Jacques-Chaquin and Préaud, eds. (1993): 85–99.

Strauss, G. (1978) *Luther's House of Learning: Indoctrination of the Young in the German Reformation* (London).

Tambiah, S. J. (1985) 'The magical power of words', in S. J. Tambiah *Culture, Thought, and Social Action: An Anthropological Perspective* (London): 17–59.

Tausiet, M. (2000) *Ponzoña en los ojos: Brujería y superstición en Aragón en el siglo XVI* (Zaragoza).

Thomas, K. V. (1971) *Religion and the Decline of Magic: Studies in Popular Beliefs in Sixteenth and Seventeenth Century England* (London).

Thomas, K. V. (1975) 'An anthropology of religion and magic', *Journal of Interdisciplinary History*, 6: 91–109.

Thorndike, L. (1923–58) *A History of Magic and Experimental Science*, 8 vols (New York).

Trevor-Roper, H. R. (1967) 'The European witch-craze of the sixteenth and seventeenth centuries', in H. R. Trevor-Roper, *Religion, the Reformation and Social Change* (London): 90–192.

Tuck, R. (1993) *Philosophy and Government 1572–1651* (Cambridge).

Valentia, G. de (1591/97) *Commentariorum Theologicorum*, 4 vols (Ingolstadt).

Vickers, B. (1979) 'Frances Yates and the writing of history', *Journal of Modern History*, 51: 287–316.

Vickers, B. (1984) 'Analogy versus identity: the rejection of occult symbolism, 1580–1680', in B. Vickers, ed. *Occult and Scientific Mentalities in the Renaissance* (Cambridge): 95–163.

Vidal, J. (1987) 'Le Parlement de Toulouse et la répression de la sorcellerie au milieu du XVIIe siècle', in *Hommages à Gérard Boulvert* (Nice): 511–27.

Voltmer, R., and Weisenstein, K. (1996) *Das Hexenregister des Claudius Musiel (Trierer Hexenprozesse, 2)* (Trier).

Waardt, H. de (1991) *Toverij en Samenleving: Holland 1500–1800* (The Hague): 335–9, English summary.

Waardt, H. de (1993) 'From cunning man to natural healer', in H. Binneveld and R. Dekker, eds. *Curing and Insuring: Essays on Illness in Past Times: The Netherlands, Belgium, England and Italy, 16th–20th Centuries* (Hilversum): 33–41.

Waardt, H. de (1997) 'Breaking the boundaries: irregular healers in eighteenth-century Holland', in M. Gijswijt-Hofstra, H. Marland and H. de Waardt, eds. *Illness and Healing Alternatives in Western Europe* (London and New York): 141–60.

Walker, A. M., and Dickerman, E. H. (1991) ' "A woman under the influence": a case of alleged possession in sixteenth-century France', *Sixteenth Century Journal*, 22: 535–54.

Walker, D. P. (1958) *Spiritual and Demonic Magic from Ficino to Campanella* (London).

Walker, D. P. (1981) *Unclean Spirits: Possession and Exorcism in France and England in the Late Sixteenth and Early Seventeenth Centuries* (London).

Webster, C. (1975) *The Great Instauration: Science, Medicine and Reform 1626–1660* (London).

Webster, C. (1982) *From Paracelsus to Newton: Magic and the Making of Modern Science* (Cambridge).

West, R. H. (c. 1984) *Reginald Scot and Renaissance Writings on Witchcraft* (Boston).

Weyer, J. (1991) *Witches, Devils, and Doctors in the Renaissance: Johann Weyer, De praestigiis daemonum*, ed. G. Mora, trans. J. Shea (Binghamton, NY).

Willis, D. (1995) *Malevolent Nurture: Witch-Hunting and Maternal Power in Early Modern England* (London).

Wilson, S. (2000) *The Magical Universe: Everyday Ritual and Magic in Pre-Modern Europe* (London and New York).

Wootton, D. (2001) 'Reginald Scot / Abraham Fleming / The Family of Love', in Clark, ed. (2001): 119–38.

Yates, F. A. (1964) *Giordano Bruno and the Hermetic Tradition* (London).

Yates, F. A. (1967) 'The Hermetic tradition in Renaissance science', in C. S. Singleton, ed. *Art, Science, and History in the Renaissance* (Baltimore): 255–74.

Yates, F. A. (1972) *The Rosicrucian Enlightenment* (London).

Zambelli, P. (1974) 'Le problème de la magie naturelle à la Renaissance', in L. Szezucki, ed. *Magia, Astrologia e Religione nel Rinascimento* (Warsaw): 48–82.

Zambelli, P. (1988) 'Scholastic and humanist views of Hermeticism and witchcraft', in I. Merkel and A. G. Debus, eds. *Hermeticism and the Renaissance: Intellectual History and the Occult in Early Modern History* (London): 126–53.

Index

CPSIA information can be obtained at www.ICGtesting.com
Printed in the USA
BVOW081920151112

305687BV00002B/5/A